GOLD RUSH

How to Collect, Invest & Profit with Gold Coins

Edited by Arlyn Sieber
Contributing Editor Mitchel Battino

©2007 Krause Publications

Published by

krause publications

An Imprint of F+W Publications

700 East State Street • Iola, WI 54990-0001
715-445-2214 • 888-457-2873
www.krausebooks.com

Our toll-free number to place an order or obtain
a free catalog is (800) 258-0929.

Library of Congress Control Number: 2007924540

ISBN-13: 978-0-89689-566-9
ISBN-10: 0-89689-566-1

Designed by Kay Sanders
Edited by Arlyn Sieber

Printed in China

CONTENTS

GOLD RUSH!

Few words evoke the dreams of the pioneer spirit and westward expansion of North America in both the mid-1800s with California, and the late 1890s with the Alaska and Yukon claims.

Gold has been a symbol of value throughout history. This volume of *Gold Rush*! A new book by Arlyn Sieber and Mitchell Battino brings into focus the coins, which are commonly available to collectors and investors, as gold also needs to be considered from an investment perspective too.

Prior to World War I, most national economies were on a gold standard. Gold coins circulated, and the national paper money issues were backed by gold reserves in either coin or bullion. Since that time, economies began to change, and since World War II, gold coins have become a novelty. In the late 1960s, bullion coins began to be minted, and by the early 1980s, several counties – Austria, Australia, China, Canada, Great Britain, South Africa and the United States were striking coins of a high purity, a nominal face value, and in a traditional coin design rather than ingot form.

So, the authors present listings culled from the seminal work on modern coinage of the world, Krause Publications' *Standard Catalog of World Coins*. Presented in an easy to follow format profuse with illustrations, one could choose the various ways to collect, either by commemorative, circulating or bullion issues. Prices are presented based on a gold price of $650. A helpful chart to make adjustments from this "spot price" is on pages 268-271.

Enjoy the *Gold Rush* too!

George S. Cuhaj
Editor
Standard Catalog of World Coins

We Buy, Sell, & Auction

THE VERY BEST IN COINS & PAPER MONEY

If you are interested in U.S., World, or Ancient Coins, Federal Paper Money, World Bank Notes, Confederate Currency, Obsolete or Colonial Currency, we offer a large selection of choice coins and paper money for immediate sale. If you are thinking of selling or consigning your coins or paper money to auction, why not do what many leading dealers and collectors have done? Contact Smythe for competitive prices and prompt, professional service. Why do people choose us? They recognize that there are no substitutes for our decades of numismatic experience, our first-class numismatic research facilities, our world-class catalogs, and our unquestioned reputation for integrity.

Call us at **800-622-1880**, visit us at our website, **www.smytheonline.com**, or e-mail us at **info@smytheonline.com**, and let us help you achieve your objectives.

Mitchell A. Battino, AAA
Senior Numismatist, Certified Appraiser
Specialist, U.S. and World Gold Coins

CHAPTER 1

GLOWING DAWN

It provides none of the basic necessities required for human survival. Yet gold has been one of the most cherished substances for as far back as historians can document civilizations. It is a symbol of material wealth. It is a symbol of royalty. It is coveted as an adornment. When configured into standard sizes and shapes as coins, it has also been valued as a medium of exchange.

In its base form, gold is an element found in a variety of rocks. It is principally found in either lode deposits or placer deposits. Lode deposits are found in mineralized rocks and are mined. Placer deposits are sometimes called "secondary deposits" because they are derived from the lode deposits. Gold is more dense than the rock enclosing it in a lode deposit. When erosion or other deterioration causes the enclosing rock to fall away, the gold can be washed away in small pieces – flakes or even larger nuggets. Placer deposits conjure images of scraggly 19th-century prospectors panning a Western stream for a windfall.

Maybe it was a glint of gold in a stream that caught the eye of the first human to recover the metal, value it, and go back in search of more. In the Periodic Table of Elements, gold's symbol is "Au," which is derived from the Latin word *aurum*, meaning "glowing dawn." As humans recovered more of the metal and worked with it, they discovered it was durable and retained its luster over time. Medieval alchemists called it a "noble" metal because it does not oxidize under normal conditions.

They also discovered that gold was malleable and could be worked and shaped into decorative forms. There is no greater evidence of ancient civilizations' lust for gold than the tomb of Tutankhamen, discovered in 1922 by English archaeologist Howard Carter. Egypt's boy king of the 1300s B.C. died at the age of 18 to 20. His tomb was a gold treasure trove of unimaginable proportions – gold figurines, gold funerary objects, the king's famous gold death mask, and much more.

In time, gold and other precious metals became mediums of exchange – items of value that could be traded for goods and services that did contribute to basic needs. At first, gold traded in base form; each quantity had to be weighed and tested for purity with each transaction. The kingdom of Lydia, which was located in part of modern-day Turkey, is credited with producing the first coins in 700-650 B.C. They were made of electrum, a natural alloy of silver and gold found in the region's rivers. King Croesus of Lydia is credited with producing the first pure-gold coin about a hundred years later.

The science of gold
Symbol: Au
Atomic number: 79
Atomic weight: 196.9665
Specific gravity: 19.3 (pure gold)

Burial fit for a king
In addition to the treasure trove in his tomb, King Tutankhamen's mummy itself was covered with treasures. The 143 precious objects tucked between the bandages included golden finger-stalls, sandals, gold rings, necklaces, bracelets, diadems, daggers, pendants, pectorals, and amulets cut from gold leaf. There were also two plain straps of golden leaves on the body's breast, a symbol of godliness.
Source: Tutankhamen, Life and Death of a Pharaoh

Great Britain,
5 guineas Charles II,
ruled 1660-1685.

Soft as gold

Gold is soft enough
to scratch with a
fingernail. A block of
gold about the size of
a sugar cube can be
beaten into a translu-
cent film some 27 feet
on one side.
Source: Gale Encyclopedia of Science.

The concept of coinage gave new form to gold and other precious metals. Coins were produced in standard sizes and purity, if but crudely at first, thus eliminating the need to determine the precious metal's value with each transaction. Civilizations that followed, including the Greeks and Romans, continued to advance the concept of coinage. Advancements in coinage methods allowed for more elaborate designs to be placed on coins, such as images of rulers and other icons of a people and nation. Thus, coins became symbols of sovereignty and nationalism.

Nations continued to strike gold coins for circulation in the centuries that followed and continued their quest to find more of the precious metal. In the 15th and 16th centuries, that quest led to exploration of the New World by Europe's most powerful nations. Hernando Cortés, for example, conquered Mexico for Spain and claimed Emperor Montezuma II's gold as his reward. In December 1606, three ships loaded with supplies and men of various skills left the London-area docks and headed down the Thames for the open water of the Atlantic. Their destination was Virginia in the New World. Their goal was exploration and riches – "to get the pearl and gold." Their ultimate accomplishment was the first permanent English settlement in North America – the Jamestown colony.

Gold issues remained a staple of world coinage into the 1600s and 1700s. In the 1800s, paper money became an economical substitute for precious-metal coinage, but the paper issues remained backed by gold or silver. Nations guaranteed that the paper issues could be exchanged for precious-metal coinage – either gold or silver. A guarantee of exchange in gold became known as the "gold standard." It required that nations retain a certain amount of gold so they could meet demand for redemption of paper issues. It prevented nations from printing an unlimited supply of paper money and thus stabilized monetary systems. Major trading nations agreed to fix the price of gold at $20.67 a troy ounce. This meant that a U.S. gold $20 coin had to contain 0.9677 ounces of gold for its intrinsic value to match its face value.

Ultimately, however, the system proved to be too inflexible. Nations could not adjust their money supply in response to economic conditions. The financial demands of World War I caused many nations to abandon the gold standard. They continued to

GOLD RUSH

strike gold coins for circulation into the 20th century before abandoning the yellow metal and eventually all circulating precious-metal coinage later in the 1900s.

Today, gold plays a diminished but still important role in the world economy. The International Monetary Fund, which has 184 member countries and is based in Washington, D.C., holds 103.4 million troy ounces of gold at designated depositories. The IMF promotes "international monetary cooperation, exchange stability, and orderly exchange arrangements" among its members. The IMF says gold provides "fundamental strength to its balance sheet," but it no longer is the common denominator in determining exchange rates and is no longer used in transactions between the IMF and its members.

The United States is an IMF member and also retains its own gold reserves. They are stored at the U.S. mints in Denver and Philadelphia, the San Francisco Assay Office, the West Point Bullion Depository in New York, and, the most famous one of all, the Fort Knox Bullion Depository in Kentucky. The Fort Knox facility was completed in December 1936 and consists of a two-story basement and attic building constructed of granite, steel, and concrete. The U.S. Mint says the gold stored in the depository is in the form of bars of almost pure gold. The bars measure 7 inches by 3 5/8 inches by 1 3/4 inches and contain 400 troy ounces of gold each.

Many countries today issue gold commemorative coins and gold bullion coins. The commemoratives are legal tender but are not intended for circulation. They are sold at a premium above face value directly by the national mint issuing the coin. The U.S. Mint, for example, strikes and sells gold commemorative coins, as mandated by laws authorizing specific issues. Bullion coins are also legal tender and have a face value, but they are usually bought and sold solely for their precious-metal content. Gold bullion coins come in various sizes from a quarter troy ounce to one troy ounce and offer private citizens a convenient medium for owning the precious metal.

Gold is weighed in troy ounces. A troy ounce (31.103 grams) is slightly heavier than an avoirdupois ounce (28.350 grams). Twelve troy ounces equal one troy pound. When used in coinage, gold is alloyed with a small amount of other metal to facilitate production. The purity of gold in a coin is called "fineness," which is expressed in parts per thousand. For example, a one-ounce American Eagle gold bullion coin is 0.9167 fine, which

Lydia, gold stater of King Croesus

Rich as Croesus

Croesus was king of Lydia when the kingdom struck the world's first pure gold coins. The kingdom was rich in natural deposits of precious metals, which made its kings rich, thus the saying "rich as Croesus."
Source: Illustrated Encyclopedia of World Coins.

The price of gold
1850 -- $18.93
1855 -- $18.93
1860 -- $18.93
1865 -- $18.93
1870 -- $18.93
1875 -- $18.94
1880 -- $18.94
1885 -- $18.94
1890 -- $18.94
1895 -- $18.93
1900 -- $18.96
1905 -- $18.92
1910 -- $18.92
1915 -- $18.99
1920 -- $20.68
1925 -- $20.64
1930 -- $20.65
1935 -- $34.84
1940 -- $33.85
1945 -- $34.71
1950 -- $34.72
1955 -- $35.03
1960 -- $35.27
1965 -- $35.12
1970 -- $36.02
1975 -- $160.86
1980 -- $615.00
1985 -- $317.00
1990 -- $383.51
1995 -- $383.79
2000 -- $279.11
2005 -- $444.74

Average daily price. Source: National Mining Association.

means it has 916.7 parts of pure gold for every 1,000 parts of total metal in the coin.

Gold coins with collectible or numismatic value sell for a premium above their gold bullion value. The extent of the premium depends on the coin's grade or condition, its rarity, and the demand for the coin in the collector market. Premiums over gold value can vary from a few percentage points for bullion coins to several hundred percent for high-quality or rare collectible coins. If the premium is high, the coin is not affected as much by fluctuating market prices for gold bullion. If the premium is low, the coin's value is more likely to be affected by the ups and downs of the gold bullion market.

Just as their ancient predecessors made transactions easier, gold coins today are an attractive means for investing in precious metals because of their standard sizes and known gold content. They also provide the satisfaction and enjoyment of pursuing a collecting hobby.

Local coin dealers base their prices on the world gold markets when buying and selling gold bullion coins or gold coins whose values are affected by their bullion content. The benchmark price per troy ounce worldwide is the twice-daily fixings of the London Bullion Market Association. The fixings allow association market participants to buy and sell large quantities of gold over the counter at a single quoted price. They also provide a reference price for many small, private transactions at local outlets, such as coin shops.

The fixing is based on the price at which gold has been trading and is a balance between dealers' buy and sell orders. Many trades worldwide are settled at the London p.m. fix. In New York, gold trades daily on the New York Mercantile Exchange from 8:20 a.m. to 1:30 p.m. "New York spot" is the price at which gold is trading at any given moment during normal trading hours and is another way to determine a gold coin's value. "New York close," or the day's last price, is also a benchmark for some gold trades.

A number of Web sites and financial news services publish the London fixings and New York spot prices throughout the trading day as well as historical charts and data. The

GOLD RUSH

price of gold is published in most daily news-papers, too. The London and New York exchanges also operate futures markets, where contracts for future delivery of gold in standard form can be purchased.

Factors that can affect the price of gold include supply, demand, the rate of inflation, the U.S. dollar's value against other major currencies, local and inter-national economic conditions, and major world events. Because gold is priced in U.S. dollars, it often, although not always, has an inverse relationship to the dollar's value. If the dollar rises against other major currencies, the price of gold tends to fall. Conversely, if the dollar decreases in value, gold often rises.

Great Britain, 1839
5 pounds, proof.

For many years, gold was considered a hedge against infla-tion. Inflation decreases the dollar's buying power, but gold tends to hold its value by increasing in price during high inflation. Although this is the trend, it is not always the case. The world economy is now more complicated. Markets are connected among many countries, where many factors can influence the price of gold. Gold's future value, therefore, is difficult to predict.

In the United States, gold ownership was restricted to coins with collectible value from 1933 until 1974. On January 31, 1934, the United States raised its official price of gold to $35 a troy ounce. The official price was raised again to $38 a troy ounce in 1971 and $42.22 a troy ounce in 1973. U.S. restric-tions on private ownership of gold were lifted in 1974, and the price of gold was now determined by the free market.

Gold prices rose steadily, reaching a high of $852 a troy ounce in January 1980. The post-1980 low of $256 an ounce was set in May 2001. Since then, gold has trended upward, reaching $725 an ounce in May 2006. In early 2007, gold traded for $610 to $685 a troy ounce, with increased daily vola-tility reflecting world events.

Karats vs. carats

"Karat" is an expres-sion of gold's purity in parts per 24. For example, 14-karat gold, commonly used in jewelry, consists of 14 parts of pure gold and 10 parts of other metals. "Carat" is a unit of weight for precious stones, such as diamonds, equal to 200 milligrams.

CHAPTER 2

THE JOY OF COLLECTING

Each denomination and series of coins – be they British sovereigns, Japanese yen, U.S. silver dollars, or any of the other thousands of available issues – present unique considerations and characteristics for collectors and investors. Gold coins are no exception. But there are universal tips that apply to coin collecting in general and set the foundation for a rewarding hobby and investing experience.

COLLECT WHAT YOU LIKE

Collectors should pursue a particular issue, type, design, or denomination because they like it. They should not pursue particular coins solely because they seem to be popular among others or because others have said that is what they should collect.

A particular coin type may have sentimental value to a collector. The collector may recall spending coins with a certain design as a youth and now wants to collect that design to fulfill a nostalgic yearning. Or the collector may have been given an old coin by a grandparent or other relative and now wants to collect other coins of the same design and denomination.

A collector may be interested in genealogy, and that may spark an interest in coins from the collector's ancestral homeland. Or the collector may simply be interested in the history of a particular country or era and pursue a collection that reflects that interest. A U.S. collector, for example, may be interested in Native American history and may pursue the many issues that carry Native American images.

Or a collector may simply like a particular denomination or coin design and not be able to explain why. Whatever may spark the interest in a particular coin, collecting what the collector likes increases the enjoyment whenever a new piece is added or the collection is admired.

HAVE A ROAD MAP

A coin collection can be whatever an individual collector wants it to be. A collector may long to own just a single gold coin, for example, and a piece with a design and price the collector likes may fulfill that longing. Pursuing a set, however, provides a focus and direction for collecting and can be more valuable than just a haphazard accumulation of coins.

Again, a set can be whatever a collector wants it to be, but the two most common methods for forming sets are (1) to collect one example of each date and mint mark in a particular series and (2) to collect one example of each "type" within a particular series, denomination, or composition.

The first method – by date and mint mark – is the more traditional

Coin directory

American Numismatic Association, 818 North Cascade Avenue, Colorado Springs, CO 80903-3279. (719) 632-2646. www.money.org.

of the two and was the focus of many collectors in the emerging numismatic hobby of the early 20th century. In the 1930s, the Whitman Publishing Company of Racine, Wisconsin, introduced its "penny board," which was a large cardboard holder that contained a slot for each date and mint mark of Lincoln cents, from 1909 to the current year. Collectors attempted to fill each slot in the board by searching circulating coins for an example of each date and mint mark.

Most coin series, however, have one or two "key dates" that make forming a complete date and mint mark collection of a particular series challenging. The key dates have lower mintages than other dates and mint marks in the series and are difficult to find. Few collectors filling in Whitman penny boards, for example, actually found a 1909-S example with designer Victor David Brenner's initials ("VDB") on the reverse. In today's coin market, asking prices for key dates reflect their rarity.

That is why many collectors turn to "type sets" for an achievable goal to their hobby pursuits. The goal of a type set is to acquire one example of each design within either a denomination, composition, time period, or some combination of the three. A type set of 20th-century U.S. half dollars, for example, would consist of a Barber type (1892-1915), Walking Liberty type (1916-1947), Franklin type (1948-1963), and Kennedy type (1965-present).

The advantage to collecting by type is that it gives collectors more flexibility in forming a set and finding examples that fit their individual hobby budgets. A collector pursuing a 20th-century U.S. half-dollar type set, for example, does not have to purchase the key-date 1921-S to fulfill the set's Walking Liberty requirement. A more affordable 1945-S in a top grade will do.

BUY THE BEST YOU CAN AFFORD

A coin's "grade," or state of preservation, is another key component to its value. The higher the grade, the higher the value.

There is nothing wrong with a set of well-worn Buffalo nickels if it is the best a collector can afford and brings the collector enjoyment. But the higher the grade and rarity of a particular coin, the greater the chances it will increase in value over time.

Also, collectors should strive for some uniformity in grade among individual pieces in a set. A type set that ranges from a well-worn VG-8 to a pristine MS-65 will not be as pleasing to the eye as one with consistently nice XF-40 to AU-50 pieces.

HANDLE COINS PROPERLY

The less a coin is handled the better, but sometimes it is

necessary to pick it up when it is not in a holder and examine it. During those times, a coin should be held by its edges and between the handler's thumb and forefinger. Handlers should not touch the coin's obverse or reverse surfaces.

Coins should also be handled over some type of soft padding so they will not be damaged if dropped accidentally.

DO NOT CLEAN COINS

Cleaning a coin can greatly reduce its value. Most cleaners and any type of rubbing action are abrasive and will damage the coin's obverse and reverse surfaces. If some type of substance on a coin really bothers a collector, the collector should consult an expert to see what, if anything, can be done about it.

A coin's grade is not based on how shiny it is. Grading refers to the amount of wear on a coin.

STORE COINS PROPERLY AND SECURELY

Long-term storage of collectible coins requires a sturdy, inert holder made specifically for coins. There are many types of holders available. Some are inexpensive and are fine for inexpensive coins in circulated grades and for short-term storage.

Dealers often sell coins in inexpensive 2-inch by 2-inch cardboard holders with Mylar windows. The holders consist of two pieces of cardboard, and the coin is sandwiched in between so it shows through the window. The pieces are held together with staples. The holders are fine for short-term storage but are not airtight. Also, collectors should be careful when removing the staples from a cardboard holder so the sharp edges do not scratch the coin inside.

Dealers may also sell coins in 2-inch by 2-inch plastic "flips." The flips consist of a plastic pouch that holds the coin and another plastic section that folds down over the pouch. Flips, too, should be considered only for short-term storage. The older ones contain polyvinylchloride, which can break down over time and leave a green slime on a coin's surface. Newer ones are made from the safer Mylar but are brittle and prone to splitting.

Hard-plastic holders – particularly those that are airtight and watertight – are the best for long-term storage of more valuable coins. They consist of two or three parts that screw together with the coin sandwiched in between but visible through a window.

Dealers today oftentimes sell gold coins in "slabs," hobby slang for hard-plastic holders issued by third-party grading services. For a fee, dealers and collectors can submit coins to the grading services to obtain a professional, unbiased opinion on the coins'

Coin glossary
Edge: The cylindrical surface of a coin between the two sides. The edge can be plain, reeded, ornamented, or lettered.

An Official Whitman® Guidebook

The Official AMERICAN NUMISMATIC ASSOCIATION

Grading Standards for United States Coins

6th EDITION
EVERY COIN, EVERY GRADE, CIRCULATED TO MINT STATE

1864

Edited by **Kenneth Bressett**
With narrative by Q. David Bowers

Books can help collectors learn how to grade coins.

Coin glossary
Obverse: The front or "heads" side of a coin.

grades. The service then encapsulates the coins in the holders and labels them with the coin's date, mint mark, denomination, grade, and a unique serial number. The grading-service holders are also suitable for long-term storage.

Collectors should also consider security. At the least, a fireproof home safe in a low-humidity environment should be used to store coins of any value. Secure home storage allows collectors to look at their coins whenever they want to, but a bank safety-deposit box provides added protection from theft and flood or fire damage.

Either way, stored coins should be checked several times a year for signs of spotting or discoloration. The holders should also be checked for signs of deterioration, rust, mildew, or other problems.

CHECK YOUR INSURANCE

Collectors should contact their agents to see if their standard homeowners' policies provide more than just a nominal amount of coverage for loss of collectible coins. Agents may be able to provide specific coverage for coins. Also, the American Numismatic Association offers collection insurance to its members at group rates.

LEARN ABOUT COINS

Coin collecting and investing should include an ongoing but enjoyable and rewarding quest for knowledge on the subject. Collectors and investors should read books, magazines, and value guides on coins. They should visit coin shops and museums with coin displays. They should consider joining a local, state, or regional coin club or the national American Numismatic Association to meet fellow collectors and learn from them.

Value guides – such as the ones appearing in this and other books and periodicals published by Krause Publications – provide independent information on the current retail prices for coins. Studying them familiarizes collectors and investors with what is rare, what is common, and the approximate prices they can expect to pay when acquiring coins.

LEARN TO GRADE

Slabs have added some stability to the subjective practice of grading coins, or quantifying the amount of wear on a coin and its overall condition. But even an expert, third-party opinion remains just that – an opinion.

Collectors should study one or more books on grading, such as *The Official American Numismatic Association Grading Standards for United States Coins*, and learn to make their own judgments on

GOLD RUSH

a coin's condition, its relationship to its value, and what they are willing to pay for that coin. Collectors should take advantage of opportunities to examine lots of coins at shows, shops, museums, displays, and club meetings. They should learn the key points of grading one or more individual series and then compare those key points among the coins they see in real life.

WHERE TO BUY COINS

Just about every city of any size has one or more local coin shops, usually owned and staffed by a dealer who started as a collector. Larger shops and collectible-coin businesses may have a large staff of employees who are also knowledgeable and experienced in buying and selling collectible gold coins.

Mexico, 8 escudos, 1825-1870.

The aforementioned shows, held in cities large and small, give collectors and investors the chance to shop the offerings of many dealers at one location. Shows sponsored by local, state, and regional coin-collecting clubs also feature non-commercial exhibits and seminars, which provide important educational opportunities for collectors and investors. Coin-collecting periodicals – such as *Coins* magazine, *Numismatic News*, and *World Coin News* – list upcoming coin shows throughout the country. The events listings in local newspapers may also include coin shows. Among the nation's largest shows are the twice-annual conventions of the American Numismatic Association, which are held in various cities throughout the United States.

Mail order is also a time-tested method for purchasing coins. The coin-collecting periodicals mentioned above are also marketplaces for coins through advertisements from dealers across the country. The advertising dealers offer a return policy so collectors and investors can examine coins firsthand before committing to the purchase.

Auctions are another time-tested and fun way to acquire coins. Large and small auction houses nationwide stage sales regularly, oftentimes in conjunction with a major show. Several weeks before the auction, they usually offer catalogs picturing and describing each coin in the sale. The catalogs themselves are educational tools for collectors and investors.

Attending a coin auction is exciting and educational, too, but it is not necessary to attend the sale in person to bid on coins. Larger auction companies usually allow collectors and investors to also bid by mail, fax, telephone, or on-line. Potential buyers should check the sale terms before bidding. Most auction companies today charge a buyer's premium of 15 percent of the selling price – an additional expense for buyers that must be considered when they bid on coins.

Coin glossary
Reverse: The backside or "tails" side of a coin, opposite from the side with the coin's principal design figure.

CHAPTER 3

HISTORY OF THE GOLD-COIN WORLD

Gold has been a valued substance for as long as history can determine, and it was used in some of the first coins struck, in Asia Minor in the 600s B.C. The Persian Empire (546-334 B.C.) owned much of the world's gold at the time and struck large quantities of gold coins called "darics." Few of them, however, survive today. Carthage, a powerful city and state in North Africa, also was a major player in gold coinage at the time. The Phoenician empire took advantage of gold deposits on the Iberian Peninsula and struck coins called "staters" in electrum – an alloy of gold and silver.

After its origins in Asia Minor, the concept of coinage spread throughout Europe, but it took a while for gold to catch on as a coinage metal on the continent. Greece mined little gold compared to Persia's vast holdings, and what gold it did own was held in reserve rather than turned into coins. Persia's prolific daric was the primary gold coin circulating in Greek city-states. Most Greek coins were silver; gold was used for coinage only when silver supplies were depleted.

Rome, aureus,
Augustus Caesaer

Silver continued to be the focus of European coinage as the Roman Empire ascended to power in the late fourth and third centuries B.C. Rome accumulated great wealth in gold through its conquests, including the vast deposits of the Iberian Peninsula, formerly held by Carthage. But like the Greeks, the Romans held most of their gold in reserve and struck gold coins only in emergencies. The first Roman gold coin was a stater struck in 215 B.C. to help finance the Second Punic War against Carthage.

In the second and first centuries B.C., the Roman senate granted Roman generals the right to strike coins from captured silver and gold so they could pay their soldiers. A Roman general in Asia Minor, L. Cornelius Sull, struck a gold "aureus" to commemorate a victory – the first Roman gold coin struck in quantity.

Rome, aureus,
Emperor Nero

Byzantine Empire, nomisma.

Great Britain, angel, Philip & Mary, ruled 1554-1558.

Julius Caesar continued his military right to strike coins after becoming dictator of the empire in the late first century B.C. His aureus was the first Roman gold coin not struck out of necessity and made circulating gold coinage more common.

In the first century A.D., Emperor Nero further expanded gold coinage by continuing to strike an aureus and adding a gold quinarius, which was half the value of an aureus. Both coins used almost pure gold and were issued in large quantities.

Gold coins continued to go through various debasements and reforms over the next 200 to 300 years, but they now enjoyed widespread circulation in the Roman empire and found their way to other lands through trade. After the empire was split, its eastern faction, the Byzantine Empire, continued to supply Europe with gold coins as the metal became scarce in western Europe. Officially, the Byzantine gold coin was called a "nomisma," but in western Europe, it was commonly called a "bezant," or "coin of Byzantium."

In time, however, the nomisma also fell victim to debasement, which reflected the declining state of the Byzantine Empire. The empire officially ended when Constantinople fell to the Turks in 1453.

As the modern map of western Europe started to take shape during the Middle Ages, gold coins were an important part of the continent's development. In the 1200s, Venice and Florence in Italy were important cities for world trade. Venice issued a gold "ducat" coin, and Florence issued a gold "florin" coin. Both coins were known for their purity and were widely accepted in international trade.

In France, Louis IX started the country's first regal gold coinage with the introduction of the "ecu" in 1266. His successors followed with similar gold coins struck in larger quantities. In England, Edward III, who ruled from 1327 to 1377, started the country's first regular gold coinage when he introduced a "florin" in 1344. A heavier "noble" gold coin followed shortly thereafter, and a smaller "angel" gold coin was introduced in 1464. They were followed

GOLD RUSH

Great Britain, sovereign, Henry VIII, ruled 1509-1547.

by the famous and intricately designed "sovereign" gold coin, introduced by Henry VII (1485-1509).

Other lands followed with their own versions of gold coins – the "gulden" in present-day Germany, the "cavalier d'or" in The Netherlands, among others.

The Renaissance years of the 14th, 15th, and 16th centuries saw advances in coin production and design. Previously, all coins were hand struck. A worker placed a planchet on top of a die and hammered away until a suitable design impression appeared. It is believed that the Italians were the first to use some type of machinery in coin production. Water or horses powered machinery that rolled metal into an even thickness so consistent planchets could be produced. Donato Bramante (1444-1514) is believed to have invented the screw press, which pressed the die into a planchet to produce the image on the coin.

Henry II (1547-1559) of France installed machinery at the Paris mint to produce coins. He was also the first monarch to place his portrait on a gold coin. Portraits and other images on coins became more natural and realistic as design methods advanced. All English coins were struck by machine beginning in 1662.

In the 1500s, gold and silver from the New World flowed into Europe. Spain in particular benefited from its colonial riches. Its mint in Mexico City produced the first coins

The marks of the French

In addition to the dates and mint marks customary on western coinage, French coins also contain two or three small privy marks. One is for the engraver general, who was responsible for the dies that struck the coins. The second is for the director of the mint that struck the coin. A third mark for the local engraver may also appear.

Great Britain, 5 guineas, James II, ruled 1685-1688.

Check the mint marks

Many Spanish colonial mints struck coins similar to regular Spanish issues until the 1820s. The colonial issues are distinguished from the regular issues by their mint marks.

A wealth of mints

Mexico's first republic, established in 1823, used 14 different mints to strike coins. All the mints used the same basic designs but many variations exist depending on the mint.

struck in the New World in 1536 — several small-denomination silver pieces. Spain's Charles I, however, prohibited the striking of gold coins in the New World. Gold was shipped back to Seville, where it was struck into coins bearing an "S" mint mark. The 22-karat gold Spanish "pistole" became the new standard for international trade.

The Spanish ban on minting gold coins abroad ended in 1675. The Mexico City mint was the first to produce gold coins; Lima followed shortly afterward. Meanwhile, the flow of gold from the New World to the Old World slowed greatly in the 1600s.

In the 1700s, ducats, issued by various European countries, became the most prominent gold coins. Late in the century, the French republic, after the 1792 revolution, issued few gold coins. But Napoleon Bonaparte changed that after taking power. He issued large numbers of gold 20-franc and 40-franc pieces.

Some have called the approximately 100 years from Napoleon's downfall to the outbreak of World War I the golden age of gold coins. They circulated widely in many countries as commerce flourished for many of those years and the world was at relative peace.

In 1817, Great Britain introduced a new sovereign that was 0.917 fine and contained 0.2354 ounces of gold. A half sovereign containing 0.1177 ounces of gold was introduced the same year.

Some German coins had taken on commemorative qualities by marking royal events starting in the 17th century. That continued into the 19th century. Among the gold commemoratives was an 1841 4-ducat marking the 25th anniversary of King Wilhelm's reign.

GOLD RUSH

Gold coinage played varying roles in the development of other lands. For centuries, China relied on cast coins made from base metals. Locally produced gold coinage did not appear in the country until the late 19th century. Chinese cash coins also circulated in Japan, which was a relative latecomer to coinage. A uniform coinage, which included some gold, did not appear in Japan until the 16th century.

In contrast, Russia took advantage of its large gold deposits to produce more than 50 million 5-rouble coins during the reign of Nicholas I (1825-1855). The Arab empire introduced the "dinar" in the 7th century. It emulated the Byzantine gold solidus, a stalwart of the Mediterranean economy. In the 15th century, the Ottoman Empire rose to power in the region after the Byzantine Empire fell. The Ottomans struck their first gold coin – the "altun" – in 1478. Their coinage emulated the size and weight of Europe's most popularly circulating coins.

India has a long coinage history that some believe dates back as far as the early Greeks. The country's Gupta kings of the late third century produced mostly gold coins along with some silver and bronze. India's gold-coinage tradition continued for many centuries later.

In the 20th century, circulating gold coinage fell victim to modern economic pressures and was discontinued. Remnants of various nations' gold coinage heritage, however, can still be found in modern-day bullion coins and commemoratives. Great Britain, for example, still issues gold sovereigns in traditional weights and specifications as bullion coins and commemoratives. Among them was a 2002 issue to mark the golden jubilee of Queen Elizabeth II's reign.

Few common citizens of the Middle Ages or Renaissance years, or even into the 19th century, may have actually possessed a gold coin of their era. But the examples of these coins that still survive today are important artifacts of the world's economic development and the lands and leaders that participated in it.

Switzerland, 100 francs, 1925.

The Chinese coinage crises

China nearly ceased the striking of coins in the 1930s and '40s because of war and uncontrollable inflation. The land relied on large amounts of paper currency issued by nationalist, communist, and Japanese occupation authorities.

Coins as awards

Russian gold ducats struck prior to Peter I (1689-1725) are believed to have been awards for military personnel rather than coinage intended for circulation. The higher the rank of the person receiving the award, the bigger the coin.

CHAPTER 4

THE JOY OF COLLECTING WORLD GOLD COINS

World gold coins offer a vast scope of collecting opportunities. There are a multitude of countries from which to choose, each with its unique history, designs, and gold-coin traditions. There are a multitude of sizes from which to choose. There are a multitude of price ranges; even some gold coins going back as far as the 1600s are affordable for many collectors. And there are a multitude of strategies collectors and investors can use to build their collections.

When deciding which gold coins to acquire, a collector should start with the basic guidelines that apply to any coin-collecting pursuit: Collect what you like, have a road map, and buy the best you can afford. The basic tenet that a collection can be whatever a collector wants it to be also applies to gold coins. Following, however, are some tips and comments on traditional collecting strategies and their application to world gold coins.

Great Britain, sovereign, 1826, George IV, ruled 1820-1830.

BY SERIES

The traditional coin-collecting pursuit of acquiring one example of each date and mint mark within a particular series may seem daunting at first considering the vast scope of world gold coins. Some denominations and designs within those denominations span several decades or even a century or more. But the task becomes less daunting with a further breakdown of a particular series.

For example, Great Britain introduced new gold half sovereign and sovereign coins in 1817. The half sovereign was struck through 1915, and the sovereign was struck through 1917 and again in 1925. Proof-only versions of each were struck in 1937. The sovereign was struck again from 1957 through 1968. Modern collector versions of the half sovereign were struck starting in 1980 and of the sovereign starting in 1974.

A collector could focus on one or the other denomination starting in 1817 and continuing through 1915 for the half sovereign and 1925 for the sovereign. Assembling a complete collection of either denomination would require time and prudent management of a collecting budget, but most

individual dates within those series are affordable for many collectors.

To get started, a collector could focus on acquiring one example of each design type within one of the series or one example of each monarch depicted within the series. Once that goal is completed, the collector could then start filling in the other dates in the series. Eventually, a collection of one or even both series could be completed.

This same breakdown and step-by-step approach can be applied to many other series in world gold coinage.

France, 1864, 20 francs, Napoleon III, ruled 1852-1870.

BY COUNTRY

Collectors sometimes focus on coins of a particular country because of some emotional nexus with that land. It may have been their ancestors' homeland, or they may simply like the coin designs and history of a particular country.

Many strategies can be pursued within the scope of collecting by country. A collector may attempt to acquire one example of each ruler whose image appeared on the country's gold coinage or focus on the coinage of one particular ruler. Or the collector may pursue one example of each gold denomination or design type produced.

Any of the collecting goals could also be narrowed to a certain period – a particular century, for example, or range of years with some historical or personal significance.

Italy, 20 lire, 1873, Viottorio Emanuele II, ruled 1861-1878.

BY REGION

A gold-coin collection could also focus on a particular continent or geographic region within that continent. Examples of the former include coins of South America or the Middle East. Examples of the latter include coins

GOLD RUSH

of the German States, the Iberian Peninsula, or colonies of a particular country.

Assembling a complete collection of all coins of a particular region is not practical for most collectors, so a further breakdown in collecting goals are in order. That could include focusing on a particular ruler, period, denomination, or some combination thereof. It could also include some form of type collecting – one coin of each ruler, for example.

BY EMPIRE

A coin collection can be a virtual history book of an empire. It would document the dates of the empire's rise to power and fall or contraction of power. It would document the rulers that reigned over the empire. And it would document the various lands that fell under the empire's domain, including the dates of conquest and the dates of loss or independence.

Argentina, argentino (5 pesos), 1887.

BY ERA

Some collectors focus on gold coins of a particular era. It could be a certain century, the reign of a certain monarch, an era with personal significance to a collector, or an important historical time.

For example, a collector could focus on the age of exploration and colonization of the New World. Gold coins of this era could include those produced in the colonies and those produced in the mother land with gold shipped back from the colonies. It could also include the first coins produced by newly independent nations as they broke away from their colonial status.

There are many other possibilities limited only to a collector's imagination and his or her historical interests.

Venezuela, 10 bolivares, 1930.

Great
Britain, sovereign
(1887-1892), Victo-
ria, ruled 1837-1901.

Great Britain, sov-
ereign (1957-1968),
Elizabeth II, ruled
since 1952.

ONE PER COUNTRY

Another common collecting strategy is to acquire one example of the coinage of as many countries as possible. Narrowing the focus here could include a particular geographic region, century, or era.

It could also include a particular coin type issued across geographical boundaries. For example, many countries issued gold trade coins called ducats. A collector could focus on acquiring one ducat from each country that issued this type. Some countries issued coins with the same or similar specifications to coins issued in other countries. For example, France's 20-franc piece of the 1800s had the same specifications as Italy's 20-lira coin of the same era (6.4516 grams total weight, 0.900-fine gold, 0.1867 ounces of gold). A collector could pursue examples of these international specifications by either series or type.

BY THEME

Modern commemorative and circulation coinage designs gave rise to collecting coins with a common theme. Examples include coins that depict animals or ships, coins from one or more countries that commemorate a certain event, or coins of a certain date, such as 2000.

Modern coinage can complement a collection of the classics. For example, a collection of coins from the era of exploration could be accessorized by modern coins that commemorate anniversaries associated with those explorations.

A collection can also be built around a certain event. For example, Great Britain and many lands still associated with the British monarchy issued commemorative coins to mark the golden jubilee of Queen Elizabeth II's reign in 2002. These recent coins could be combined with coins from the 1950s that first depicted the queen.

BY COLLECTOR'S CHOICE

As noted above, various aspects of the listed strategies overlap and can be combined and mixed to form a goal that interests an individual collector. The result should be a gold-coin collection that is affordable and attainable for the collector, and a collection that brings enjoyment and satisfaction.

CHAPTER 5

CLASSIC WORLD GOLD COINS

AUSTRALIA

Australia's rich mineral deposits include gold, which provided for extensive mintage of trade coinage in the land as a British colony and later as a commonwealth. The half sovereign and sovereign coinage is readily available and affordable. Prices for many individual dates and mint marks in circulated grades are based on the bullion value of their gold content. Coins without mint marks were struck at Sydney and are designated in the listings with an "(sy)". Coins with an S mint mark were also struck at Sydney. Other mint marks are M for Melbourne and P for Perth. The British monarch, as Australia's head of state, continued to be depicted on Australian coins after establishment of the commonwealth.

KM# 5

KM# 1 1/2 SOVEREIGN
3.9940 g., 0.9170 Gold .1177 oz. AGW   **Ruler:** Victoria **Obv:** Fillet head left **Rev:** Crowned AUSTRALIA within wreath

Date	Mintage	F	VF	XF	Unc	BU
1855(sy)	21,000	8,500	16,500	45,000	95,000	—
1856(sy)	478,000	500	1,750	4,500	12,500	—

KM# 3 1/2 SOVEREIGN
3.9940 g., 0.9170 Gold .1177 oz. AGW   **Ruler:** Victoria **Obv:** Head left, hair tied with banksia wreath **Rev:** AUSTRALIA within wreath

Date	Mintage	F	VF	XF	Unc	BU
1857(sy)	537,000	250	350	4,500	10,000	—
1857(sy) Proof	—	Value: 85,000				
1858(sy)	483,000	250	350	5,000	14,500	—
1858(sy) (Error)	—	—	—	—	—	—
1859(sy)	341,000	250	350	5,500	18,000	—
1860(sy)	156,000	450	1,750	12,000	30,000	—
1861(sy)	186,000	250	375	5,000	12,500	—
1862(sy)	210,000	250	375	5,500	15,000	—
1863(sy)	348,000	250	350	5,500	15,000	—
1864(sy)	141,000	250	650	7,000	20,000	—
1865(sy)	62,000	300	650	6,500	18,500	—
1866(sy)	154,000	275	600	5,500	17,500	—
1866(sy) Proof	—	Value: 60,000				

KM# 5 1/2 SOVEREIGN
3.9940 g., 0.9170 Gold .1177 oz. AGW **Ruler:** Victoria **Obv:** Young head left **Rev:** Crowned shield, mint mark below

Date	Mintage	F	VF	XF	Unc	BU
1871S	180,000	85.00	165	1,650	10,000	—
1871S Proof	—	Value: 50,000				
1872S	356,000	85.00	165	1,650	10,000	—
1873M	165,000	85.00	165	1,850	11,250	—
1875S	252,000	85.00	165	1,650	10,000	—
1877M	140,000	100	200	1,850	11,250	—
1879S	220,000	85.00	165	1,350	8,500	—
1880S	80,000	85.00	185	2,250	12,250	—
1880S Proof	—	Value: 45,000				
1881S	62,000	85.00	185	2,500	13,500	—
1881M	42,000	95.00	225	2,750	15,500	—
1881 Proof	—	Value: 45,000				
1882S	52,000	125	250	3,750	25,000	—
1882M	106,000	85.00	175	1,750	10,000	—
1883S	220,000	80.00	155	1,100	6,750	—
1883S Proof	—	Value: 45,000				
1884M	48,000	95.00	225	3,250	20,000	—
1884M Proof	—	Value: 45,000				
1885M	11,000	250	550	5,500	35,000	—
1886S	82,000	85.00	165	1,750	11,500	—
1886M	38,000	85.00	175	2,250	12,500	—
1886 Proof	—	Value: 45,000				
1887S	134,000	85.00	165	1,550	10,000	—
1887S Proof	—	Value: 45,000				
1887M	64,000	125	250	3,750	27,500	—

What do the slashes mean?

Slashes in dates indicate an "overdate." This occurs when one or more digits of the date are re-engraved over a date on an old die to save on dies or correct an error. Portions of the old date can still be seen under the new one.

KM# 9 1/2 SOVEREIGN
3.9940 g., 0.9170 Gold .1177 oz. AGW **Ruler:** Victoria **Obv:** Jubilee head left **Rev:** Crowned shield, mint mark below

Date	Mintage	F	VF	XF	Unc	BU
1887S	Inc. above	80.00	120	375	3,500	—
1887S Proof	—	Value: 50,000				
1887M	Inc. above	90.00	130	450	4,750	—
1887M Proof	—	Value: 50,000				
1888M Proof	—	Value: 52,500				
1889S	64,000	90.00	130	675	6,750	—
1889M Proof	—	Value: 52,500				
1890M Proof	—	Value: 52,500				
1891S With J.E.B.	154,000	100	160	975	9,500	—
1891S Without J.E.B.	Inc. above	90.00	130	675	6,750	—
1891M Proof	—	Value: 52,500				

Date	Mintage	F	VF	XF	Unc	BU
1892S Proof	—	Value: 52,500				
1892M Proof	—	Value: 52,500				
1893S Proof	—	Value: 52,500				
1893M	110,000	80.00	120	600	6,250	—
1893M Proof	—	Value: 45,000				

KM# 12 1/2 SOVEREIGN
3.9940 g., 0.9170 Gold .1177 oz. AGW **Ruler:** Victoria **Obv:** Veiled head left **Obv. Designer:** Thomas Brock **Rev:** St. George slaying dragon, mint mark above date

Date	Mintage	F	VF	XF	Unc	BU
1893S	250,000	75.00	100	500	2,750	—
1893S Proof	—	Value: 50,000				
1893M	—	10,000	—	—	—	—
1893M Proof	—	Value: 52,500				
1894M Proof	—	Value: 52,500				
1895M Proof	—	Value: 52,500				
1896M	218,000	80.00	130	600	3,250	—
1896M Proof	—	Value: 45,000				
1897S	230,000	75.00	100	500	3,000	—
1897M Proof	—	Value: 52,500				
1898M Proof	—	Value: 52,500				
1899M	90,000	80.00	130	800	3,250	—
1899M Proof	—	Value: 45,000				
1899P Proof	—	—	—	—	—	—
1900S	260,000	75.00	100	500	3,000	—
1900M	113,000	80.00	130	800	3,250	—
1900M Proof	—	Value: 45,000				
1900P	119,000	80.00	130	800	3,250	—
1901M Proof	—	Value: 55,000				
1901P Proof	—	Value: 70,000				
Note: Imperfect proofs worth substantially less.						

KM# 7 SOVEREIGN
7.9881 g., 0.9170 Gold .2354 oz. AGW **Ruler:** Victoria **Obv:** Young head left, mint mark below **Rev:** St. George slaying dragon **Note:** Mintage figures include St. George and shield types. No separate mintage figures are known.

Date	Mintage	F	VF	XF	Unc	BU
1871S	2,814,000	BV	200	1,250	5,000	—
1871S Proof	—	Value: 50,000				

Date	Mintage	F	VF	XF	Unc	BU
1872S	1,815,000	—	BV	275	2,200	—
1872M	748,000	BV	325	1,750	6,000	—
1873S	1,478,000	—	BV	250	2,500	—
1873M	752,000	—	BV	225	2,000	—
1873M Proof	—	Value: 45,000				
1874S	1,899,000	—	BV	225	2,500	—
1874M	1,373,000	—	BV	200	2,000	—
1874M Proof	—	Value: 45,000				
1875S	2,122,000	—	BV	225	1,850	—
1875M	1,888,000	—	BV	225	1,500	—
1875M Proof	—	Value: 45,000				
1876S	1,613,000	—	BV	160	1,750	—
1876M	2,124,000	—	BV	160	1,250	—
1877S Rare	2	—	—	—	—	—
1877M	1,487,000	—	BV	160	1,150	—
1878M	2,171,000	—	BV	160	1,150	—
1879S	1,366,000	175	300	1,650	5,500	—
1879M	2,740,000	—	BV	160	1,000	—
1880S	1,459,000	—	BV	225	1,850	—
1880S Proof	—	Value: 45,000				
1880M	3,053,000	—	BV	160	1,150	—
1881S	1,360,000	—	BV	225	1,500	—
1881M	2,324,000	—	BV	160	1,150	—
1881M Proof	—	Value: 45,000				
1882S	1,298,000	—	BV	160	1,250	—
1882M	2,466,000	—	BV	160	1,250	—
1883S	1,108,000	BV	175	600	3,000	—
1883M	2,050,000	—	BV	160	1,000	—
1883M Proof	—	Value: 45,000				
1884S	1,595,000	—	BV	160	1,000	—
1884M	2,942,000	—	BV	160	950	—
1884M Proof	—	Value: 45,000				
1885S	1,486,000	—	BV	160	1,150	—
1885M	2,957,000	—	BV	160	1,000	—
1885M Proof	—	Value: 45,000				
1886S	1,677,000	—	BV	160	1,150	—
1886M	2,902,000	—	BV	160	950	—
1886M Proof	—	Value: 45,000				
1887S	1,000,000	—	BV	225	1,350	—
1887M	1,915,000	—	BV	225	1,350	—
1887M Proof	—	Value: 45,000				

KM# 6 SOVEREIGN

7.9881 g., 0.9170 Gold .2354 oz. AGW **Ruler:** Elizabeth II **Obv:** Young head left, date below **Rev:** Mint mark below crowned shield **Note:** Mintage figures include St. George and shield types. No separate mintage figures are known. Mint mark placement varies.

Date	Mintage	F	VF	XF	Unc	BU
1871S Incuse ww	2,814,000	—	BV	200	1,250	—
1871S Raised ww	Inc. above	—	BV	200	1,250	—
1871S Proof	—	Value: 50,000				
1872S	1,815,000	—	BV	200	1,500	—
1872/1M	748,000	225	475	1,250	2,250	—
1872M	Inc. above	—	BV	200	1,250	—
1873S	1,478,000	—	BV	200	1,250	—
1874M	1,373,000	—	BV	225	2,000	—
1875S	2,122,000	—	BV	200	1,000	—
1875S Proof	—	Value: 50,000				
1877S	1,590,000	—	BV	200	1,000	—
1878S	1,259,000	—	BV	200	1,000	—
1879S	1,366,000	—	BV	200	1,000	—
1880S	1,459,000	—	BV	200	1,000	—
1880S Proof	—	Value: 50,000				
1880M	3,053,000	700	1,850	4,250	9,500	—
1880M Proof	—	Value: 50,000				
1881S	1,360,000	—	BV	200	1,450	—
1881M	2,324,000	BV	175	325	1,500	—
1882S	1,298,000	—	BV	200	1,450	—
1882M	2,466,000	—	BV	200	1,450	—
1883S	1,108,000	—	BV	185	950	—
1883S Proof	—	Value: 50,000				
1883M	2,049,999	200	325	1,000	3,750	—
1883M Proof	—	Value: 50,000				
1884S	1,595,000	—	BV	185	1,000	—
1884M	2,942,000	—	BV	185	1,000	—
1884M Proof	—	Value: 50,000				
1885S	1,486,000	—	BV	185	950	—
1885M	2,957,000	—	BV	185	950	—
1885M Proof	—	Value: 50,000				
1886S	1,677,000	—	BV	185	1,000	—
1886S Proof	—	Value: 50,000				
1886M	2,902,000	3,750	7,500	11,500	30,000	—
1886M Proof	—	Value: 75,000				
1887S	1,000,000	—	BV	285	2,000	—
1887S Proof	—	Value: 50,000				
1887M	1,915,000	750	1,650	4,000	10,000	—
1887M Proof	—	Value: 50,000				

KM# 10 SOVEREIGN

7.9881 g., 0.9170 Gold .2354 oz. AGW **Ruler:** Victoria **Obv:** Jubilee head left **Rev:** St. George slaying dragon, mint mark above date **Note:** Designers initials on reverse omitted on some pieces 1880S-1882S and 1881M-1882M. Mint mark placement varies.

Date	Mintage	F	VF	XF	Unc	BU
1887S	1,002,000	BV	185	450	1,150	—
1887S Proof	—	Value: 40,000				
1887M	940,000	—	BV	165	275	—
1887M Proof	—	Value: 40,000				
1888S	2,187,000	—	BV	160	245	—
1888M	2,830,000	—	BV	160	245	—
1888M Proof	—	Value: 40,000				
1889S	3,262,000	—	BV	160	245	—
1889M	2,732,000	—	BV	160	245	—
1889M Proof	—	Value: 40,000				
1890S	2,808,000	—	BV	160	245	—
1890M	2,473,000	—	BV	160	245	—
1890M Proof	—	Value: 40,000				
1891S	2,596,000	—	BV	160	245	—
1891M	2,749,000	—	BV	160	245	—
1892S	2,837,000	—	BV	160	245	—
1892M	3,488,000	—	BV	160	245	—
1893S	1,498,000	—	BV	160	245	—
1893S Proof	—	Value: 40,000				
1893M	1,649,000	—	BV	160	245	—
1893M Proof	—	Value: 40,000				

KM# 13 SOVEREIGN

7.9881 g., 0.9170 Gold .2354 oz. AGW **Ruler:** Victoria **Obv:** Older veiled head left **Rev:** St. George slaying the dragon

Date	Mintage	F	VF	XF	Unc	BU
1893S	1,346,000	—	BV	155	225	—
1893S Proof	—	Value: 40,000				
1893M	1,914,000	—	BV	155	225	—
1893M Proof	—	Value: 40,000				
1894S	3,067,000	—	BV	155	200	—
1894S Proof	—	Value: 40,000				
1894M	4,166,000	—	BV	155	200	—
1894M Proof	—	Value: 40,000				
1895S	2,758,000	—	BV	155	200	—
1895M	4,165,000	—	BV	155	200	—
1895M Proof	—	Value: 40,000				
1896S	2,544,000	—	BV	155	200	—

What do the listed sale results mean? Some coins are too rare and come up for sale too seldomly to estimate values in different grades. In those instances, the most recent known auction or private-sale result for an example of the coin is listed. Included are the coin's date, the transaction date, the coin's grade, and the price realized.

Date	Mintage	F	VF	XF	Unc	BU
1896M	4,456,000	—	BV	155	200	—
1896M Proof	—		Value: 40,000			
1897S	2,532,000	—	BV	155	225	—
1897M	5,130,000	—	BV	155	200	—
1897M Proof	—		Value: 40,000			
1898S	2,548,000	—	BV	155	225	—
1898M	5,509,000	—	BV	155	200	—
1898M Proof	—		Value: 40,000			
1899S	3,259,000	—	BV	155	185	—
1899M	5,579,000	—	BV	155	185	—
1899M Proof	—		Value: 40,000			
1899P	690,000	BV	250	900	2,250	—
1899P Proof	—		Value: 45,000			
1900S	3,586,000	—	BV	155	185	—
1900M	4,305,000	—	BV	155	185	—
1900M Proof	—		Value: 40,000			
1900P	1,886,000	—	BV	155	220	—
1901S	3,012,000	—	BV	155	220	—
1901M	3,987,000	—	BV	155	220	—
1901M Proof	—		Value: 45,000			
1901P	2,889,000	—	BV	155	220	—
1901P Proof	—		Value: 45,000			

AUSTRIA

Franz Joseph I reigned from 1848 to 1916 and was the penultimate ruler of the Austro-Hungarian empire. Austria became a republic following World War I. His image appears on a long run of gold coins. Some issues remain affordable despite low mintages. Mint marks: A – Vienna. B – Kremnica. D – Salzburg. E – Karlsburg. G – Graz. M – Milan. V – Venice.

KM# 2167 DUCAT
3.4909 g., 0.9860 Gold .1106 oz. AGW **Ruler:** Franz II (I) **Obv:** Laureate head right **Obv. Legend:** FRANCISCVS II D. G. ROM... **Rev:** Crowned imperial double eagle **Rev. Legend:** ...D. LOTH. VEN. SAL.

Date	Mintage	F	VF	XF	Unc	BU
1804A	—	325	650	1,000	1,750	—
1805A	—	325	650	1,000	1,750	—
1806A	—	300	600	900	1,600	—
1806B	—	325	650	1,000	1,750	—
1806C	—	750	1,500	2,250	3,000	—
1806D	—	325	650	1,000	1,750	—

KM# 2168 DUCAT

3.4909 g., 0.9860 Gold .1106 oz. AGW **Ruler:** Franz II (I) **Obv:**
Laureate head right **Rev:** Crowned imperial double eagle **Rev.**
Legend: ... D. LO. SAL. WIRC.

Date	Mintage	F	VF	XF	Unc	BU
1806A	—	160	250	375	550	—
1806D	—	750	1,250	1,500	2,000	—
1807A	—	125	200	275	450	—
1807C	—	180	275	425	650	—
1808A	—	125	200	275	450	—
1808D Rare	—	—	—	—	—	—
1809A	—	125	200	275	450	—
1809B	—	160	250	375	575	—
1809D	—	500	700	950	1,200	—
1810A	—	125	200	275	450	—

KM# 2169 DUCAT

3.4909 g., 0.9860 Gold .1106 oz. AGW **Ruler:** Franz II (I) **Rev.**
Legend: ...LO: WI: ET IN. FR: DVX.

Date	Mintage	F	VF	XF	Unc	BU
1811A	—	85.00	125	200	300	—
1811B	—	85.00	125	200	300	—
1812A	—	85.00	125	200	300	—
1812B	—	85.00	125	200	300	—
1812G Rare	—	—	—	—	—	—
1813A	—	100	140	225	325	—
1813B	—	85.00	125	200	300	—
1813E	—	100	140	225	325	—
1813G Rare	—	—	—	—	—	—
1814A	—	85.00	125	200	300	—
1814B	—	100	140	225	325	—
1814E	—	100	140	225	325	—
1814G Rare	—	—	—	—	—	—
1815A	—	85.00	125	200	300	—
1815B	—	85.00	125	200	300	—
1815E	—	85.00	125	200	300	—
1815G	—	100	150	250	350	—

KM# 2170 DUCAT

3.4909 g., 0.9860 Gold .1106 oz. AGW **Ruler:** Franz II (I) **Obv:**
Laureate bust right **Rev:** Crowned imperial double eagle **Rev.**
Legend: ...GAL. LOD. IL. REX. A. A.

Date	Mintage	F	VF	XF	Unc	BU
1816A	—	85.00	125	200	300	—
1817A	—	85.00	125	200	300	—

Date	Mintage	F	VF	XF	Unc	BU
1818A	—	85.00	125	200	300	—
1818B	—	85.00	125	200	300	—
1818E	—	85.00	125	200	300	—
1818G	—	100	140	225	325	—
1819A	—	85.00	125	200	300	—
1819B	—	100	140	225	325	—
1819E	—	85.00	125	200	300	—
1819G	—	100	140	225	325	—
1819V	—	350	525	700	1,050	—
1820A	—	85.00	125	200	300	—
1820B	—	85.00	125	200	300	—
1820E	—	85.00	125	200	300	—
1820G	—	85.00	125	200	300	—
1821A	—	85.00	125	200	300	—
1821B	—	85.00	125	200	300	—
1821E	—	85.00	125	200	300	—
1821G	—	85.00	125	200	300	—
1822A	—	85.00	125	200	300	—
1822B	—	85.00	125	200	300	—
1822E	—	85.00	125	200	300	—
1822G	—	85.00	125	200	300	—
1823A	—	85.00	125	200	300	—
1823B	—	85.00	125	200	300	—
1823E	—	85.00	125	200	300	—
1823G	—	85.00	125	200	300	—
1824A	—	85.00	125	200	300	—
1824B	—	85.00	125	200	300	—
1824E	—	85.00	125	200	300	—
1824G	—	100	140	225	325	—
1824V	—	350	525	700	1,050	—

KM# 2171 DUCAT
3.4909 g., 0.9860 Gold .1106 oz. AGW   **Ruler:** Franz II (I) **Obv:** Ribbons on wreath forward across neck **Rev:** Crowned imperial double eagle

Date	Mintage	F	VF	XF	Unc	BU
1825A	—	85.00	125	200	300	—
1825B	—	100	135	225	325	—
1825E	—	110	160	250	375	—
1825G	—	—	—	—	—	—
1826A	—	85.00	125	200	300	—
1826B	—	110	160	250	375	—

Date	Mintage	F	VF	XF	Unc	BU
1826E	—	90.00	130	200	300	—
1826G Rare	—	—	—	—	—	—
1827A	—	85.00	125	200	300	—
1827B	—	110	160	250	375	—
1827E	—	110	160	250	375	—
1828A	—	100	140	225	325	—
1828B	—	85.00	125	200	300	—
1828E	—	85.00	125	200	300	—
1829A	—	85.00	125	180	275	—
1829B	—	85.00	125	200	300	—
1829E	—	85.00	125	200	300	—
1830A	—	85.00	125	180	275	—
1830B	—	100	130	200	300	—
1830E	—	90.00	130	200	300	—
1831A	—	1,100	1,600	2,400	3,200	—

KM# 2172 DUCAT

3.4909 g., 0.9860 Gold .1106 oz. AGW **Ruler:** Franz II (I) **Obv:** Ribbons on wreath behind neck **Rev:** Crowned imperial double eagle

Date	Mintage	F	VF	XF	Unc	BU
1831A	—	110	160	250	375	—
1832A	—	100	120	200	300	—
1832B	—	100	120	200	300	—
1833A	—	100	120	200	300	—
1833B	—	100	120	200	300	—
1833E	—	110	160	250	375	—
1834A	—	100	120	200	300	—
1834B	—	100	120	200	300	—
1834E	—	110	160	250	375	—
1835A	—	100	120	200	300	—
1835B	—	100	120	200	300	—
1835E	—	110	160	250	375	—

KM# 2261 DUCAT

3.5000 g., 0.9860 Gold 0.111 oz. AGW **Ruler:** Ferdinand I **Obv:** Laureate bust right **Obv. Legend:** FERDINANDVS I. D.G. AVSTRIAE. IMPERATOR. **Rev:** Crowned imperial double eagle **Rev. Legend:** HVNG. BOH. LOMB. ET VEN. - GAL. LOD. IL. REX. A. A.

Date	Mintage	F	VF	XF	Unc	BU
1835 A	—	275	500	800	1,200	—
1835 E	—	275	500	800	1,200	—
1836 A	—	160	275	450	650	—
1836 E	—	200	325	525	800	—

KM# 2262 DUCAT
3.4909 g., 0.9860 Gold .1106 oz. AGW **Ruler:** Ferdinand I **Obv:**
Laureate head right **Rev:** Crowned imperial double eagle

Date	Mintage	F	VF	XF	Unc	BU
1837A	—	BV	80.00	130	200	—
1837B	—	80.00	115	190	275	—
1837E	—	80.00	115	190	275	—
1838A	—	BV	80.00	180	275	—
1838B	—	80.00	115	190	275	—
1838E	—	80.00	115	190	275	—
1839A	—	BV	80.00	130	200	—
1839B	—	80.00	115	200	275	—
1839E	—	80.00	115	200	275	—
1840A	—	BV	80.00	130	200	—
1840B	—	BV	80.00	130	200	—
1840E	—	BV	80.00	140	225	—
1840V	—	475	650	975	1,275	—
1841A	—	BV	80.00	130	200	—
1841B	—	BV	80.00	110	180	—
1841E	—	BV	80.00	110	180	—
1841V	—	250	350	525	725	—
1842A	—	75.00	100	160	250	—
1842B	—	100	130	200	350	—
1842E	—	BV	80.00	110	180	—
1842V	—	200	275	700	1,000	—
1843A	—	BV	80.00	110	180	—
1843B	—	BV	80.00	130	200	—
1843E	—	BV	80.00	130	200	—
1843V	—	200	275	700	1,350	—
1844A	—	BV	80.00	110	180	—
1844B	—	BV	80.00	110	180	—
1844E	—	BV	80.00	110	180	—
1844V	—	200	275	700	1,350	—
1845A	—	BV	80.00	110	180	—
1845B	—	BV	80.00	110	180	—
1845E	—	BV	80.00	130	200	—
1845V	—	200	275	700	1,200	—
1846A	—	BV	80.00	130	200	—
1846B	—	BV	80.00	130	200	—
1846E	—	BV	80.00	130	200	—
1846V	—	200	275	700	1,000	—
1847A	—	BV	80.00	110	180	—
1847B	—	BV	80.00	110	180	—

What do the prices mean?

The prices listed are the approximate retail values for coins in the various grades listed. These are the approximate prices collectors can expect to pay when purchasing coins on the open market. The prices are guides only; actual selling prices on the open market will vary. The prices are compiled by Krause Publications' staff of independent market analysts, who monitor auction results and other sources for pricing information.

Date	Mintage	F	VF	XF	Unc	BU
1847E	—	80.00	100	180	250	—
1847V	—	250	350	550	775	—
1848A	—	BV	80.00	110	180	—
1848B	—	BV	80.00	110	180	—
1848E	—	BV	80.00	110	180	—
1848V	—	250	350	550	775	—

KM# 2268 DUCAT

3.4909 g., 0.9860 Gold .1106 oz. AGW **Ruler:** Franz Joseph I
Subject: 50th Jubilee **Obv:** Laureate head left **Rev:** Second date
below eagle

Date	Mintage	F	VF	XF	Unc	BU
1848/1898A	27,000	150	250	350	500	—
1849/1898A	2,292	500	1,000	1,300	1,800	—
1850/1898A	2,292	500	1,000	1,300	1,800	—
1851/1898A	2,292	500	1,000	1,300	1,800	—

KM# 2263 DUCAT

3.4909 g., 0.9860 Gold .1106 oz. AGW **Ruler:** Franz Joseph I
Obv: Laureate head right **Rev:** Crowned imperial double eagle

Date	Mintage	F	VF	XF	Unc	BU
1852A	—	80.00	100	160	225	—
1853A	—	90.00	120	180	250	—
1853B	114,000	90.00	110	180	250	—
1853E	—	100	130	200	250	—
1854A	—	BV	80.00	120	180	—
1854B	87,000	110	135	225	350	—
1854E	—	100	130	200	250	—
1854V	—	350	600	1,000	1,750	—
1855A	—	BV	80.00	120	180	—
1855B	133,000	160	225	350	550	—
1855E	—	90.00	110	180	250	—
1855V	—	250	450	800	1,200	—
1856A	—	BV	80.00	140	200	—
1856B	121,000	80.00	110	180	250	—
1856E	—	BV	80.00	140	200	—
1856V	—	250	450	800	1,200	—
1857A	—	BV	80.00	130	180	—
1857B	86,000	BV	80.00	130	200	—
1857E	—	100	140	225	350	—
1857V	—	250	450	800	1,200	—
1858A	—	BV	80.00	110	160	—
1858B	71,000	100	130	180	250	—

Date	Mintage	F	VF	XF	Unc	BU
1858E	—	90.00	110	180	250	—
1858M	—	300	1,000	2,000	2,750	—
1858V	—	250	450	800	1,200	—
1859A	—	BV	80.00	110	160	—
1859B	34,000	BV	80.00	140	200	—
1859E	—	BV	80.00	110	180	—
1859V	—	250	450	800	1,200	—

KM# 2264 DUCAT
3.4909 g., 0.9860 Gold .1106 oz. AGW **Ruler:** Franz Joseph I
Obv: Laureate head right **Rev:** Crowned imperial double eagle

Date	Mintage	F	VF	XF	Unc	BU
1860A	—	75.00	100	140	225	—
1860B	56,000	85.00	120	180	275	—
1860E	—	100	140	200	325	—
1860V	—	250	400	800	1,200	—
1861A	—	BV	80.00	120	200	—
1861B	121,000	75.00	100	160	250	—
1861E	—	90.00	120	200	325	—
1861V	—	325	800	1,750	2,500	—
1862A	—	BV	80.00	120	225	—
1862B	68,000	BV	90.00	140	225	—
1862E	—	75.00	100	160	225	—
1862V	—	200	400	800	1,200	—
1863A	—	BV	80.00	120	225	—
1863B	58,000	BV	80.00	120	225	—
1863E	—	BV	80.00	120	225	—
1863V	—	175	375	600	1,000	—
1864A	—	75.00	100	160	250	—
1864B	99,000	80.00	120	180	275	—
1864E	—	75.00	100	160	250	—
1864V	—	275	800	1,750	2,500	—
1865A	—	75.00	100	160	250	—
1865B	81,000	75.00	100	160	250	—
1865E	—	75.00	100	160	250	—
1865V	—	250	475	800	1,200	—

KM# 2265 DUCAT
3.4909 g., 0.9860 Gold .1106 oz. AGW **Ruler:** Franz Joseph
I **Obv:** Head right with heavier side whiskers **Rev:** Crowned
imperial double eagle

Date	Mintage	F	VF	XF	Unc	BU
1866A	—	80.00	115	200	350	—

Date	Mintage	F	VF	XF	Unc	BU
1866B	76,000	80.00	140	225	400	—
1866E	—	80.00	115	200	350	—
1866V	—	275	575	1,100	1,700	—

KM# 2266 DUCAT
3.4909 g., 0.9860 Gold .1106 oz. AGW **Ruler:** Franz Joseph I
Obv: Laureate head right **Rev:** Crowned imperial double eagle

Date	Mintage	F	VF	XF	Unc	BU
1867A	—	BV	90.00	130	180	—
1867B	112,000	BV	100	140	200	—
1867E	—	75.00	110	160	225	—
1868A	—	BV	90.00	130	180	—
1869A	—	BV	90.00	130	180	—
1870A	—	BV	90.00	130	180	—
1871A	—	BV	90.00	130	180	—
1872A	—	BV	90.00	130	180	—

KM# 2267 DUCAT
3.4909 g., 0.9860 Gold .1106 oz. AGW **Ruler:** Franz Joseph I
Obv: Laureate head right, heavy whiskers **Rev:** Crowned imperial double eagle **Note:** 996,721 pieces were struck from 1920-1936.

Date	Mintage	F	VF	XF	Unc	BU
1872	460,000	BV	100	125	175	—
1873	516,000	BV	100	125	175	—
1874	353,000	BV	100	125	175	—
1875	184,000	BV	100	125	175	—
1876	680,000	BV	80.00	125	150	—
1877	823,000	BV	80.00	125	175	—
1878	281,000	BV	80.00	125	175	—
1879	362,000	BV	80.00	125	175	—
1880	341,000	BV	100	150	225	—
1881	477,000	BV	80.00	125	175	—
1882	390,000	BV	100	125	175	—
1883	409,000	BV	100	125	175	—
1884	238,000	BV	80.00	125	175	—
1885	257,000	BV	80.00	125	150	—
1886	291,000	BV	80.00	125	150	—
1887	223,000	BV	80.00	100	150	—
1888	309,000	BV	80.00	100	150	—
1889	335,000	BV	80.00	100	150	—
1890	374,000	BV	80.00	100	150	—
1891	325,000	BV	80.00	100	150	—
1901	348,621	BV	100	125	175	—
1902	311,471	BV	100	125	175	—

KM# 2267

Date	Mintage	F	VF	XF	Unc	BU
1903	380,014	BV	100	125	175	—
1904	517,118	BV	100	125	175	—
1905	391,534	BV	125	150	200	—
1906	491,574	BV	125	150	200	—
1907	554,205	BV	125	175	250	—
1908	408,832	BV	80.00	125	175	—
1909	366,318	BV	80.00	100	150	—
1910	440,424	BV	80.00	100	150	—
1911	590,826	BV	80.00	100	125	—
1912	494,991	BV	80.00	100	125	—
1913	319,926	BV	80.00	100	125	—
1914	378,241	BV	80.00	100	125	—
1915 Restrike	—	—	—	—	BV+ 10%	—
1915 Restrike, Proof	—	BV+5%				
1951 Error for 1915	—	75.00	125	150	225	—

CANADA

British-produced sovereigns circulated in Canada in the 19th century. Late in the century, gold was discovered in the Yukon, and a mint was established in Ottawa in 1908. Its first gold coins were more British sovereigns struck from dies prepared in London, but the coins were distinguished by a C mint mark for Ottawa. The Ottawa-produced sovereigns continued to be struck until 1919 along side gold decimal coins in 1912, 1913, and 1914.

KM# 14 SOVEREIGN
Weight: 7.9881 g. **Composition:** 0.9170 Gold .2354 oz. AGW
Ruler: Edward VII **Reverse:** St. George slaying dragon, mint mark below horse's rear hooves

Date	Mintage	F-12	VF-20	XF-40	AU-50	MS-60	MS-63
1908C	636	1,250	1,850	2,350	2,600	2,850	4,000
1909C	16,273	160	200	245	285	500	1,600
1910C	28,012	BV	185	225	265	500	2,000

KM# 20 SOVEREIGN
Weight: 7.9881 g. **Composition:** 0.9170 Gold 0.2354 oz. AGW
Ruler: George V **Reverse:** St. George slaying dragon, mint mark below horse's rear hooves

Date	Mintage	F-12	VF-20	XF-40	AU-50	MS-60	MS-63
1911C	256,946	—	—	BV	155	160	180
1913C	3,715	550	700	950	1,200	1,500	3,000
1914C	14,871	175	225	350	450	600	950
1916C About 20 known	—	8,000	12,500	15,750	17,750	20,000	27,500

KM# 20

KM# 27

Date	Mintage	F-12	VF-20	XF-40	AU-50	MS-60	MS-63
Note: Stacks' A.G. Carter Jr. Sale 12-89 Gem BU realized $82,500							
1917C	58,845	—	—	BV	160	175	500
1918C	106,514	—	—	BV	160	175	750
1919C	135,889	—	—	BV	160	175	650

KM# 26 5 DOLLARS
Weight: 8.3592 g. **Composition:** 0.9000 Gold 0.2419 oz. AGW
Ruler: George V **Obverse:** Crowned bust left **Obv. Designer:**
E. B. MacKennal **Reverse:** Arms within wreath, date and
denomination below **Rev. Designer:** W. H. J. Blakemore

Date	Mintage	F-12	VF-20	XF-40	AU-50	MS-60	MS-63
1912	165,680	BV	160	175	200	250	550
1913	98,832	BV	160	175	200	250	600
1914	31,122	175	275	350	425	650	2,000

KM# 27 10 DOLLARS
Weight: 16.7185 g. **Composition:** 0.9000 Gold 0.4838 oz. AGW
Ruler: George V **Obverse:** Crowned bust left **Obv. Designer:**
E. B. MacKennal **Reverse:** Arms within wreath, date and
denomination below **Rev. Designer:** W. H. J. Blakemore

Date	Mintage	F-12	VF-20	XF-40	AU-50	MS-60	MS-63
1912	74,759	BV	320	360	400	550	2,000
1913	149,232	BV	325	375	400	600	2,600
1914	140,068	BV	330	400	450	700	2,750

CUBA

Cuba finally gained independence from Spain in 1902.
Many of its gold issues from the first republic (1902-1962) are
affordable despite relatively low mintages.

KM# 16 PESO
1.6718 g., 0.9000 Gold .0483 oz. AGW **Obv:** National arms
within wreath, denomination below **Rev:** Head of Jose Marti
right, date below

Date	Mintage	F	VF	XF	Unc	BU
1915	6,850	50.00	100	150	275	600
1915 Proof	140	Value: 1,750				
1916	11,000	50.00	100	150	300	700
1916 Proof	100	Value: 2,500				

KM# 17 2 PESOS
3.3436 g., 0.9000 Gold .0967 oz. AGW **Obv:** National arms within
wreath, denomination below **Rev:** Head right, date below

Date	Mintage	F	VF	XF	Unc	BU
1915	10,000	70.00	90.00	175	500	1,000
1915 Proof	100	Value: 3,000				

Date	Mintage	F	VF	XF	Unc	BU
1916	150,000	65.00	75.00	90.00	200	450
1916 Proof; Rare	8	—	—	—	—	—

KM# 18 4 PESOS
6.6872 g., 0.9000 Gold .1935 oz. AGW **Obv:** National arms within wreath, denomination below **Rev:** Head right, date below

Date	Mintage	F	VF	XF	Unc	BU
1915	6,300	135	175	375	1,100	1,600
1915 Proof	100	Value: 3,000				
1916	129,000	125	135	160	500	750
1916 Proof	90	Value: 4,500				

KM# 19 5 PESOS
8.3592 g., 0.9000 Gold .2419 oz. AGW **Obv:** National arms within wreath, denomination below **Rev:** Head right, date below

Date	Mintage	F	VF	XF	Unc	BU
1915	696,000	—	BV	165	210	475
1915 Proof	—	Value: 3,200				
1916	1,132,000	—	BV	160	200	450
1916 Proof	—	Value: 6,500				
Note: American Numismatic Rarities Eliasberg sale 4-05, Proof 65 realized $13,800.						

KM# 18

KM# 20 10 PESOS
16.7185 g., 0.9000 Gold .4838 oz. AGW **Obv:** National arms within wreath, denomination below **Rev:** Head right, date below

Date	Mintage	F	VF	XF	Unc	BU
1915	95,000	—	BV	330	550	800
1915 Proof	—	Value: 7,500				
1916	1,169,000	—	BV	320	400	750
1916 Proof, Rare	—	—	—	—	—	—
Note: David Akers John Jay Pittman sale 8-99 very choice Proof realized $19,550, choice Proof realized $14,950. American Numismatic Rarities Eliasberg sale 4-05, Proof 62 realized $29,900.						

KM# 21 20 PESOS
33.4370 g., 0.9000 Gold .9676 oz. AGW **Subject:** Jose Marti **Obv:** National arms within wreath, denomination below **Rev:** Head right, date below

Date	Mintage	F	VF	XF	Unc	BU
1915	57,000	BV	675	800	1,500	3,000
1915 Proof; Rare	—	—	—	—	—	—
Note: David Akers John Jay Pittman sale 8-99 very choice proof 1915 realized $11,500.						
1916 Proof; Rare	10	—	—	—	—	—
Note: David Akers John Jay Pittman sale 8-99 nearly choice Proof 1916 realized $43,125.						

KM# 791.1

DENMARK

Denmark, a constitutional monarchy, introduced decimal coinage in 1874, and the system continues today. In the late 1800s and continuing into the 1900s, the system included 10-kroner and 20-kroner coins. The 20-kroner contains just over a quarter-ounce of gold.

KM# 790.1 10 KRONER
4.4803 g., 0.9000 Gold .1296 oz. AGW **Ruler:** Christian IX
Obv: Head right **Rev:** Seated figure left with shield and porpoise

Date	Mintage	F	VF	XF	Unc	BU
1873(h) HC/CS	369,000	BV	90.00	155	275	—
1874(h) HC/CS	Inc. above	BV	95.00	165	300	—
1877(h) HC/CS	98,000	BV	125	180	375	—
1890(h) HC/CS	151,000	BV	90.00	155	250	—

KM# 790.2 10 KRONER
4.4803 g., 0.9000 Gold .1296 oz. AGW **Ruler:** Christian IX
Obv: Head right **Rev:** Seated figure left with shield and porpoise

Date	Mintage	F	VF	XF	Unc	BU
1898(h) HC/VBP	100,000	BV	95.00	165	270	—
1900(h) HC/VBP	204,000	BV	85.00	110	200	—

KM# 809 10 KRONER
4.4803 g., 0.9000 Gold .1296 oz. AGW **Ruler:** Frederik VIII
Obv: Head left with titles **Rev:** Draped crowned national arms above date, value, mint mark and initials VBP

Date	Mintage	F	VF	XF	Unc	BU
1908(h) VBP; GJ	308,000	—	100	120	140	—
1909(h) VBP; GJ	153,000	—	100	120	140	—

KM# 816 10 KRONER
4.4803 g., 0.9000 Gold .1296 oz. AGW **Ruler:** Christian X
Obv: Head right with title, date, mint mark, initials VBP. Initials AH at neck **Rev:** Draped crowned national arms above date, value, mint mark and initials VBP

Date	Mintage	F	VF	XF	Unc	BU
1913(h) AH/ GJ	312,000	—	100	120	135	—
1917(h) AH/ GJ	132,000	—	100	130	145	—

KM# 791.1 20 KRONER
8.9606 g., 0.9000 Gold .2592 oz. AGW **Ruler:** Christian IX
Obv: Head right **Rev:** Seated figure left with shield and porpoise

Date	Mintage	F	VF	XF	Unc	BU
1873(h) HC/CS	1,153,000	—	BV	180	230	—
1874(h) HC/CS	Inc. above	800	1,500	2,250	3,500	—
1876(h) HC/CS	351,000	—	BV	190	280	—
1877(h) HC/CS	Inc. above	—	BV	285	380	—
1890(h) HC/CS	102,000	—	BV	285	380	—

KM# 791.2 20 KRONER

8.9606 g., 0.9000 Gold .2592 oz. AGW **Ruler:** Christian IX
Obv: Head right **Rev:** Seated figure left with shield and porpoise

Date	Mintage	F	VF	XF	Unc	BU
1900(h) CS/VBP	100,000	—	BV	230	340	—

KM# 810 20 KRONER

8.9606 g., 0.9000 Gold .2592 oz. AGW **Ruler:** Frederik VIII
Obv: Head left, with titles **Rev:** Crowned and mantled arms above date, value, mint mark and initials VBP

Date	Mintage	F	VF	XF	Unc	BU
1908(h) VBP; GJ	243,000	—	175	210	250	—
1909(h) VBP; GJ	365,000	—	180	220	260	—
1910(h) VBP; GJ	200,000	—	200	225	275	—
1911(h) VBP; GJ	183,000	—	180	220	260	—
1912(h) VBP; GJ	184,000	—	180	220	260	—

KM# 817.1 20 KRONER

8.9606 g., 0.9000 Gold .2592 oz. AGW **Ruler:** Christian X
Obv: Head right with title, date, mint mark, initials VBP, initials AH at neck **Rev:** Crowned and mantled arms above date, value, mint mark and initials VBP

Date	Mintage	F	VF	XF	Unc	BU
1913(h) AH/GJ	815,000	—	175	210	250	—
1914(h) AH/GJ	920,000	—	175	210	250	—
1915(h) AH/GJ	532,000	—	180	215	255	—
1916(h) AH/GJ	1,401,000	—	180	220	265	—
1917(h) AH/GJ	Inc. above	—	180	220	260	—

KM# 817.2 20 KRONER

8.9606 g., 0.9000 Gold .2592 oz. AGW **Ruler:** Christian X
Obv: Head right with title, date, mint mark, and initials HCN, initials AH at neck **Rev:** Crowned and mantled arms above date, value, mint mark, and initials HCN **Note:** 1926-1927 dated 20 Kroners were not released for circulation.

Date	Mintage	F	VF	XF	Unc	BU
1926(h) HCN	358,000	—	—	3,000	6,000	—
1927(h) HCN	Inc. above	—	—	3,000	6,000	—

KM# 817.3 20 KRONER

8.9606 g., 0.9000 Gold .2592 oz. AGW **Ruler:** Christian X
Obv: Head right with title, date, mint mark, and initials HCN. Initials AH at neck **Rev:** Crowned and mantled arms above date, value, mint mark and initials HCN **Note:** The 1930- 1931 dated 20 Kroners were not released for circulation.

Date	Mintage	F	VF	XF	Unc	BU
1930(h) N	1,285,000	—	—	3,000	6,000	—
1931(h) N	Inc. above	—	—	3,000	6,000	—

FINLAND

Finland was a grand duchy under the Russian Empire from 1809 until gaining independence on December 6, 1917. Gold coins of 10 markkaa and 20 markkaa were issued during this time.

KM# 8.1 10 MARKKAA
3.2258 g., 0.9000 Gold .0933 oz. AGW **Ruler:** Alexander II
Obv: Narrow eagle **Rev:** Denomination and date within circle
Note: Regal issues

Date	Mintage	F	VF	XF	Unc	BU
1878 S	254,000	100	150	175	200	—

KM# 8.2 10 MARKKAA
3.2258 g., 0.9000 Gold .0933 oz. AGW, 18.9 mm.
Ruler: Nicholas II **Obv:** Crowned imperial double eagle holding orb and scepter **Rev:** Denomination and date within circle, fineness around **Note:** Regal issues

Date	Mintage	F	VF	XF	Unc	BU
1879/0 S	—	1,500	3,000	5,000	—	—
Note: Only a few pieces known						
1879 S	200,000	100	150	175	200	—
1881 S	100,000	120	160	200	240	—
1882 S	386,000	100	150	175	200	—
1904 L	102,000	250	350	400	500	—
1905 L	43,000	1,500	2,000	2,800	3,000	—
1913 L	396,000	100	150	175	200	—

KM# 9.1 20 MARKKAA
6.4516 g., 0.9000 Gold .1867 oz. AGW **Ruler:** Alexander II
Obv: Narrow eagle **Rev:** Denomination and date within circle
Note: Regal issues

Date	Mintage	F	VF	XF	Unc	BU
1878 S	Est. 235,000	150	180	220	270	—
Note: Some specimens may appear as prooflike; Proofs were never made officially by the mint						

KM# 9.2 20 MARKKAA
6.4516 g., 0.9000 Gold .1867 oz. AGW, 21.3 mm.
Ruler: Nicholas II **Obv:** Crowned imperial double eagle holding orb and scepter **Rev:** Denomination and date within circle, fineness around **Note:** Regal issues.

Date	Mintage	F	VF	XF	Unc	BU
1879 S	300,000	150	180	200	220	—
1880 S	90,000	350	500	600	750	—
1891 L	91,000	170	200	220	250	—

KM# 9.2

GOLD RUSH

Date	Mintage	F	VF	XF	Unc	BU
1903 L	112,000	150	180	210	230	—
1904 L	188,000	150	180	200	220	—
1910 L	201,000	150	180	200	220	—
1911 L	161,000	150	180	200	220	—
1912 L	881,000	2,500	4,500	6,000	7,000	—
1912 S	Inc. above	150	180	200	220	—
1913 S	214,000	150	180	200	220	—

FRANCE

Through all of France's political upheaval of the 19th century, the country's gold 20-franc coin remained stalwart. Introduced by Napoleon, it continued to be struck in the same specifications by subsequent political regimes into the 20th century. Accompanying it for many years was a larger 40-franc and later 50-franc and 100-franc pieces introduced by Napoleon III.

KM# 706.3 20 FRANCS
6.4516 g., 0.9000 Gold .1867 oz. AGW **Ruler:** Louis XVIII
Obv: Uniformed bust right **Rev:** Crowned arms within wreath

Date	Mintage	F	VF	XF	Unc	BU
1814K	63,000	BV	150	200	600	—
1815K	30,000	BV	150	200	600	—

KM# 706.4 20 FRANCS
6.4516 g., 0.9000 Gold .1867 oz. AGW **Ruler:** Louis XVIII
Obv: Uniformed bust right **Rev:** Crowned arms within wreath

Date	Mintage	F	VF	XF	Unc	BU
1814L	45,000	BV	150	200	600	—
1815L	34,000	BV	150	200	600	—

KM# 706.5 20 FRANCS
6.4516 g., 0.9000 Gold .1867 oz. AGW **Ruler:** Louis XVIII
Obv: Uniformed bust right **Rev:** Crowned arms within wreath

Date	Mintage	F	VF	XF	Unc	BU
1814Q	29,000	130	175	250	650	—
1815Q	39,000	BV	150	200	600	—

KM# 706.6 20 FRANCS
6.4516 g., 0.9000 Gold .1867 oz. AGW **Ruler:** Louis XVIII
Obv: Uniformed bust right **Rev:** Crowned arms within wreath

Date	Mintage	F	VF	XF	Unc	BU
1814W	60,000	BV	150	200	600	—
1815W	88,000	BV	150	200	600	—

KM# 706.1 20 FRANCS
6.4516 g., 0.9000 Gold .1867 oz. AGW **Ruler:** Louis XVIII
Obv: Uniformed bust right **Obv. Legend:** LOUIS XVIII ROI DE
FRANCE **Rev:** Crowned arms within wreath **Note:** Engraver:
Tiolier.

Date	Mintage	F	VF	XF	Unc	BU
1814A	2,684,000	BV	130	150	425	—
1815A	2,113,000	BV	130	150	425	—

KM# 706.2 20 FRANCS
6.4516 g., 0.9000 Gold .1867 oz. AGW **Ruler:** Louis XVIII
Obv: Uniformed bust right **Rev:** Crowned arms within wreath

Date	Mintage	F	VF	XF	Unc	BU
1815B	1,539	300	600	1,200	1,500	—

KM# 829 5 FRANCS
1.6929 g., 0.9000 Gold .0467 oz. AGW **Obv:** Laureate head
right **Rev:** Denomination within wreath **Edge Lettering:** DIEU
PROTEGE LA FRANCE

Date	Mintage	F	VF	XF	Unc	BU
1878A Proof	30		Value: 6,500			
1889A Proof	40		Value: 5,250			

KM# 830 10 FRANCS
3.2258 g., 0.9000 Gold .0933 oz. AGW **Obv:** Laureate head
right **Rev:** Denomination within wreath

Date	Mintage	F	VF	XF	Unc	BU
1878A Proof	30		Value: 5,250			
1889A Proof	100		Value: 4,750			
1895A	214,000	—	BV	75.00	200	—
1896A	585,000	—	BV	75.00	150	—
1899A	1,600,000	—	BV	75.00	150	—

KM# 846 10 FRANCS
3.2258 g., 0.9000 Gold .0933 oz. AGW

Date	Mintage	F	VF	XF	Unc	BU
1899	699,000	—	BV	75.00	120	—
1899 Matte Proof	—		Value: 900			
1900	1,570,000	—	BV	75.00	95.00	115
1900 Proof	—		Value: 800			
1901	2,100,000	—	BV	65.00	85.00	125
1901	2,100,000	—	BV	65.00	85.00	125
1905	1,426,000	—	BV	65.00	85.00	125
1905	1,426,000	—	BV	65.00	85.00	125
1906	3,665,000	—	BV	65.00	85.00	125

GOLD RUSH

Date	Mintage	F	VF	XF	Unc	BU
1907	3,364,000	—	BV	65.00	85.00	125
1908	1,650,000	—	BV	65.00	85.00	125
1909	599,000	—	BV	70.00	120	255
1910	2,110,000	—	BV	65.00	85.00	125
1911	1,881,000	—	BV	65.00	85.00	125
1912	1,756,000	—	BV	65.00	85.00	125
1914	3,041,000	—	BV	65.00	85.00	125

KM# 825 20 FRANCS

6.4516 g., 0.9000 Gold .1867 oz. AGW **Obv:** Standing Genius writing the Constitution, rooster at right, fasces at left
Rev: Denomination above date within circular wreath

Date	Mintage	F	VF	XF	Unc	BU
1871A	2,508,000	—	BV	125	140	—
1874A	1,216,000	—	BV	125	140	—
1875A	11,746,000	—	BV	125	140	—
1876A	8,825,000	—	BV	125	140	—
1877A	12,759,000	—	BV	125	140	—
1878A	9,189,000	—	BV	125	140	—
1878A Proof	30	Value: 5,000				
1879A	1,038,000	—	BV	125	140	—
1886A	985,000	—	BV	125	140	—
1887A	1,231,000	—	BV	125	140	—
1887A Proof	—	Value: 5,250				
1888A	28,000	—	BV	150	275	—
1889A	873,000	—	BV	125	140	—
1889A Proof	100	Value: 4,250				
1890A	1,030,000	—	BV	125	140	—
1891A	871,000	—	BV	125	140	—
1892A	226,000	—	BV	125	140	—
1893A	2,517,000	—	BV	125	140	—
1894A	491,000	—	BV	125	140	—
1895A	5,293,000	—	BV	125	140	—
1896A	5,330,000	—	BV	125	140	—
1897A	11,069,000	—	BV	125	140	—
1898A	8,866,000	—	BV	125	140	—

KM# 825

KM# 847 20 FRANCS

6.4516 g., 0.9000 Gold .1867 oz. AGW **Edge Lettering:** DIEU PROTEGE LA FRANCE

Date	Mintage	F	VF	XF	Unc	BU
1899A	1,500,000	—	—	BV	140	170
1899A Proof	—	Value: 1,250				
1900A	615,000	—	—	BV	140	165
1900A Proof	Inc. above	Value: 1,000				

Date	Mintage	F	VF	XF	Unc	BU
1901A	2,643,000	—	—	BV	140	185
1901A	2,643,000	—	—	BV	140	185
1902A	2,394,000	—	—	BV	140	185
1902A	2,394,000	—	—	BV	140	185
1903A	4,405,000	—	—	BV	140	185
1904A	7,706,000	—	—	BV	140	185
1905A	9,158,000	—	—	BV	140	185
1906A	14,613,000	—	—	BV	140	185

KM# 857 20 FRANCS
6.4516 g., 0.9000 Gold .1867 oz. AGW **Obv:** Oak leaf wreath encircles liberty head right **Rev:** Rooster divides denomination, date below **Edge Lettering:** LIBERTE EGALITE FRATERNITE **Note:** All dates from 1907-1914 have been officially restruck.

Date	Mintage	F	VF	XF	Unc	BU
1906	—	—	—	BV	130	165
1907	17,716,000	—	—	BV	130	165
1908	6,721,000	—	—	BV	130	165
1909	9,637,000	—	—	BV	130	165
1910	5,779,000	—	—	BV	130	165
1911	5,346,000	—	—	BV	130	165
1912	10,332,000	—	—	BV	130	165
1913	12,163,000	—	—	BV	130	165
1914	6,518,000	—	—	BV	130	165

KM# 831 50 FRANCS
16.1290 g., 0.9000 Gold .4467 oz. AGW **Obv:** Standing Genius writing the Constitution, rooster at right, fasces at left **Rev:** Denomination above date within circular wreath

Date	Mintage	F	VF	XF	Unc	BU
1878A	5,294	400	700	1,350	2,000	—
1887A	301	550	1,250	2,250	3,700	—
1889A Proof	100	Value: 7,000				
1896A	800	500	900	1,800	2,800	—
1900A	200	650	1,500	2,500	4,500	—
1900A Proof	—	Value: 8,000				
1904A	20,000	325	550	900	1,650	—

KM# 832 100 FRANCS
32.2581 g., 0.9000 Gold .9335 oz. AGW **Obv:** Standing Genius writing the Constitution, rooster on right, fasces on left **Rev:** Denomination above date within circular wreath **Edge Lettering:** DIEU PROTEGE LA FRANCE

Date	Mintage	F	VF	XF	Unc	BU
1878A	13,000	—	BV	650	700	1,000
1878A Proof	30	Value: 14,000				

KM# 831

GOLD RUSH

Date	Mintage	F	VF	XF	Unc	BU
1879A	39,000	—	BV	650	700	1,000
1881A	22,000	—	BV	650	700	1,000
1882A	37,000	—	BV	650	700	1,000
1885A	2,894	—	675	850	1,150	—
1886A	39,000	—	BV	650	800	1,000
1887A	234	850	1,750	3,500	6,500	—
1889A Proof	100	Value: 12,000				
1894A	143	1,250	2,750	2,750	10,000	—
1896A	400	750	1,100	650	5,500	—
1899A	10,000	750	BV	525	800	1,000
1900A	20,000	450	475	525	675	1,000
1900A Proof	—	Value: 5,000				
1901A	10,000	—	BV	625	800	1,200
1901A	10,000	—	BV	625	800	1,200
1902A	10,000	—	BV	625	800	1,200
1902A	10,000	—	BV	625	800	1,200
1903A	10,000	—	BV	625	800	1,200
1904A	20,000	—	BV	625	800	1,200
1905A	10,000	—	BV	625	800	1,200
1906A	30,000	—	BV	626	800	1,200

KM# 858 100 FRANCS

32.2581 g., 0.9000 Gold .9335 oz. AGW   **Obv:** Standing Genius writing the constitution, rooster on right, column on the left **Rev:** Denomination and date within wreath
Edge Lettering: LIBERTE EGALITE FRATERNITE

Date	Mintage	F	VF	XF	Unc	BU
1907A	20,000	—	—	BV	645	900
1908A	23,000	—	—	BV	645	900
1909A	20,000	—	—	BV	645	900
1910A	20,000	—	—	BV	645	900
1911A	30,000	—	—	BV	645	900
1912A	20,000	—	—	BV	645	900
1913A	30,000	—	—	BV	645	900
1914A Rare	1,281	—	—	—	—	—

KM# 880 100 FRANCS

6.5500 g., 0.9000 Gold .1895 oz. AGW   **Obv:** Winged head left **Rev:** Denomination above grain sprig, date below, laurel and oak branches flank **Note:** Without mint mark.

Date	Mintage	F	VF	XF	Unc	BU
1929	50	—	—	2,500	4,000	—
1932	Est. 50	—	—	3,250	4,750	—

Date	Mintage	F	VF	XF	Unc	BU
1933	Est. 300	—	—	1,650	2,500	—
1934 Rare	—	—	—	—	—	—
1935	6,102,000	—	—	500	800	—
1936	7,689,000	—	—	500	800	—

GERMAN STATES

Before the German Empire was formed in 1871, "Germany" was little more than a geographic expression referring to an area consisting of hundreds of effectively autonomous states. After the empire was formed, the states continued to have the right to strike gold and silver coins with values higher than 1 mark. Hamburg officially became a free city in 1510 but was occupied by France during the Napoleonic years. It joined the North German Confederation in 1861 and the empire in 1871. Prussia was one of the most powerful German states and a kingdom itself, created in 1701. It lost territory to Napoleon in 1806 but regained the captured lands and more in 1813. When the German Empire was created, the king of Prussia was named king of the larger empire. The German Empire and Prussian kingdom ended when World War I ended. Saxony also was one of the most powerful states in central Europe by the 1500s and became a kingdom in 1806. At the Congress of Vienna in 1815, it was forced to cede half of its territories to Prussia.

Hamburg

KM# 291 5 MARK
1.9910 g., 0.9000 Gold .0576 oz. AGW **Obv:** Helmeted arms with lion supporters **Obv. Legend:** FREIE UND HANSESTADT HAMBURG **Rev:** Crowned imperial eagle **Rev. Legend:** DEUTSCHES REICH 1977, 5 MARK below

Date	Mintage	F	VF	XF	Unc	BU
1877J	441,000	200	300	400	600	800
1877J Proof; Rare	—	—	—	—	—	—

KM# 285 10 MARK
3.9820 g., 0.9000 Gold .1152 oz. AGW **Obv:** Helmeted ornate arms **Obv. Legend:** FREIE UND HANSESTADT HAMBURG **Rev:** Type I **Rev. Legend:** DEUTSCHES REICH

Date	Mintage	F	VF	XF	Unc	BU
1873B	25,000	600	1,300	2,000	3,500	4,500
1873B Proof; Rare	—	—	—	—	—	—

What do the grade headings mean?
See the grading section in the appendix for information on the various grades listed.

GOLD RUSH

KM# 286 10 MARK
3.9820 g., 0.9000 Gold .1152 oz. AGW **Obv:** Helmeted ornate arms **Obv. Legend:** FREIE UND HANSESTADT HAMBURG **Rev:** Type II **Rev. Legend:** DEUTSCHES REICH

Date	Mintage	F	VF	XF	Unc	BU
1874B	50,000	450	800	1,500	2,500	3,000

KM# 288 10 MARK
3.9820 g., 0.9000 Gold .1152 oz. AGW **Obv:** Helmeted arms with lion supporters **Obv. Legend:** FREIE UND HANSESTADT HAMBURG **Rev:** Crowned imperial eagle **Rev. Legend:** DEUTSCHES REICH

Date	Mintage	F	VF	XF	Unc	BU
1875J	608,000	85.00	125	250	400	500
1875J Proof	—	Value: 1,000				
1876J	6,321	550	850	1,350	1,750	2,000
1877J	221,000	85.00	125	200	350	450
1879J	255,000	85.00	125	225	400	500
1880J	139,000	85.00	125	200	350	450
1888J	163,000	85.00	125	200	350	450

KM# 292 10 MARK
3.9820 g., 0.9000 Gold .1152 oz. AGW **Obv:** Helmeted arms with lion supporters **Obv. Legend:** FREIE UND HANSESTADT HAMBURG **Rev:** Crowned imperial eagle, type II **Rev. Legend:** DEUTSCHES REICH

Date	Mintage	F	VF	XF	Unc	BU
1890J	245,000	90.00	150	225	350	400
1893J	246,000	90.00	150	225	350	400
1896J	164,000	90.00	150	225	350	400
1898J	344,000	90.00	150	225	350	400
1900J	82,000	90.00	150	225	350	450
1901J	82,000	90.00	150	175	385	500
1902J	41,000	120	225	350	650	1,000
1903J	310,000	90.00	150	175	350	500
1905J	164,000	90.00	150	175	350	500
1906J	164,000	90.00	150	175	350	500
1907J	111,000	90.00	150	175	350	500
1908J	32,000	150	300	450	800	1,300
1909J	122,000	90.00	150	175	350	500
1909J Proof	—	Value: 1,600				
1910J	41,000	120	225	300	600	1,000
1910J Proof	—	Value: 2,000				
1911J	75,000	95.00	175	250	300	800
1911J Proof	—	Value: 6,000				
1912J	48,000	145	245	350	500	1,000

KM# 292

Date	Mintage	F	VF	XF	Unc	BU
1912J Proof	—			Value: 2,000		
1913J	41,000	145	245	300	400	1,000
1913J Proof	—			Value: 2,000		

KM# 289 20 MARK
7.9650 g., 0.9000 Gold .2304 oz. AGW **Obv:** Helmeted arms with lion supporters **Obv. Legend:** FREIE UND HANSESTADT HAMBURG **Rev:** Crowned imperial eagle, type II **Rev. Legend:** DEUTSCHES REICH

Date	Mintage	F	VF	XF	Unc	BU
1875J	313,000	—	160	190	285	350
1876J	1,723,000	—	BV	155	250	325
1877J	1,324,000	—	BV	160	250	325
1878J	2,008,000	—	BV	160	250	325
1879J	104,000	225	375	700	1,250	1,500
1880J	120,000	BV	165	275	400	500
1881J	500	10,000	15,000	20,000	30,000	35,000
1883J	125,000	—	BV	175	300	400
1884J	639,000	—	BV	175	300	400
1887J	251,000	—	BV	165	300	375
1889J	14,000	400	900	1,250	1,800	2,200

KM# 295 20 MARK
7.9650 g., 0.9000 Gold .2304 oz. AGW **Obv:** Helmeted arms with lion supporters **Obv. Legend:** FREIE UND HANSESTADT HAMBURG Rev: Crowned imperial eagle, type III **Rev. Legend:** DEUTSCHES REICH

Date	Mintage	F	VF	XF	Unc	BU
1893J	815,000	—	BV	180	225	300
1894J	501,000	—	BV	180	225	300
1895J	501,000	—	BV	180	225	300
1897J	500,000	—	BV	180	225	300
1899J	1,002,000	—	BV	160	200	275
1900J	501,000	—	BV	170	225	300
1908J Rare	14	—	—	—	75,000	—
1913J	491,000	—	BV	160	200	275
1913J Proof	—			Value: 1,000		

Prussia
KM# 507 5 MARK
1.9910 g., 0.9000 Gold .0576 oz. AGW **Ruler:** Wilhelm I **Obv:** Head right **Obv. Legend:** WILHELM DEUTSCHER KAISER KONIG V. PREUSSEN **Rev:** Crowned imperial eagle **Rev. Legend:** DEUTSCHES REICH date, 5 MARK below

Date	Mintage	F	VF	XF	Unc	BU
1877A	1,217,000	125	200	300	500	650

Date	Mintage	F	VF	XF	Unc	BU
1877A Proof	—	Value: 1,300				
1877B	517,000	125	200	300	500	650
1877B Proof	—	Value: 1,200				
1877C	688,000	125	200	300	500	650
1878A	502,000	125	200	300	500	650
1878A Proof	—	Value: 1,300				

KM# 502 10 MARK

3.9820 g., 0.9000 Gold .1152 oz. AGW **Ruler:** Wilhelm I
Obv: Head right **Obv. Legend:** WILHELM DEUTSCHER KAISER
KONIG V. PREUSSEN **Rev:** Crowned imperial eagle **Rev. Legend:**
DEUTSCHES REICH

Date	Mintage	F	VF	XF	Unc	BU
1872A	3,123,000	BV	85.00	110	200	250
1872A Proof	—	Value: 1,600				
1872B	1,418,000	BV	95.00	120	225	275
1872C	1,747,000	BV	85.00	130	275	325
1873A	3,016,000	—	BV	90.00	200	250
1873A Proof	—	Value: 1,600				
1873B	2,273,000	BV	100	125	275	325
1873C	2,295,000	BV	95.00	120	275	325

KM# 504 10 MARK

3.9820 g., 0.9000 Gold .1152 oz. AGW **Ruler:** Wilhelm I **Obv:**
Head right **Obv. Legend:** WILHELM DEUTSCHER KAISER KONIG
V. PREUSSEN **Rev:** Type II **Rev. Legend:** DEUTSCHES REICH date,
10 MARK below

Date	Mintage	F	VF	XF	Unc	BU
1874A	833,000	BV	95.00	120	250	300
1874A Proof	—	Value: 1,100				
1874B	1,028,000	BV	95.00	120	250	300
1874C	321,000	BV	95.00	120	250	300
1874C Proof	—	Value: 1,300				
1875A	2,430,000	BV	95.00	120	250	300
1875B	456,000	BV	95.00	120	300	350
1875C	1,532,000	BV	95.00	120	250	300
1876B	2,800	1,000	1,600	2,200	3,000	3,500
1876B Proof	—	Value: 10,000				
1876C	27,000	500	1,200	1,600	2,500	3,000
1877A	851,000	BV	95.00	120	250	350
1877B	247,000	BV	105	120	350	450
1877C	328,000	BV	85.00	120	300	350
1878A	1,126,000	BV	85.00	110	250	300

Date	Mintage	F	VF	XF	Unc	BU
1878B	15,000	45,000	60,000	85,000	100,000	120,000
1878C	516,000	BV	100	130	300	350
1879A	1,012,000	BV	95.00	120	225	275
1879A Proof	—	Value: 800				
1879C	282,000	BV	125	150	300	400
1880A	1,762,000	BV	85.00	120	250	325
1882A	8,382	1,500	3,200	4,500	6,500	8,500
1883A	13,000	1,200	1,800	2,400	3,000	4,500
1883A Proof	—	Value: 10,000				
1886A	14,000	1,500	2,000	3,200	5,000	6,000
1888A	189,000	BV	95.00	130	275	325
1888A Proof	—	Value: 1,300				

KM# 514 10 MARK
3.9820 g., 0.9000 Gold .1152 oz. AGW **Ruler:** Friedrich III
March - June **Obv:** Head right **Obv. Legend:** FRIEDRICH
DEUTSCHER KAISER KONIG V. PREUSSEN **Rev:** Crowned
imperial eagle **Rev. Legend:** DEUTSCHES REICH date, 10 MARK
below

Date	Mintage	F	VF	XF	Unc	BU
1888A	876,000	BV	95.00	120	175	225
1888A Proof	—	Value: 700				

KM# 517 10 MARK
3.9820 g., 0.9000 Gold .1152 oz. AGW **Ruler:** Wilhelm II **Obv:**
Head right **Obv. Legend:** WILHELM II DEUTSCHER KAISER KONIG
V. PREUSSEN **Rev:** Type II **Rev. Legend:** DEUTSCHES REICH date,
10 MARK below

Date	Mintage	F	VF	XF	Unc	BU
1889A	24,000	1,600	3,000	3,500	4,500	6,500
1889A Proof	—	Value: 6,500				

KM# 520 10 MARK
3.9820 g., 0.9000 Gold .1152 oz. AGW **Ruler:** Wilhelm II **Obv:**
Head right **Obv. Legend:** WILHELM II DEUTSCHER KAISER KONIG
V. PREUSSEN **Rev:** Crowned imperial eagle, type III **Rev. Legend:**
DEUTSCHES REICH date, 10 MARK below

Date	Mintage	F	VF	XF	Unc	BU
1890A	1,512,000	BV	100	120	275	325
1890A Proof	—	Value: 1,000				
1892A	35,000	400	600	1,000	1,500	2,000
1893A	1,591,000	BV	100	120	275	325
1894A	18,000	550	1,100	1,450	2,000	2,500

Date	Mintage	F	VF	XF	Unc	BU
1895A	29,000	400	700	1,200	1,900	2,250
1896A	1,081,000	BV	100	120	275	325
1897A	114,000	BV	120	200	300	400
1898A	2,280,000	BV	95.00	120	275	325
1899A	300,000	BV	110	165	275	325
1900A	742,000	BV	95.00	120	275	325
1900A Proof	—	Value: 900				
1901A	702,000	BV	95.00	120	250	400
1901A Proof	—	Value: 1,300				
1902A	271,000	BV	135	185	275	425
1902A Proof	—	Value: 1,300				
1903A	1,685,000	BV	95.00	125	250	400
1903A Proof	—	Value: 1,300				
1904A	1,178,000	BV	95.00	125	250	400
1905A	1,063,000	BV	95.00	125	250	400
1905A Proof	117	Value: 1,300				
1906A	542,000	BV	100	135	265	425
1906A Proof	150	Value: 1,300				
1907A	813,000	BV	95.00	125	250	400
1907A Proof	—	Value: 1,300				
1909A	532,000	BV	100	135	265	425
1909A Proof	—	Value: 1,300				
1910A	803,000	BV	95.00	125	250	400
1911A	271,000	BV	130	180	275	400
1911A Proof	—	Value: 1,300				
1912A	542,000	BV	95.00	125	250	400
1912A Proof	—	Value: 1,300				

KM# 501 20 MARK
7.9650 g., 0.9000 Gold .2304 oz. AGW **Ruler:** Wilhelm I **Obv:**
Head right **Obv. Legend:** WILHELM DEUTSCHER KAISER KONIG
V. PREUSSEN **Rev:** Crowned imperial eagle **Rev. Legend:**
DEUTSCHES REICH

Date	Mintage	F	VF	XF	Unc	BU
1871A	502,000	125	200	275	500	750
1871A Proof	—	Value: 1,800				
1872A	7,717,000	—	BV	170	200	250
1872A Proof	2,491	Value: 1,800				
1872B	1,918,000	—	BV	180	225	275
1872C	3,056,000	—	BV	180	225	275
1873A	9,063,000	—	BV	180	225	275
1873A Proof	—	Value: 1,800				

Date	Mintage	F	VF	XF	Unc	BU
1873B	3,441,000	—	BV	180	225	275
1873C	5,228,000	—	BV	180	225	275
1873C Proof	—	Value: 1,800				

KM# 505 20 MARK
7.9650 g., 0.9000 Gold .2304 oz. AGW   **Ruler:** Wilhelm I **Obv:** Head right **Obv. Legend:** WILHELM DEUTSCHER KAISER KONIG V. PREUSSEN **Rev:** Type II **Rev. Legend:** DEUTSCHES REICH date, 20 MARK below

KM# 505

Date	Mintage	F	VF	XF	Unc	BU
1874A	762,000	—	BV	155	200	300
1874A Proof	—	Value: 1,300				
1874B	824,000	—	BV	160	225	300
1874C	88,000	—	BV	175	250	300
1875A	4,203,000	—	BV	155	200	300
1875B	Est. 1,500	180	350	600	1,200	1,600
1876A	2,673,000	—	BV	155	200	250
1876C	423,000	160	250	400	600	1,000
1877A	1,250,000	—	BV	155	200	250
1877B	501,000	—	BV	200	300	350
1877C	6,384	1,000	1,700	2,400	3,000	4,500
1878A	2,175,000	—	BV	155	200	250
1878C	82,000	160	250	400	600	900
1879A	1,022,999	—	BV	155	200	250
1881A	428,000	—	BV	155	200	250
1882A	655,000	—	BV	155	200	250
1882A Proof	—	Value: 1,500				
1883A	4,283,000	—	BV	155	200	250
1884A	224,000	—	BV	155	200	250
1885A	407,000	—	BV	155	200	250
1886A	176,000	—	BV	155	200	250
1887A	5,645,000	—	BV	155	200	250
1887A Proof	—	Value: 1,500				
1888A	534,000	—	BV	155	200	250
1888A Proof	—	Value: 1,500				

KM# 515 20 MARK
7.9650 g., 0.9000 Gold .2304 oz. AGW   **Ruler:** Friedrich III March - June **Obv:** Head right **Obv. Legend:** FRIEDRICH DEUTSCHER KAISER KONIG V. PREUSSEN **Rev:** Crowned imperial eagle **Rev. Legend:** DEUTSCHES REICH date, 20 MARK below

Date	Mintage	F	VF	XF	Unc	BU
1888A	5,364,000	—	BV	155	225	300
1888A Proof	—	Value: 900				

KM# 516 20 MARK

7.9650 g., 0.9000 Gold .2304 oz. AGW **Ruler:** Wilhelm II Obv:
Head right **Obv. Legend:** WILHELM II DEUTSCHES KAISER
KONIG V. PREUSSEN **Rev:** Crowned imperial eagle **Rev. Legend:**
DEUTSCHES REICH date, 20 MARK below

Date	Mintage	F	VF	XF	Unc	BU
1888A	756,000	—	BV	155	275	350
1888A Proof	—	Value: 1,250				
1889A	9,642,000	—	BV	155	200	275
1889A Proof	—	Value: 1,100				

KM# 521 20 MARK

7.9650 g., 0.9000 Gold .2304 oz. AGW **Ruler:** Wilhelm II **Obv:**
Head right **Obv. Legend:** WILHELM II DEUTSCHER KAISER KONIG
V. PREUSSEN **Rev:** Crowned imperial eagle, type III **Rev. Legend:**
DEUTSCHES REICH date, 20 MARK below

Date	Mintage	F	VF	XF	Unc	BU
1890A	3,695,000	—	BV	160+10%	225	275
1891A	2,752,000	—	BV	160+10%	225	275
1891A Proof	—	Value: 1,000				
1892A	1,815,000	—	BV	160+10%	225	275
1893A	3,172,000	—	BV	160+10%	225	275
1894A	5,815,000	—	BV	160+10%	225	275
1895A	4,135,000	—	BV	160+10%	225	275
1896A	4,239,000	—	BV	160+10%	225	275
1896A Proof	—	Value: 1,000				
1897A	5,394,000	—	BV	160+10%	225	275
1898A	6,542,000	—	BV	160+10%	225	275
1899A	5,873,000	—	BV	160+10%	225	275
1899A Proof	—	Value: 1,000				
1900A	5,163,000	—	BV	160+10%	225	275
1901A	5,188,000	—	BV	160+10%	225	400
1901A Proof	—	Value: 1,400				
1902A	4,138,000	—	BV	160+10%	225	400
1902A Proof	—	Value: 1,400				
1903A	2,870,000	—	BV	160+10%	225	400
1903A Proof	—	Value: 1,400				
1904A	3,453,000	—	BV	160+10%	225	400
1904A Proof	—	Value: 1,250				
1905A	4,176,000	—	BV	160+10%	225	400
1905A Proof	287	Value: 1,250				
1905J	921,000	BV+5%	BV+10%	190	300	400
1906A	7,788,000	—	BV	160+10%	250	400
1906A Proof	124	Value: 1,250				
1906J	82,000	BV+5%	290	380	600	400
1907A	2,576,000	—	BV	160+10%	225	400

KM# 521

Date	Mintage	F	VF	XF	Unc	BU
1907A Proof	—			Value: 1,250		
1908A	3,274,000	—	BV	160+10%	225	400
1908A Proof	—			Value: 1,200		
1909A	5,213,000	—	BV	160+10%	225	400
1909J	350,000	BV+5%	BV+10%	190	300	400
1909A Proof	—			Value: 1,200		
1909J Proof	—			Value: 1,750		
1910A	8,646,000	—	BV	160+10%	225	400
1910J	753,000	—	BV	160+10%	225	400
1911A	4,746,000	—	BV	160+10%	225	400
1912A	5,569,000	—	BV	160+10%	225	400
1912J	503,000	BV+3%	BV+5%	190	300	400
1913A	6,102,000	—	BV	160+10%	225	400
1913A Proof	—			Value: 1,000		

KM# 537 20 MARK
7.9650 g., 0.9000 Gold .2304 oz. AGW **Ruler:** Wilhelm II **Obv:** Uniformed bust right **Rev:** Crowned imperial eagle with shield on breast

Date	Mintage	F	VF	XF	Unc	BU
1913A	—	BV	BV+5%	180	250	300
1913A Proof	—			Value: 1,500		
1914A	2,137,000	BV	BV+5%	180	250	300
1914A Proof	—			Value: 1,500		
1915A	1,271,000	—	1,100	1,400	2,000	2,500

Saxony

KM # 1239 5 MARK
1.9910 g., 0.9000 Gold .0576 oz. AGW **Ruler:** Albert **Rev:** Type I

Date	Mintage	F	VF	XF	Unc	BU
1877E	402,000	175	275	375	550	750
1877E Proof	—			Value: 1,000		

KM # 1232 10 MARK
3.9820 g., 0.9000 Gold .1152 oz. AGW **Ruler:** Johann

Date	Mintage	F	VF	XF	Unc	BU
1872E	339,000	90.00	175	285	500	800
1873E	822,000	90.00	175	285	500	800

KM # 1235 10 MARK
3.9820 g., 0.9000 Gold .1152 oz. AGW **Ruler:** Albert **Rev:** Type II

Date	Mintage	F	VF	XF	Unc	BU
1874E	48,000	450	750	1,200	2,500	3,000
1875E	528,000	70.00	120	200	400	600

Date	Mintage	F	VF	XF	Unc	BU
1877E	201,000	70.00	120	200	500	750
1878E	225,000	70.00	120	200	500	750
1879E	182,000	70.00	120	200	500	750
1881E	240,000	70.00	120	200	500	750
1888E	149,000	70.00	120	200	500	750

KM # 1247 10 MARK
3.9820 g., 0.9000 Gold .1152 oz. AGW **Ruler:** Albert **Rev:** Type III

Date	Mintage	F	VF	XF	Unc	BU
1891 E	224,000	100	160	200	450	550
1893E	224,000	100	145	200	450	550
1896E	150,000	100	160	200	450	550
1898E	313,000	100	160	225	450	550
1900E	74,000	100	160	250	450	550
1900E Proof	—			Value: 1,500		
1901E	75,000	100	160	250	450	550
1902E	37,000	100	160	250	475	575
1902E Proof	—			Value: 1,500		

KM # 1259 10 MARK
3.9820 g., 0.9000 Gold .1152 oz. AGW **Ruler:** Georg

Date	Mintage	F	VF	XF	Unc	BU
1903E	284,000	100	210	350	600	—
1903E Proof	100			Value: 1,600		
1904E	149,000	100	210	350	600	—

KM # 1264 10 MARK
3.9820 g., 0.9000 Gold .1152 oz. AGW **Ruler:** Friedrich August III

Date	Mintage	F	VF	XF	Unc	BU
1905E	112,000	120	225	285	450	—
1905E Proof	100			Value: 1,400		
1906E	75,000	120	225	285	450	—
1906E Proof	—			Value: 1,500		
1907E Proof	—			Value: 1,500		
1907E	112,000	120	225	285	450	—
1909E	112,000	120	225	285	450	—
1910E	75,000	120	225	285	450	—
1910E Proof	—			Value: 1,400		
1911E	38,000	120	225	285	450	—
1912E	75,000	120	225	285	450	—

KM # 1264

KM # 1233 20 MARK
7.9650 g., 0.9000 Gold .2304 oz. AGW **Ruler:** Johann **Rev:**
Type I

Date	Mintage	F	VF	XF	Unc	BU
1872E	890,000	120	150	200	400	650
1872E Proof	—		Value: 3,000			

KM # 1234 20 MARK
7.9650 g., 0.9000 Gold .2304 oz. AGW **Ruler:** Johann **Obv:**
Large letters in legend

Date	Mintage	F	VF	XF	Unc	BU
1873E	203,000	120	150	200	400	650

KM # 1236 20 MARK
7.9650 g., 0.9000 Gold .2304 oz. AGW **Ruler:** Albert **Rev:** Type II

Date	Mintage	F	VF	XF	Unc	BU
1874E	153,000	120	150	180	425	650
Date	**Mintage**	**VG**	**F**	**VF**	**XF**	**Unc**
1876E	482,000	120	150	180	425	650
1876E Proof	—	Value: 1,800				
1877E	1,181	8,000	15,000	20,000	30,000	40,000
1878E	1,564	9,500	17,500	27,500	35,000	45,000

KM # 1248 20 MARK
7.9650 g., 0.9000 Gold .2304 oz. AGW **Ruler:** Albert **Rev:**
Type III

Date	Mintage	F	VF	XF	Unc	BU
1894E	639,000	115	150	200	350	450
1895E	113,000	120	175	250	425	525

KM # 1260 20 MARK
7.9650 g., 0.9000 Gold .2304 oz. AGW **Ruler:** Georg **Rev:** Type III

Date	Mintage	F	VF	XF	Unc	BU
1903E	250,000	120	175	250	450	—
1903E Proof	—	Value: 1,800				

KM # 1265 20 MARK
7.9650 g., 0.9000 Gold .2304 oz. AGW **Ruler:**
Friedrich August III

Date	Mintage	VG	F	VF	XF	Unc
1905E	500,000	—	115	135	200	350
1905E Proof	86	Value: 1,500				
1913E	121,000	—	125	175	250	450
1914E	325,000	—	120	165	225	425
1914E Proof	—	Value: 1,750				

GREAT BRITAIN

In 1817, Great Britain opened a new mint on Tower Hill and introduced a new coinage. The old system was based on 21 shillings equaling 1 guinea. The new system was based on 20 shillings equaling 1 pound, or "sovereign." The classic sovereign coinage, which survived well into the 20th century as circulating coins, depicts the reigning monarch on the obverse and either a coat of arms or an image of St. George slaying a dragon on the reverse.

KM# 673 1/2 SOVEREIGN
3.9940 g., 0.9170 Gold .1177 oz. AGW **Ruler:** George III **Obv:** Laureate head right **Obv. Legend:** GEORGIUS III DEI GRATIA **Rev:** Crowned arms **Rev. Legend:** BRITANNIARUM REX FID: DEF:

Date	Mintage	F	VF	XF	Unc	BU
1817	2,080,000	110	175	400	1,000	—
1817 Proof	—	Value: 6,300				
1818/7 Rare	1,030,000	—	—	—	—	—
1818	Inc. above	110	225	400	1,050	—
1818 Proof	—	Value: 5,000				
1820	35,000	100	175	400	1,050	—

KM# 681 1/2 SOVEREIGN
3.9940 g., 0.9170 Gold .1177 oz. AGW **Ruler:** George IV **Obv:** Laureate head left **Obv. Legend:** GEORGIUS IIII D:G: BRITANNIAR: REX F:D: **Rev:** Crowned arms within flower garland

Date	Mintage	F	VF	XF	Unc	BU
1821	231,000	450	1,100	2,600	4,500	—
1821 Proof	—	Value: 8,000				

KM# 689 1/2 SOVEREIGN
3.9940 g., 0.9170 Gold .1177 oz. AGW **Ruler:** George IV **Obv:** Laureate head left **Obv. Legend:** GEORGIUS IIII D:G: BRITANNIAR: REX F:D: **Rev:** Crowned arms

Date	Mintage	F	VF	XF	Unc	BU
1823	224,000	110	250	650	1,500	—
1823	—	Value: 7,500				
1824	592,000	100	225	600	1,500	—
1825	761,000	100	225	600	1,500	—
1825 Proof	—	Value: 4,500				

KM# 700 1/2 SOVEREIGN
3.9940 g., 0.9170 Gold .1177 oz. AGW **Ruler:** George IV **Obv:** Head left **Obv. Legend:** GEORGIUS IV DEI GRATIA **Rev:** Crowned arms within cartouche **Rev. Legend:** BRITANNIARUM REX FID: DEF:

Date	Mintage	F	VF	XF	Unc	BU
1826	345,000	90.00	200	600	2,000	—
1826 Proof	—	Value: 3,750				

Date	Mintage	F	VF	XF	Unc	BU
1827	492,000	100	225	600	1,600	—
1828	1,225,000	90.00	200	600	1,200	—

KM# 716 1/2 SOVEREIGN
3.9940 g., 0.9170 Gold .1177 oz. AGW **Ruler:** William IV

Date	Mintage	F	VF	XF	Unc	BU
1831 Proof	—	Value: 3,000				

KM# 720 1/2 SOVEREIGN
3.9940 g., 0.9170 Gold .1177 oz. AGW, 18 mm. **Ruler:** William IV **Obv:** Head right **Obv. Legend:** GULIELMUS IIII D:G: BRITANNIAR: REX F:D: **Rev:** Crowned arms within cartouche

Date	Mintage	F	VF	XF	Unc	BU
1834	134,000	125	275	850	1,800	—

KM# 722 1/2 SOVEREIGN
3.9940 g., 0.9170 Gold .1177 oz. AGW, 19 mm. **Ruler:** William IV **Obv:** Head right **Obv. Legend:** GULIELMUS IIII D:G: BRITANNIAR: REX F:D: **Rev:** Crowned arms within cartouche

Date	Mintage	F	VF	XF	Unc	BU
1835	773,000	150	225	800	1,600	—
1836	147,000	250	500	1,250	2,250	—
1837	160,000	150	250	800	1,600	—

KM# 735.1 1/2 SOVEREIGN
3.9940 g., 0.9170 Gold .1177 oz. AGW **Ruler:** Victoria **Obv:** Head left **Obv. Legend:** VICTORIA DEI GRATIA **Rev:** Without die number **Rev. Legend:** BRITANNIARUM REGINA FID: DEF:

Date	Mintage	F	VF	XF	Unc	BU
1838	273,000	100	175	500	1,400	—
1839 Proof	1,230	Value: 3,000				
1841	509,000	100	175	550	1,400	—
1842	2,223,000	90.00	100	300	800	—
1843	1,252,000	100	175	500	1,400	—
1844	1,127,000	100	140	450	1,100	—
1845	888,000	300	650	1,800	3,500	—
1846	1,064,000	95.00	140	450	1,100	—
1847	983,000	90.00	100	350	1,100	—
1848	411,000	100	200	400	1,250	—
1849	845,000	95.00	140	400	1,000	—
1850	180,000	275	450	1,600	2,800	—
1851	774,000	100	140	375	1,200	—
1852	1,378,000	100	135	350	1,000	—
1853	2,709,000	95.00	135	350	1,000	—

Date	Mintage	F	VF	XF	Unc	BU
1853 Proof	—	Value: 5,500				
1854 Rare	1,125,000	—	—	—	—	—
1855	1,120,000	100	140	300	750	—
1856	2,392,000	90.00	130	300	700	—
1857	728,000	100	140	300	750	—
1858	856,000	90.00	130	300	700	—
1859	2,204,000	85.00	120	300	700	—
1860	1,132,000	90.00	130	325	750	—
1861	1,131,000	90.00	130	300	775	—
1862	—	750	1,800	4,500	11,000	—
1863	1,572,000	90.00	135	300	700	—
1880	1,008,999	80.00	100	300	600	—
1883	2,870,000	80.00	100	225	600	—
1884	1,114,000	80.00	100	225	600	—
Note: 1884 is much rarer than the mintage figure indicates						
1885/3	4,469,000	100	175	375	850	—
1885	Inc. above	80.00	110	225	550	—

KM# 735.2 1/2 SOVEREIGN
3.9940 g., 0.9170 Gold .1177 oz. AGW **Ruler:** Victoria **Obv:**
Head left **Obv. Legend:** VICTORIA DEI GRATIA **Rev:** With die
number **Rev. Legend:** BRITANNIARUM REGINA FID: DEF:

Date	Mintage	F	VF	XF	Unc	BU
1863	Inc. above	85.00	100	300	550	—
1864	1,758,000	85.00	100	225	600	—
1865	1,835,000	85.00	100	225	600	—
1866	2,059,000	85.00	100	225	600	—
1867	993,000	100	130	250	650	—
1869	1,862,000	90.00	130	250	650	—
1870	160,000	110	150	300	750	—
1871	2,063,000	90.00	150	260	600	—
1871 Proof	—	Value: 7,500				
Note: Plain edge						
1872	3,249,000	100	130	240	550	—
1873	1,927,000	100	130	260	650	—
1874	1,884,000	100	140	270	650	—
1875	516,000	100	150	280	650	—
1876	2,785,000	90.00	130	200	550	—
1877	2,197,000	90.00	130	200	550	—
1878	2,082,000	90.00	130	200	550	—
1879	35,000	125	200	400	900	—
1880	Inc. above	90.00	125	300	800	—

KM# 766 1/2 SOVEREIGN
3.9940 g., 0.9170 Gold .1177 oz. AGW **Ruler:** Victoria **Obv:** Coroneted bust left **Obv. Legend:** VICTORIA DEI GRATIA **Rev:** Without die number **Rev. Legend:** BRITANNIARUM REGINA FID: DEF:

Date	Mintage	F	VF	XF	Unc	BU
1887	872,000	BV	85.00	120	240	—
1887 Proof	797	Value: 700				
1890	2,266,000	BV	85.00	120	250	—
1891	1,079,000	BV	85.00	120	250	—
1892	13,680,000	BV	85.00	120	250	—
1893	4,427,000	BV	85.00	120	250	—

KM# 784 1/2 SOVEREIGN
3.9940 g., 0.9170 Gold .1177 oz. AGW **Ruler:** Victoria **Obv:** Mature draped bust left **Obv. Legend:** VICTORIA. DEI. GRA. BRITT. REGINA. FID. DEF. IND. IMP. **Obv. Designer:** Thomas Brock **Rev:** St. George slaying the dragon right

Date	Mintage	F	VF	XF	Unc	BU
1893	Inc. above	BV	80.00	100	180	—
1893 Proof	773	Value: 700				
1894	3,795,000	BV	80.00	100	180	—
1895	2,869,000	BV	80.00	100	180	—
1896	2,947,000	BV	80.00	100	170	—
1897	3,568,000	BV	80.00	100	170	—
1898	2,869,000	BV	80.00	100	170	—
1899	3,362,000	BV	80.00	100	170	—
1900	4,307,000	BV	80.00	100	170	—
1901	2,037,999	—	BV	90.00	170	—

KM# 804 1/2 SOVEREIGN
3.9940 g., 0.9170 Gold .1177 oz. AGW **Ruler:** Edward VII **Obv:** Head right **Rev:** St. George slaying the dragon

Date	Mintage	F	VF	XF	Unc	BU
1902	4,244,000	—	80.00	90.00	120	—
1902 Proof	15,000	Value: 225				
1903	2,522,000	—	BV	90.00	120	—
1904	1,717,000	—	BV	90.00	120	—
1905	3,024,000	—	BV	90.00	120	—
1906	4,245,000	—	BV	90.00	120	—
1907	4,233,000	—	BV	90.00	120	—
1908	3,997,000	—	BV	90.00	120	—
1909	4,011,000	—	BV	90.00	120	—
1910	5,024,000	—	BV	90.00	120	—

KM# 819 1/2 SOVEREIGN
3.9940 g., 0.9170 Gold .1177 oz. AGW **Ruler:** George V **Obv:**
Head left **Obv. Designer:** Bertram MacKennal **Rev:** St. George
slaying the dragon

Date	Mintage	F	VF	XF	Unc	BU
1911	6,104,000	—	BV	90.00	120	—
1911 Proof	3,764			Value: 350		
1912	6,224,000	—	BV	90.00	120	—
1913	6,094,000	—	BV	90.00	120	—
1914	7,251,000	—	BV	90.00	120	—
1915	2,043,000	—	BV	90.00	120	—

KM# 858 1/2 SOVEREIGN
3.9940 g., 0.9170 Gold .1177 oz. **AGW** **Ruler:** George VI **Obv:**
Head left **Obv. Designer:** T. H. Paget **Rev:** St. George slaying the
dragon

Date	Mintage	F	VF	XF	Unc	BU
1937 Proof	5,500			Value: 400		
1937 Matte Proof; Unique	—	—	—	—	—	—

KM# 674 SOVEREIGN
7.9881 g., 0.9170 Gold .2354 oz. AGW **Ruler:** George III
Obv: Laureate head right **Obv. Legend:** GEORGIUS III D.F.
BRITANNIAR. REX F.D. **Rev:** St. George slaying the dragon right

Date	Mintage	F	VF	XF	Unc	BU
1817	3,235,000	225	375	900	1,600	—
1817 Proof	—			Value: 9,000		
1818	2,347,000	250	425	1,100	1,900	—
1818 Proof	—			Value: 12,000		
1819 Rare	3,574	—	—	—	—	—
1820	932,000	250	400	1,000	1,600	—
1820 Proof	—	—	—	—	—	—

KM# 682 SOVEREIGN
7.9881 g., 0.9170 Gold .2354 oz. AGW **Ruler:** George IV
Obv: Laureate head left **Obv. Legend:** GEORGIUS IIII D:G:
BRITANNIAR: REX F:D: **Rev:** St. George slaying the dragon

Date	Mintage	F	VF	XF	Unc	BU
1821	9,405,000	225	375	1,000	1,500	—
1821 Proof	—			Value: 5,000		
1822	5,357,000	250	375	1,100	2,000	—
1823	617,000	375	1,200	3,500	8,000	—
1824	3,768,000	250	400	1,100	2,250	—
1825	4,200,000	350	1,000	2,800	6,250	—

KM# 819

KM# 696 SOVEREIGN

7.9881 g., 0.9170 Gold .2354 oz. AGW **Ruler:** George IV **Obv:** Head left **Obv. Legend:** GEORGIUS IV DEI GRATIA **Rev:** Crowned arms within cartouche **Rev. Legend:** BRITANNIARUM REX FID: DEF:

Date	Mintage	F	VF	XF	Unc	BU
1825	Inc. above	200	400	1,000	2,500	—
1825 Proof	—	Value: 5,500				
1825 Proof	—	Value: 6,500				
Note: Plain edge						
1826	5,724,000	200	350	1,000	1,600	—
1826 Proof	—	Value: 5,000				
1827	2,267,000	225	400	725	1,800	—
1828	386,000	1,800	3,500	12,000	—	—
Note: Only 6 or 7 known						
1829	2,445,000	250	425	1,000	2,000	—
1830	2,388,000	250	425	1,000	2,500	—
1830 Proof	—	—	—	—	—	—
1830 Proof	—	Value: 20,000				
Note: Plain edge						

KM# 717 SOVEREIGN

7.9881 g., 0.9170 Gold .2354 oz. AGW **Ruler:** William IV **Obv:** Head right **Obv. Legend:** GULIELMUS IIII D:G: BRITANNIAR: REX F:D: **Rev:** Crowned arms within cartouche

Date	Mintage	F	VF	XF	Unc	BU
1831	599,000	250	450	1,200	2,000	—
1831 Proof	—	Value: 6,250				
1832	3,737,000	225	350	1,000	2,700	—
1833	1,225,000	250	400	1,100	2,800	—
1835	723,000	250	400	1,200	3,000	—
1836	1,714,000	250	400	1,100	2,800	—
1837	1,173,000	275	400	1,200	2,800	—
1837 Proof	—	Value: 12,500				

KM# 736.1 SOVEREIGN

7.9881 g., 0.9170 Gold .2354 oz. AGW **Ruler:** Victoria **Obv:** Head left **Obv. Legend:** VICTORIA DEI GRATIA **Rev:** Without die number **Rev. Legend:** BRITANNIARUM REGINA FID: DEF:

Date	Mintage	F	VF	XF	Unc	BU
1838	2,719,000	160	350	800	1,750	—
1838 Proof P.E.	—	Value: 12,500				
1838 Proof	—	Value: 8,000				
1839	504,000	250	700	1,400	3,000	—
1839 Proof	—	Value: 5,500				
1841	124,000	1,600	2,800	7,200	—	—

KM# 736.1

Date	Mintage	F	VF	XF	Unc	BU
1842	4,865,000	BV	165	275	1,250	—
1843/2	5,982,000	600	—	—	—	—
1843	Inc. above	BV	175	275	1,100	—
1843 Narrow shield	Inc. above	4,500	7,000	—	—	—
1844	3,000,000	BV	175	275	1,100	—
1845	3,801,000	BV	175	275	1,200	—
1846	3,803,000	BV	175	275	1,700	—
1847	4,667,000	BV	175	275	1,200	—
1848	2,247,000	BV	BV	250	1,050	—
1849	1,755,000	BV	BV	275	1,100	—
1850	1,402,000	BV	175	300	1,350	—
1851	4,014,000	BV	BV	275	1,100	—
1852	8,053,000	BV	BV	250	1,050	—
1853 Proof	—	Value: 7,800				
1853 WW raised	10,598,000	BV	BV	250	900	—
1853 WW incuse	Inc. above	BV	BV	250	900	—
1854 WW raised	3,590,000	BV	180	355	1,250	—
1854 WW incuse	Inc. above	BV	BV	250	900	—
1855 WW raised	8,448,000	BV	200	275	950	—
1855	Inc. above	BV	BV	250	900	—
1856	4,806,000	BV	BV	200	900	—
1856 Small date	Inc. above	BV	BV	200	900	—
1857	4,496,000	BV	BV	200	900	—
1858	803,000	BV	BV	200	950	—
1859	1,548,000	BV	BV	200	900	—
1859 Small date	Inc. above	BV	BV	200	900	—
1860	2,556,000	BV	BV	250	1,100	—
1861	7,623,000	BV	BV	225	1,000	—
1862/1	—	—	—	—	—	—
1862	7,836,000	BV	BV	200	850	—
1863	5,922,000	BV	BV	200	850	—
1872	13,487,000	BV	BV	200	800	—

KM# 736.2 SOVEREIGN

7.9881 g., 0.9170 Gold .2354 oz. AGW **Ruler:** Victoria **Obv:** Head left **Obv. Legend:** VICTORIA DEI GRATIA **Rev:** Die number below wreath **Rev. Legend:** BRITANNIARUM REGINA FID: DEF:

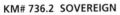

Date	Mintage	F	VF	XF	Unc	BU
1863	Inc. above	BV	BV	185	750	—
1864	8,656,000	BV	BV	180	800	—
1865	1,450,000	BV	BV	200	800	—
1866	4,047,000	BV	BV	180	750	—

Date	Mintage	F	VF	XF	Unc	BU
1868	1,653,000	BV	BV	185	750	—
1869	6,441,000	BV	BV	175	700	—
1869 Proof	—	Value: 6,500				
1870	2,190,000	BV	BV	180	700	—
1871	8,767,000	BV	BV	180	700	—
1872	Inc. above	BV	BV	180	700	—
1873	2,368,000	BV	BV	180	700	—
1874	521,000	1,500	2,500	6,500	—	—

KM# 736.3 SOVEREIGN
7.9881 g., 0.9170 Gold .2354 oz. AGW   **Ruler:** Victoria **Obv:** Additional line on lower edge of ribbon **Rev:** Without die number **Note:** Ansell variety.

Date	Mintage	F	VF	XF	Unc	BU
1859	168,000	800	1,250	3,500	6,000	—

KM# 752 SOVEREIGN
7.9881 g., 0.9170 Gold .2354 oz. AGW   **Ruler:** Victoria **Obv:** Head left **Obv. Legend:** VICTORIA D:G: BRITANNIAR: REG: F:D: **Rev:** St. George slaying the dragon

Date	Mintage	F	VF	XF	Unc	BU
1871	Inc. above	BV	BV	185	600	—
1871 Proof	—	Value: 8,500				
1872	Inc. above	BV	BV	185	600	—
1873	Inc. above	BV	BV	250	600	—
1874	Inc. above	BV	190	350	750	—
1876	3,319,000	BV	BV	225	650	—
1876 Proof	Inc. above	Value: 8,500				
1878	1,091,000	BV	BV	185	550	—
1879	20,000	200	800	1,700	5,000	—
1880	3,650,000	BV	BV	180	500	—
1880	—	BV	BV	180	500	—
Note: Without designer's initials on reverse						
1884	1,770,000	BV	160	200	550	—
1885	718,000	BV	170	240	625	—

KM# 767 SOVEREIGN
7.9881 g., 0.9170 Gold .2354 oz. AGW   **Ruler:** Victoria **Obv:** Coroneted bust left **Obv. Legend:** VICTORIA D:G: BRITT: REG: F: D: **Rev:** St. George slaying the dragon

Date	Mintage	F	VF	XF	Unc	BU
1887	1,111,000	—	BV	160	300	—
1887 Proof	797	Value: 950				

Date	Mintage	F	VF	XF	Unc	BU
1888	2,777,000	—	BV	BV	300	—
1889	7,257,000	—	BV	BV	300	—
1890	6,530,000	—	BV	BV	300	—
1891	6,329,000	—	BV	BV	300	—
1892	7,105,000	—	BV	BV	300	—

KM# 785 SOVEREIGN
7.9881 g., 0.9170 Gold .2354 oz. AGW **Ruler:** Victoria **Obv:** Mature draped bust left **Obv. Legend:** VICTORIA. DEI. GRA. BRITT. REGINA. FID. DEF. IND. IMP. **Obv. Designer:** Thomas Brock **Rev:** St. George slaying the dragon

Date	Mintage	F	VF	XF	Unc	BU
1893	6,898,000	—	—	BV	235	—
1893 Proof	773	Value: 1,100				
1894	3,783,000	—	—	BV	270	—
1895	2,285,000	—	—	BV	235	—
1896	3,334,000	—	—	BV	235	—
1898	4,361,000	—	—	BV	235	—
1899	7,516,000	—	—	BV	235	—
1900	10,847,000	—	—	BV	235	—
1901	1,579,000	—	—	BV	235	—

KM# 805 SOVEREIGN
7.9881 g., 0.9170 Gold .2354 oz. AGW **Ruler:** Edward VII **Obv:** Head right **Rev:** St. George slaying the dragon

Date	Mintage	F	VF	XF	Unc	BU
1902	4,738,000	—	—	BV	170	—
1902 Proof	15,000	Value: 350				
1903	8,889,000	—	—	BV	170	—
1904	10,041,000	—	—	BV	170	—
1905	5,910,000	—	—	BV	170	—
1906	10,467,000	—	—	BV	170	—
1907	18,459,000	—	—	BV	170	—
1908	11,729,000	—	—	BV	170	—
1909	12,157,000	—	—	BV	170	—
1910	22,380,000	—	—	BV	170	—

KM# 820 SOVEREIGN
7.9881 g., 0.9170 Gold .2354 oz. AGW **Ruler:** George V **Obv:** Head left **Obv. Designer:** Bertram MacKennal **Rev:** St. George slaying the dragon

Date	Mintage	F	VF	XF	Unc	BU
1911	30,044,000	—	—	BV	170	—

KM# 859

Date	Mintage	F	VF	XF	Unc	BU
1911 Proof	3,764	Value: 800				
1912	30,318,000	—	—	BV	170	—
1913	24,540,000	—	—	BV	170	—
1914	11,501,000	—	—	BV	170	—
1915	20,295,000	—	—	BV	170	—
1916	1,554,000	—	—	BV	185	—
1917	1,014,999	3,000	3,500	6,500	12,000	—
1925	4,406,000	—	—	BV	170	—

KM# 859 SOVEREIGN
7.9881 g., 0.9170 Gold .2354 oz. AGW **Ruler:** George VI **Obv:** Head left **Obv. Designer:** T. H. Paget **Rev:** St. George slaying the dragon

Date	Mintage	F	VF	XF	Unc	BU
1937 Proof	5,500	Value: 2,000				
1937 Matte Proof; Unique	—	—	—	—	—	—

MEXICO

Mexico was the site of advanced native civilizations 1,500 years before conquistador Hernando Cortés conquered the wealthy Aztec empire of Montezuma (1519-1521) and founded a Spanish colony, which lasted for almost 300 years. Mexico declared independence from Spain on September 16, 1810. Mexico survived routine political upheaval in ensuing years until a reform constitution of February 5, 1917, stabilized the government. Spain established a mint at Mexico City in 1535, but it did not produce gold coins until 1679. The long run of Mexican gold coinage that ensued, extending well into the 20th century, provides a wealth of opportunities for collectors and investors today.

KM# 410 PESO
1.6920 g., 0.8750 Gold .0476 oz. AGW **Obv:** Facing eagle, snake in beak **Obv. Legend:** REPUBLICA MEXICANA **Rev:** Value within 1/2 wreath

Date	Mintage	F	VF	XF	Unc	BU
1888AsL/MoM Rare	—	—	—	—	—	—
1888As L Rare	—	—	—	—	—	—

KM# 410.1 PESO
1.6920 g., 0.8750 Gold .0476 oz. AGW **Obv:** Facing eagle, snake in beak **Obv. Legend:** REPUBLICA MEXICANA **Rev:** Value within 1/2 wreath

Date	Mintage	F	VF	XF	Unc	BU
1888Ca/MoM Rare	104	—	—	—	—	—

GOLD RUSH

KM# 410.2 PESO
1.6920 g., 0.8750 Gold .0476 oz. AGW **Obv:** Facing eagle, snake in beak **Obv. Legend:** REPUBLICA MEXICANA **Rev:** Value within 1/2 wreath

Date	Mintage	F	VF	XF	Unc	BU
1873Cn P	1,221	75.00	100	150	250	—
1875Cn P	—	85.00	125	150	250	—
1878Cn G	248	100	175	225	500	—
1879Cn D	—	100	150	200	475	—
1881/0Cn D	338	100	150	200	475	—
1882Cn D	340	100	150	200	475	—
1883Cn D	—	100	150	200	475	—
1884Cn M	—	100	150	200	475	—
1886/4Cn M	277	100	150	225	500	—
1888/7Cn M	2,586	100	175	225	450	—
1888Cn M	Inc. above	65.00	100	150	265	—
1889Cn M Rare	—	—	—	—	—	—
1891/89Cn M	969	75.00	100	150	275	—
1892Cn M	780	75.00	100	150	275	—
1893Cn M	498	85.00	125	150	275	—
1894Cn M	493	80.00	125	150	275	—
1895Cn M	1,143	65.00	100	150	250	300
1896/5Cn M	1,028	65.00	100	150	250	—
1897Cn M	785	65.00	100	150	250	325
1898Cn M	3,521	65.00	100	150	225	—
1898Cn/MoM	Inc. above	65.00	100	150	250	—
1899Cn Q	2,000	65.00	100	150	225	—
1901Cn Q	Inc. above	65.00	100	150	225	—
1901/0Cn Q	2,350	65.00	100	150	225	—
1902Cn Q	2,480	65.00	100	150	225	—
1902Cn/MoQ/C	Inc. above	65.00	100	150	225	—
1904Cn H	3,614	65.00	100	150	225	—
1904Cn/Mo/ H	Inc. above	65.00	100	150	250	—
1905Cn P	1,000	—	—	—	—	—
Note: Reported, not confirmed						

KM# 410.3 PESO
1.6920 g., 0.8750 Gold .0476 oz. AGW **Obv:** Facing eagle, snake in beak **Obv. Legend:** REPUBLICA MEXICANA **Rev:** Value within 1/2 wreath

Date	Mintage	F	VF	XF	Unc	BU
1870Go S	—	100	125	150	265	—
1871Go S	500	100	175	225	475	—
1888Go R	210	125	200	250	550	—

What do the KM numbers mean?

The KM numbers refer to the Krause-Mishler system of cataloging coins, introduced in the Standard Catalog of World Coins series of reference books published by Krause Publications. The system assigns a unique number to each coin type within a country, allowing for easy and definitive reference to a particular coin by collectors. "C" numbers refer to the Craig cataloging system, and "Y" numbers refer to the Yeoman cataloging system.

Date	Mintage	F	VF	XF	Unc	BU
1890Go R	1,916	75.00	100	150	265	—
1892Go R	533	100	150	175	350	—
1894Go R	180	150	200	250	550	—
1895Go R	676	100	150	175	325	—
1896/5Go R	4,671	65.00	100	150	250	—
1897/6Go R	4,280	65.00	100	150	250	—
1897Go R	Inc. above	65.00	100	150	250	—
1898Go R	5,193	65.00	100	150	250	750
Note: Regular obverse						
1898Go R	Inc. above	75.00	100	150	250	750
Note: Mule, 5 Centavos obverse, normal reverse						
1899Go R	2,748	65.00	100	150	250	—
1900/800Go R	864	75.00	125	150	285	—

KM# 410.4 PESO

1.6920 g., 0.8750 Gold .0476 oz. AGW **Obv:** Facing eagle, snake in beak **Obv. Legend:** REPUBLICA MEXICANA **Rev:** Value within 1/2 wreath

Date	Mintage	F	VF	XF	Unc	BU
1875Ho R Rare	310	—	—	—	—	—
1876Ho F Rare	—	—	—	—	—	—
1888Ho G/MoM Rare	—	—	—	—	—	—

KM# 410.5 PESO

1.6920 g., 0.8750 Gold .0476 oz. AGW **Obv:** Facing eagle, snake in beak **Obv. Legend:** REPUBLICA MEXICANA **Rev:** Value within 1/2 wreath

Date	Mintage	F	VF	XF	Unc	BU
1870Mo C	2,540	45.00	65.00	95.00	185	—
1871Mo M/C	1,000	55.00	100	150	250	—
1872Mo M/C	3,000	45.00	65.00	95.00	185	—
1873/1Mo M	2,900	45.00	65.00	100	200	—
1873Mo M	Inc. above	45.00	65.00	95.00	185	—
1874Mo M	—	45.00	65.00	95.00	185	—
1875Mo B/M	—	45.00	65.00	95.00	185	250
1876/5Mo B/M	—	45.00	65.00	95.00	185	—
1877Mo M	—	45.00	65.00	95.00	185	—
1878Mo M	2,000	45.00	65.00	95.00	185	—
1879Mo M	—	45.00	65.00	95.00	185	—
1880/70Mo M	—	45.00	65.00	95.00	185	—
1881/71Mo M	1,000	45.00	65.00	95.00	185	—
1882/72Mo M	—	45.00	65.00	95.00	185	—
1883/72Mo M	1,000	45.00	65.00	95.00	185	—

Date	Mintage	F	VF	XF	Unc	BU
1884Mo M	—	45.00	65.00	95.00	185	—
1885/71Mo M	—	45.00	65.00	95.00	185	—
1885Mo M	—	45.00	65.00	95.00	185	—
1886Mo M	1,700	45.00	65.00	95.00	185	—
1887Mo M	2,200	45.00	65.00	95.00	185	—
1888Mo M	1,000	45.00	65.00	95.00	185	—
1889Mo M	500	100	150	200	285	—
1890Mo M	570	100	150	200	285	—
1891Mo M	746	100	150	200	285	—
1892/0Mo M	2,895	45.00	65.00	95.00	185	—
1893Mo M	5,917	45.00	65.00	95.00	185	—
1894/3MMo	—	45.00	65.00	95.00	185	—
1894Mo M	6,244	45.00	65.00	95.00	185	—
1895Mo M	8,994	45.00	65.00	95.00	185	—
1895Mo B	Inc. above	45.00	65.00	95.00	185	—
1896Mo B	7,166	45.00	65.00	95.00	185	—
1896Mo M	Inc. above	45.00	65.00	95.00	185	—
1897Mo M	5,131	45.00	65.00	95.00	185	—
1898/7Mo M	5,368	45.00	65.00	95.00	185	—
1899Mo M	9,515	45.00	65.00	95.00	185	—
1900/800Mo M	9,301	45.00	65.00	95.00	185	—
1900/880Mo M	Inc. above	45.00	65.00	95.00	185	—
1900/890Mo M	Inc. above	45.00	65.00	95.00	185	—
1900Mo M	Inc. above	45.00	65.00	95.00	185	—
1901Mo M Small date	Inc. above	45.00	65.00	95.00	185	—
1901/801Mo M Large date	8,293	45.00	65.00	95.00	185	—
1902Mo M Large date	11,000	45.00	65.00	95.00	185	—
1902Mo M Small date	Inc. above	45.00	65.00	95.00	185	—
1903Mo M Large date	10,000	45.00	65.00	95.00	185	—
1903Mo M Small date	Inc. above	55.00	85.00	125	200	—
1904Mo M	9,845	45.00	65.00	95.00	185	—
1905Mo M	3,429	45.00	65.00	95.00	185	—

KM# 410.6 PESO
1.6920 g., 0.8750 Gold .0476 oz. AGW   **Obv:** Facing eagle, snake in beak **Obv. Legend:** REPUBLICA MEXICANA **Rev:** Value within 1/2 wreath

Date	Mintage	F	VF	XF	Unc	BU
1872Zs H	2,024	125	150	175	275	—
1875/3Zs A	—	125	150	200	325	—
1878Zs S	—	125	150	175	275	—
1888Zs Z	280	175	225	325	700	—
1889Zs Z	492	150	175	225	450	—
1890Zs Z	738	150	175	225	450	—

KM# 411 2-1/2 PESOS
4.2300 g., 0.8750 Gold .1190 oz. AGW **Obv:** Facing eagle, snake in beak **Obv. Legend:** REPUBLICA MEXICANA **Rev:** Value within 1/2 wreath

Date	Mintage	F	VF	XF	Unc	BU
1888As/MoL Rare	—	—	—	—	—	—

KM# 411.2 2-1/2 PESOS
4.2300 g., 0.8750 Gold .1190 oz. AGW **Obv:** Facing eagle, snake in beak **Rev:** Value within 1/2 wreath

Date	Mintage	F	VF	XF	Unc	BU
1888Do C Rare	—	—	—	—	—	—

KM# 411.3 2-1/2 PESOS
4.2300 g., 0.8750 Gold .1190 oz. AGW **Obv:** Facing eagle, snake in beak **Obv. Legend:** REPUBLICA MEXICANA **Rev:** Value within 1/2 wreath

Date	Mintage	F	VF	XF	Unc	BU
1871Go S	600	1,250	2,000	2,500	3,250	—
1888Go/MoR	110	1,750	2,250	2,750	3,500	—

KM# 411.4 2-1/2 PESOS
4.2300 g., 0.8750 Gold .1190 oz. AGW **Obv:** Facing eagle, snake in beak **Obv. Legend:** REPUBLICA MEXICANA **Rev:** Value within 1/2 wreath

Date	Mintage	F	VF	XF	Unc	BU
1874Ho R Rare	—	—	—	—	—	—
1888Ho G Rare	—	—	—	—	—	—

KM# 411.5 2-1/2 PESOS
4.2300 g., 0.8750 Gold .1190 oz. AGW **Obv:** Facing eagle, snake in beak **Rev:** Value within 1/2 wreath

Date	Mintage	F	VF	XF	Unc	BU
1870Mo C	820	150	250	350	750	—
1872Mo M/C	800	150	250	350	750	—
1873/2Mo M	—	200	350	750	1,350	—
1874Mo M	—	200	350	750	1,350	—
1874Mo B/M	—	200	350	750	1,350	—
1875Mo B	—	200	350	750	1,350	—
1876Mo B	—	250	500	1,000	1,850	—
1877Mo M	—	200	350	750	1,350	—
1878Mo M	400	200	350	750	1,350	—
1879Mo M	—	200	350	750	1,350	—
1880/79Mo M	—	200	350	750	1,350	—
1881Mo M	400	200	350	750	1,350	—
1882Mo M	—	225	400	850	1,500	2,000
1883/73Mo M	400	200	350	750	1,350	—

Mint Marks of Mexico

As - Alamos
Ca - Chihuahua
Cn - Culiacan
Do - Durango
Ga - Guadalajara
Go - Guanajuato
Ho - Hermosilla
Mo - Mexico City
Zs - Zacatecas

Date	Mintage	F	VF	XF	Unc	BU
1884Mo M	—	250	500	1,000	1,600	—
1885Mo M	—	400	850	1,750	3,000	—
1886Mo M	400	200	350	750	1,350	—
1887Mo M	400	200	350	750	1,350	—
1888Mo M	540	200	350	750	1,350	—
1889Mo M	240	150	300	525	950	—
1890Mo M	420	200	350	750	1,350	—
1891Mo M	188	200	350	750	1,350	—
1892Mo M	240	200	350	750	1,350	—

KM# 411.6 2-1/2 PESOS
4.2300 g., 0.8750 Gold .1190 oz. AGW **Obv:** Facing eagle, snake in beak **Obv. Legend:** REPUBLICA MEXICANA **Rev:** Value within 1/2 wreath

Date	Mintage	F	VF	XF	Unc	BU
1872Zs H	1,300	200	350	500	1,200	—
1873Zs H	—	175	325	475	900	—
1875/3Zs A	—	200	350	750	1,350	—
1877Zs S	—	200	350	750	1,350	—
1878Zs S	300	200	350	750	1,350	—
1888Zs/MoS	80	300	500	1,000	1,800	—
1889Zs/Mo Z	184	250	450	950	1,600	—
1890Zs Z	326	200	350	750	1,350	—

KM# 412 5 PESOS
8.4600 g., 0.8750 Gold .2380 oz. AGW **Obv:** Facing eagle, snake in beak **Obv. Legend:** REPUBLICA MEXICANA **Rev:** Radiant cap above scales

Date	Mintage	F	VF	XF	Unc	BU
1875As L	—	—	—	—	—	—
1878As L	383	900	1,700	3,000	4,500	—

KM# 412.1 5 PESOS
8.4600 g., 0.8750 Gold .2380 oz. AGW **Obv:** Facing eagle, snake in beak **Obv. Legend:** REPUBLICA MEXICANA **Rev:** Radiant cap above scales

Date	Mintage	F	VF	XF	Unc	BU
1888Ca M Rare	120	—	—	—	—	—

KM# 412.2 5 PESOS
8.4600 g., 0.8750 Gold .2380 oz. AGW **Obv:** Facing eagle, snake in beak **Obv. Legend:** REPUBLICA MEXICANA **Rev:** Radiant cap above scales

Date	Mintage	F	VF	XF	Unc	BU
1873Cn P	—	300	600	1,000	2,000	—

Date	Mintage	F	VF	XF	Unc	BU
1874Cn P	—	—	—	—	—	—
1875Cn P	—	300	500	800	1,750	—
1876Cn P	—	300	500	800	1,750	—
1877Cn G	—	300	500	800	1,750	—
1882Cn Rare	174	—	—	—	—	—
1888Cn M	—	500	1,000	1,350	2,000	—
1890Cn M	435	250	500	750	1,600	—
1891Cn M	1,390	250	400	500	1,000	—
1894Cn M	484	250	500	750	1,600	—
1895Cn M	142	500	750	1,500	2,500	—
1900Cn Q	1,536	175	300	400	900	—
1903Cn Q	1,000	175	300	400	750	—

KM# 412.3 5 PESOS
8.4600 g., 0.8750 Gold .2380 oz. AGW **Obv:** Facing eagle, snake in beak **Obv. Legend:** REPUBLICA MEXICANA **Rev:** Radiant cap above scales

Date	Mintage	F	VF	XF	Unc	BU
1873/2Do P	—	700	1,250	1,800	3,000	—
1877Do P	—	700	1,250	1,800	3,000	—
1878Do E	—	700	1,250	1,800	3,000	—
1879/7Do B	—	700	1,250	1,800	3,000	—
1879Do B	—	700	1,250	1,800	3,000	—

KM# 412.4 5 PESOS
8.4600 g., 0.8750 Gold .2380 oz. AGW **Obv:** Facing eagle, snake in beak **Obv. Legend:** REPUBLICA MEXICANA **Rev:** Radiant cap above scales

Date	Mintage	F	VF	XF	Unc	BU
1871Go S	1,600	400	800	1,250	2,250	—
1887Go R	140	600	1,200	1,600	3,000	—
1888Go R Rare	65	—	—	—	—	—
1893Go R Rare	16	—	—	—	—	—

KM# 412.5 5 PESOS
8.4600 g., 0.8750 Gold .2380 oz. AGW **Obv:** Facing eagle, snake in beak **Obv. Legend:** REPUBLICA MEXICANA **Rev:** Radiant cap above scales

Date	Mintage	F	VF	XF	Unc	BU
1874Ho R	—	1,750	2,500	3,000	4,500	—
1877Ho R	990	750	1,250	2,000	3,000	—
1877Ho A	Inc. above	650	1,100	1,750	2,750	—
1888Ho G Rare	—	—	—	—	—	—

KM# 412.6 5 PESOS
8.4600 g., 0.8750 Gold .2380 oz. AGW **Obv:** Facing eagle, snake in beak **Obv. Legend:** REPUBLICA MEXICANA **Rev:** Radiant cap above scales

Date	Mintage	F	VF	XF	Unc	BU
1870Mo C	550	200	400	600	1,500	—
1871/69Mo M	1,600	175	300	400	650	—
1871Mo M	Inc. above	175	300	400	650	—
1872Mo M	1,600	175	300	400	650	—
1873/2Mo M	—	200	400	550	850	—
1874Mo M	—	200	400	550	850	—
1875/3Mo B/M	—	200	400	550	950	—
1875Mo B	—	200	400	550	950	—
1876/5Mo B/M	—	200	400	550	1,000	—
1877Mo M	—	250	450	750	1,650	—
1878/7Mo M	400	200	400	550	1,250	—
1878Mo M	Inc. above	200	400	550	1,250	—
1879/8Mo M	—	200	400	550	1,250	—
1880Mo M	—	200	400	550	1,250	—
1881Mo M	—	200	400	550	1,250	—
1882Mo M	200	250	450	750	1,650	—
1883Mo M	200	250	450	750	1,650	—
1884Mo M	—	250	450	750	1,650	—
1886Mo M	200	250	450	750	1,650	—
1887Mo M	200	250	450	750	1,650	—
1888Mo M	250	200	400	550	1,650	—
1889Mo M	190	250	450	750	1,650	—
1890Mo M	149	250	450	750	1,650	—
1891Mo M	156	250	450	750	1,650	—
1892Mo M	214	250	450	750	1,650	—
1893Mo M	1,058	200	400	500	800	—
1897Mo M	370	200	400	550	1,000	—
1898Mo M	376	200	400	550	1,000	—
1900Mo M	1,014	175	300	400	650	1,000
1901Mo M	1,071	175	300	400	650	—
1902Mo M	1,478	175	300	400	650	—
1903Mo M	1,162	175	300	400	650	—
1904Mo M	1,415	175	300	400	650	—
1905Mo M	563	200	400	550	1,500	—

KM# 412.7 5 PESOS
8.4600 g., 0.8750 Gold .2380 oz. AGW **Obv:** Facing eagle, snake in beak **Obv. Legend:** REPUBLICA MEXICANA **Rev:** Radiant cap above scales

Date	Mintage	F	VF	XF	Unc	BU
1874Zs A	—	250	500	750	1,500	—
1875Zs A	—	200	400	500	1,000	—
1877Zs S/A	—	200	400	550	1,000	—
1878/7Zs S/A	—	200	400	550	1,000	—
1883Zs S	—	175	300	450	700	—
1888Zs Z	70	1,000	1,500	2,000	3,000	—
1889Zs Z	373	200	300	500	850	—
1892Zs Z	1,229	175	300	450	700	—

KM# 413 10 PESOS
16.9200 g., 0.8750 Gold .4760 oz. AGW **Obv:** Facing eagle, snake in beak **Obv. Legend:** REPUBLICA MEXICANA **Rev:** Radiant cap above scales

Date	Mintage	F	VF	XF	Unc	BU
1874As DL Rare	—	—	—	—	—	—
1875As L	642	600	1,250	2,500	3,500	—
1878As L	977	500	1,000	2,000	3,000	—
1879As L	1,078	500	1,000	2,000	3,000	—
1880As L	2,629	500	1,000	2,000	3,000	—
1881As L	2,574	500	1,000	2,000	3,000	—
1882As L	3,403	500	1,000	2,000	3,000	—
1883As L	3,597	500	1,000	2,000	3,000	—
1884As L Rare	—	—	—	—	—	—
1885As L	4,562	500	1,000	2,000	3,000	—
1886As L	4,643	500	1,000	2,000	3,000	—
1887As L	3,667	500	1,000	2,000	3,000	—
1888As L	4,521	500	1,000	2,000	3,000	—
1889As L	5,615	500	1,000	2,000	3,000	—
1890As L	4,920	500	1,000	2,000	3,000	—
1891As L	568	500	1,000	2,000	3,000	—
1892As L	—	—	—	—	—	—
1893As L	817	500	1,000	2,000	3,000	—
1894/3As L	1,658	—	—	—	—	—
1894As L	Inc. above	500	1,000	2,000	3,000	—
1895As L	1,237	500	1,000	2,000	3,000	—

KM# 413.1 10 PESOS
16.9200 g., 0.8750 Gold .4760 oz. AGW **Obv:** Facing eagle, snake in beak **Obv. Legend:** REPUBLICA MEXICANA **Rev:** Radiant cap above scales

Date	Mintage	F	VF	XF	Unc	BU
1888Ca M	175	—	—	7,500	—	—

KM# 413.2 10 PESOS
16.9200 g., 0.8750 Gold .4760 oz. AGW **Obv:** Facing eagle, snake in beak **Obv. Legend:** REPUBLICA MEXICANA **Rev:** Radiant cap above scales

Date	Mintage	F	VF	XF	Unc	BU
1881Cn D	—	400	600	1,000	1,750	—
1882Cn D	874	400	600	1,000	1,750	—
1882Cn E	Inc. above	400	600	1,000	1,750	—
1883Cn D	221	—	—	—	—	—
1883Cn M	Inc. above	400	600	1,000	1,750	—
1884Cn D	—	400	600	1,000	1,750	—
1884Cn M	—	400	600	1,000	1,750	—
1885Cn M	1,235	400	600	1,000	1,750	—
1886Cn M	981	400	600	1,000	1,750	—
1887Cn M	2,289	400	600	1,000	1,750	—
1888Cn M	767	400	600	1,000	1,750	—
1889Cn M	859	400	600	1,000	1,750	—
1890Cn M	1,427	400	600	1,000	1,750	—
1891Cn M	670	400	600	1,000	1,750	—
1892Cn M	379	400	600	1,000	1,750	—
1893Cn M	1,806	400	600	1,000	1,750	—
1895Cn M	179	500	1,000	1,500	2,500	—
1903Cn Q	774	400	600	1,000	1,750	—

KM# 413.3 10 PESOS
16.9200 g., 0.8750 Gold .4760 oz. AGW **Obv:** Facing eagle, snake in beak **Obv. Legend:** REPUBLICA MEXICANA **Rev:** Radiant cap above scales

Date	Mintage	F	VF	XF	Unc	BU
1872Do P	1,755	350	500	800	1,250	—
1873/2Do P	1,091	350	500	850	1,350	—
1873/2Do M/P	Inc. above	350	550	900	1,450	—
1874Do M	—	350	550	900	1,450	—
1875Do M	—	350	550	900	1,450	—
1876Do M	—	450	750	1,250	2,000	—
1877Do P	—	350	550	900	1,450	—
1878Do E	582	350	550	900	1,450	—
1879/8Do B	—	350	550	900	1,450	—
1879Do B	—	350	550	900	1,450	—
1880Do P	2,030	350	550	900	1,450	3,750
1881/79Do P	2,617	350	550	900	1,450	—
1882Do P Rare	1,528	—	—	—	—	—
1882Do C	Inc. above	350	550	900	1,450	—
1883Do C	793	450	750	1,250	2,000	—
1884Do C	108	450	750	1,250	2,000	—

KM# 413.4 10 PESOS
16.9200 g., 0.8750 Gold .4760 oz. AGW **Obv:** Facing eagle, snake in beak **Obv. Legend:** REPUBLICA MEXICANA **Rev:** Radiant cap above scales

Date	Mintage	F	VF	XF	Unc	BU
1870Ga C	490	500	800	1,000	1,750	—
1871Ga C	1,910	400	800	1,250	2,250	—
1872Ga C	780	500	1,000	2,000	2,500	—
1873Ga C	422	500	1,000	2,000	3,000	—
1874/3Ga C	477	500	1,000	2,000	3,000	—
1875Ga C	710	500	1,000	2,000	3,000	—
1878Ga A	183	600	1,200	2,500	3,500	—
1879Ga A	200	600	1,200	2,500	3,500	—
1880Ga S	404	500	1,000	2,000	3,000	—
1881Ga S	239	600	1,200	2,500	3,500	—
1891Ga S	196	600	1,200	2,500	3,500	—

KM# 413.5 10 PESOS
16.9200 g., 0.8750 Gold .4760 oz. AGW **Obv:** Facing eagle, snake in beak **Obv. Legend:** REPUBLICA MEXICANA **Rev:** Radiant cap above scales

Date	Mintage	F	VF	XF	Unc	BU
1872Go S	1,400	2,000	4,000	6,500	10,000	—
1887Go R Rare	80	—	—	—	—	—
Note: Stack's Rio Grande Sale 6-93, P/L AU realized, $12,650						
1888Go R Rare	68	—	—	—	—	—

KM# 413.6 10 PESOS
16.9200 g., 0.8750 Gold .4760 oz. AGW **Obv:** Facing eagle, snake in beak **Obv. Legend:** REPUBLICA MEXICANA **Rev:** Radiant cap above scales

Date	Mintage	F	VF	XF	Unc	BU
1874Ho R Rare	—	—	—	—	—	—
1876Ho F Rare	357	—	—	—	—	—
1878Ho A	814	1,750	3,000	3,500	5,500	—
1879Ho A	—	1,000	2,000	2,500	4,000	—
1880Ho A	—	1,000	2,000	2,500	4,000	—
1881Ho A Rare	—	—	—	—	—	—
Note: American Numismatic Rarities Eliasberg sale 4-05, MS-62 realized $34,500.						

KM# 413.7 10 PESOS
16.9200 g., 0.8750 Gold .4760 oz. AGW **Obv:** Facing eagle, snake in beak **Obv. Legend:** REPUBLICA MEXICANA **Rev:** Radiant cap above scales

Date	Mintage	F	VF	XF	Unc	BU
1870Mo C	480	500	900	1,200	2,000	—

Date	Mintage	F	VF	XF	Unc	BU
1872/1Mo M/C	2,100	350	550	900	1,350	—
1873Mo M	—	400	600	950	1,450	—
1874/3Mo M	—	400	600	950	1,450	—
1875Mo B/M	—	400	600	950	1,450	—
1876Mo B Rare	—	—	—	—	—	—
1878Mo M	300	400	600	950	1,450	—
1879Mo M	—	—	—	—	—	—
1881Mo M	100	500	1,000	1,600	2,500	—
1882Mo M	—	400	600	950	1,450	—
1883Mo M	100	600	1,000	1,600	2,500	—
1884Mo M	—	600	1,000	1,600	2,500	—
1885Mo M	—	400	600	950	1,450	—
1886Mo M	100	600	1,000	1,600	2,500	—
1887Mo M	100	600	1,000	1,625	2,750	—
1888Mo M	144	450	750	1,200	2,000	—
1889Mo M	88	600	1,000	1,600	2,500	—
1890Mo M	137	600	1,000	1,600	2,500	—
1891Mo M	133	600	1,000	1,600	2,500	—
1892Mo M	45	600	1,000	1,600	2,500	—
1893Mo M	1,361	350	550	900	1,350	—
1897Mo M	239	400	600	950	1,450	—
1898/7Mo M	244	425	625	1,000	1,750	—
1900Mo M	733	400	600	950	1,450	—
1901Mo M	562	350	500	800	1,250	—
1902Mo M	719	350	500	800	1,250	—
1903Mo M	713	350	500	800	1,250	—
1904Mo M	694	350	500	800	1,250	—
1905Mo M	401	400	600	950	1,500	—

KM# 413.8 10 PESOS
16.9200 g., 0.8750 Gold .4760 oz. AGW   **Obv:** Facing eagle, snake in beak **Obv. Legend:** REPUBLICA MEXICANA **Rev:** Radiant cap above scales

Date	Mintage	F	VF	XF	Unc	BU
18700a E	4,614	400	600	900	1,600	—
18710a E	2,705	400	600	950	1,650	—
18720a E	5,897	400	600	850	1,500	—
18730a E	3,537	400	600	850	1,500	—
18740a E	2,205	400	600	1,200	1,850	—
18750a E	312	450	750	1,400	2,250	—
18760a E	766	450	750	1,400	2,250	—
18770a E	463	450	750	1,400	2,250	—
18780a E	229	450	750	1,400	2,250	—
18790a E	210	450	750	1,400	2,250	—

Date	Mintage	F	VF	XF	Unc	BU
18800a E	238	450	750	1,400	2,250	—
18810a E	961	400	600	1,200	2,000	—
18820a E	170	600	1,000	1,500	2,500	—
18830a E	111	600	1,000	1,500	2,500	—
18840a E	325	450	750	1,400	2,250	—
18850a E	370	450	750	1,400	2,250	—
18860a E	400	450	750	1,400	2,250	—
18870a E	—	700	1,250	2,250	4,000	—
18880a E	—	—	—	—	—	—

KM# 413.9 10 PESOS
16.9200 g., 0.8750 Gold .4760 oz. AGW **Obv:** Facing eagle, snake in beak **Obv. Legend:** REPUBLICA MEXICANA **Rev:** Radiant cap above scales

Date	Mintage	F	VF	XF	Unc	BU
1871Zs H	2,000	350	500	800	1,250	—
1872Zs H	3,092	325	500	750	1,150	—
1873Zs H	936	400	600	950	1,450	—
1874Zs H	—	400	600	950	1,450	—
1875/3Zs A	—	400	600	1,000	1,750	—
1876/5Zs S	—	400	600	1,000	1,750	—
1877Zs S/H	506	400	600	1,000	1,750	—
1878Zs S	711	400	600	1,000	1,750	—
1879/8Zs S	—	450	750	1,400	2,250	—
1879Zs S	—	450	750	1,400	2,250	—
1880Zs S	2,089	350	550	950	1,450	—
1881Zs S	736	400	600	1,000	1,750	—
1882/1Zs Z	—	400	600	1,000	1,750	2,500
1882Zs S	1,599	350	550	950	1,450	—
1883/2Zs S	256	400	600	1,000	1,750	—
1884/3Zs S	—	350	550	950	1,600	—
1884Zs S	—	350	550	950	1,600	—
1885Zs S	1,588	350	550	950	1,450	—
1886Zs S	5,364	350	550	950	1,450	—
1887Zs Z	2,330	350	550	950	1,450	—
1888Zs Z	4,810	350	550	950	1,450	—
1889Zs Z	6,154	300	500	750	1,250	—
1890Zs Z	1,321	350	550	950	1,450	—
1891Zs Z	1,930	350	550	950	1,450	—
1892Zs Z	1,882	350	550	950	1,450	—
1893Zs Z	2,899	350	550	950	1,450	—
1894Zs Z	2,501	350	550	950	1,450	—
1895Zs Z	1,217	350	550	950	1,450	—

KM# 414 20 PESOS
33.8400 g., 0.8750 Gold .9520 oz. AGW **Obv:** Facing eagle,
snake in beak **Rev:** Radiant cap above scales

Date	Mintage	F	VF	XF	Unc	BU
1876As L Rare	276	—	—	—	—	—
1877As L Rare	166	—	—	—	—	—
1878As L	—	—	—	—	—	—
1888As L Rare	—	—	—	—	—	—

KM# 414.2 20 PESOS
33.8400 g., 0.8750 Gold .9520 oz. AGW **Obv:** Facing eagle,
snake in beak **Obv. Legend:** REPUBLICA MEXICANA **Rev:** Radiant
cap above scales

Date	Mintage	F	VF	XF	Unc	BU
1870Cn E	3,749	BV	685	950	2,000	—
1871Cn P	3,046	BV	685	950	2,000	—
1872Cn P	972	BV	685	950	2,000	—
1873Cn P	1,317	BV	685	950	2,000	—
1874Cn P	—	BV	685	950	2,000	—
1875Cn P	—	600	1,200	1,800	2,500	—
1876Cn P	—	BV	685	950	2,000	—
1876Cn G	—	BV	685	950	2,000	—
1877Cn G	167	600	1,000	1,500	3,000	—
1878Cn Rare	842	—	—	—	—	—
1881/0Cn D	2,039	—	—	—	—	—
1881Cn D	Inc. above	BV	685	950	2,000	—
1882/1Cn D	736	BV	685	950	2,000	—
1883Cn M	1,836	BV	685	950	2,000	—
1884Cn M	—	BV	685	950	2,000	—
1885Cn M	544	BV	685	950	2,000	—
1886Cn M	882	BV	685	950	2,000	—
1887Cn M	837	BV	685	950	2,000	—
1888Cn M	473	BV	685	950	2,000	—
1889Cn M	1,376	BV	685	950	2,000	—
1890Cn M	—	800	1,750	3,500	8,750	—
1891Cn M	237	BV	900	1,200	2,250	—
1892Cn M	526	BV	685	950	2,000	—
1893Cn M	2,062	BV	685	950	2,000	—
1894Cn M	4,516	BV	685	950	2,000	—
1895Cn M	3,193	BV	685	950	2,000	—
1896Cn M	4,072	BV	685	950	2,000	—
1897/6Cn M	959	BV	685	950	2,000	—
1897Cn M	Inc. above	BV	685	950	2,000	—
1898Cn M	1,660	BV	685	950	2,000	—

KM# 414.3

Date	Mintage	F	VF	XF	Unc	BU
1899Cn M	1,243	BV	685	950	2,000	—
1899Cn Q	Inc. above	BV	900	1,200	2,250	—
1900Cn Q	1,558	BV	685	950	2,000	—
1901Cn Q	Inc. above	BV	685	950	2,000	—
1901/0Cn Q	1,496	—	—	—	—	—
1902Cn Q	1,059	BV	685	950	2,000	—
1903Cn Q	1,121	BV	685	950	2,000	—
1904Cn H	4,646	BV	685	950	2,000	—
1905Cn P	1,738	BV	900	1,200	2,250	—

KM# 414.3 20 PESOS
33.8400 g., 0.8750 Gold .9520 oz. AGW **Obv:** Facing eagle, snake in beak **Obv. Legend:** REPUBLICA MEXICANA **Rev:** Radiant cap above scales

Date	Mintage	F	VF	XF	Unc	BU
1870Do P	416	1,000	1,500	2,000	2,500	—
1871/0Do P	1,073	1,000	1,750	2,250	2,750	—
1871Do P	Inc. above	1,000	1,500	2,000	2,500	—
1872/1Do PT	—	1,500	3,000	4,500	7,000	—
1876Do M	—	1,000	1,500	2,000	2,500	—
1877Do P	94	1,500	2,250	2,750	3,250	—
1878Do Rare	258	—	—	—	—	—

KM# 414.4 20 PESOS
33.8400 g., 0.8750 Gold .9520 oz. AGW **Obv:** Facing eagle, snake in beak **Obv. Legend:** REPUBLICA MEXICANA **Rev:** Radiant cap above scales

Date	Mintage	F	VF	XF	Unc	BU
1870Go S	3,250	BV	665	900	1,500	—
1871Go S	20,000	BV	665	900	1,500	2,200
1872Go S	18,000	BV	665	900	1,500	—
1873Go S	7,000	BV	665	900	1,500	—
1874Go S	—	BV	665	900	1,500	—
1875Go S	—	BV	665	900	1,500	—
1876Go S	—	BV	665	900	1,500	—
1876Go M/S	—	—	—	—	—	—
1877Go M/S Rare	15,000	—	—	—	—	—
1877Go R	Inc. above	BV	665	900	1,500	—
1877Go S Rare	Inc. above	—	—	—	—	—
1878/7Go M/S	13,000	675	1,250	2,000	2,800	—
1878Go M	Inc. above	675	1,250	2,000	2,800	—
1878Go S	Inc. above	BV	665	900	1,500	—
1879Go S	8,202	BV	800	1,200	2,300	—

GOLD RUSH

Date	Mintage	F	VF	XF	Unc	BU
1880Go S	7,375	BV	665	900	1,500	—
1881Go S	4,909	BV	665	900	1,500	—
1882Go S	4,020	BV	665	900	1,500	—
1883/2Go B	3,705	BV	750	1,150	2,250	—
1883Go B	Inc. above	BV	665	900	1,500	—
1884Go B	1,798	BV	665	900	1,500	—
1885Go R	2,660	BV	665	900	1,500	—
1886Go R	1,090	625	800	1,250	2,500	—
1887Go R	1,009	625	800	1,250	2,500	—
1888Go R	1,011	625	800	1,250	2,500	—
1889Go R	956	625	800	1,250	2,500	—
1890Go R	879	625	800	1,250	2,500	—
1891Go R	818	625	800	1,250	2,500	—
1892Go R	730	625	800	1,250	2,500	—
1893Go R	3,343	BV	665	1,000	2,000	—
1894/3Go R	6,734	BV	665	900	1,500	—
1894Go R	Inc. above	BV	665	900	1,500	—
1895/3Go R	7,118	BV	665	900	1,500	—
1895Go R	Inc. above	BV	665	900	1,500	—
1896Go R	9,219	BV	665	900	1,500	5,750
1897/6Go R	6,781	BV	665	900	1,500	—
1897Go R	Inc. above	BV	665	900	1,500	—
1898Go R	7,710	BV	665	900	1,500	—
1899Go R	8,527	BV	665	900	1,500	—
1900Go R	4,512	550	800	1,250	2,350	—

KM# 414.5 20 PESOS
33.8400 g., 0.8750 Gold .9520 oz. AGW   **Obv:** Facing eagle, snake in beak **Obv. Legend:** REPUBLICA MEXICANA **Rev:** Radiant cap above scales

Date	Mintage	F	VF	XF	Unc	BU
1874Ho R Rare	—	—	—	—	—	—
1875Ho R Rare	—	—	—	—	—	—
1876Ho F Rare	—	—	—	—	—	—
1888Ho g Rare	—	—	—	—	—	—

KM# 414.6 20 PESOS
33.8400 g., 0.8750 Gold .9520 oz. AGW   **Obv:** Facing eagle, snake in beak **Obv. Legend:** REPUBLICA MEXICANA **Rev:** Radiant cap above scales

Date	Mintage	F	VF	XF	Unc	BU
1870Mo C	14,000	BV	665	850	1,500	—
1871Mo M	21,000	BV	665	850	1,500	—

Date	Mintage	F	VF	XF	Unc	BU
1872/1Mo M	11,000	BV	665	850	1,650	—
1872Mo M	Inc. above	BV	665	850	1,500	—
1873Mo M	5,600	BV	665	850	1,500	—
1874/2Mo M	—	BV	665	850	1,500	—
1874/2Mo B	—	BV	700	1,000	1,650	—
1875Mo B	—	BV	650	900	1,600	—
1876Mo B	—	BV	650	900	1,600	—
1876Mo M	—	—	—	—	—	—
Note: Reported, not confirmed						
1877Mo M	2,000	BV	700	1,100	2,000	—
1878Mo M	7,000	BV	650	900	1,600	—
1879Mo M	—	BV	650	900	1,750	—
1880Mo M	—	BV	650	900	1,750	—
1881/0Mo M	11,000	BV	665	850	1,500	—
1881Mo M	Inc. above	BV	665	850	1,500	—
1882/1Mo M	5,800	BV	665	850	1,500	—
1882Mo M	Inc. above	BV	665	850	1,500	—
1883/1Mo M	4,000	BV	665	850	1,500	—
1883Mo M	Inc. above	BV	665	850	1,500	—
1884/3Mo M	—	BV	650	900	1,600	—
1884Mo M	—	BV	650	900	1,600	—
1885Mo M	6,000	BV	650	900	1,750	—
1886Mo M	10,000	BV	665	850	1,500	—
1887Mo M	12,000	625	800	1,500	2,500	—
1888Mo M	7,300	BV	665	850	1,450	—
1889Mo M	6,477	650	850	1,650	3,750	—
1890Mo M	7,852	BV	665	850	1,550	—
1891/0Mo M	8,725	BV	665	850	1,550	—
1891Mo M	Inc. above	BV	665	850	1,550	—
1892Mo M	11,000	BV	665	850	1,500	—
1893Mo M	15,000	BV	665	850	1,500	—
1894Mo M	14,000	BV	665	850	1,500	—
1895Mo M	13,000	BV	665	850	1,500	—
1896Mo B	14,000	BV	665	850	1,500	—
1897/6Mo M	12,000	BV	665	850	1,500	—
1897Mo M	Inc. above	BV	665	850	1,500	—
1898Mo M	20,000	BV	665	850	1,500	—
1899Mo M	23,000	BV	665	850	1,500	—
1900Mo M	21,000	BV	665	850	1,500	—
1901Mo M	29,000	BV	665	850	1,500	—
1902Mo M	38,000	BV	665	850	1,500	—

Date	Mintage	F	VF	XF	Unc	BU
1903/2Mo M	31,000	BV	665	850	1,500	—
1903Mo M	Inc. above	BV	665	850	1,500	—
1904Mo M	52,000	BV	665	850	1,500	—
1905Mo M	9,757	BV	665	850	1,500	—

KM# 414.7 20 PESOS
33.8400 g., 0.8750 Gold .9520 oz. AGW **Obv:** Facing eagle, snake in beak **Obv. Legend:** REPUBLICA MEXICANA **Rev:** Radiant cap above scales

Date	Mintage	F	VF	XF	Unc	BU
18700a E	1,131	750	1,500	2,500	5,000	—
18710a E	1,591	750	1,500	2,500	5,000	—
18720a E	255	1,000	1,750	3,000	7,000	—
18880a E	170	2,000	3,000	5,000	—	—

KM# 414.8 20 PESOS
33.8400 g., 0.8750 Gold .9520 oz. AGW **Obv:** Facing eagle, snake in beak **Rev:** Radiant cap above scales

Date	Mintage	F	VF	XF	Unc	BU
1871Zs H	1,000	3,500	6,500	7,000	9,000	—
1875Zs A	—	4,000	6,000	7,500	9,500	—
1878Zs S	441	4,000	6,000	7,500	9,500	—
1888Zs Z Rare	50	—	—	—	—	—
1889Zs Z	640	3,500	5,500	7,000	9,000	—

KM# 414.1 20 PESOS
33.8400 g., 0.8750 Gold .9520 oz. AGW **Obv:** Facing eagle, snake in beak **Rev:** Radiant cap above scales **Note:** Mint mark CH, Ca.

Date	Mintage	F	VF	XF	Unc	BU
1872CH M	995	BV	700	1,000	2,500	—
1873CH M	950	BV	700	1,000	2,500	—
1874CH M	1,116	BV	685	950	2,500	—
1875CH M	750	BV	700	1,000	2,500	—
1876CH M	600	BV	800	1,250	2,750	—
1877CH Rare	55	—	—	—	—	—
1882CH M	1,758	BV	685	950	2,500	—
1883CH M	161	700	1,000	1,500	3,000	—
1884CH M	496	BV	700	1,000	2,500	—
1885CH M	122	700	1,000	1,500	3,000	—
1887Ca M	550	BV	700	1,000	2,500	—
1888Ca M	351	BV	700	1,000	2,500	—
1889Ca M	464	BV	700	1,000	2,500	—

Date	Mintage	F	VF	XF	Unc	BU
1890Ca M	1,209	BV	685	950	2,500	—
1891Ca M	2,004	BV	665	900	2,250	—
1893Ca M	418	BV	700	950	2,500	—
1895Ca M	133	700	1,000	1,500	3,000	—

KM# 461 2 PESOS
1.6666 g., 0.9000 Gold .0482 oz. AGW, 13 mm. **Obv:** National arms **Rev:** Date above value within wreath **Note:** Mint mark Mo.

Date	Mintage	F	VF	XF	Unc	BU
1919	1,670,000	—	BV	35.00	65.00	—
1920/10	—	BV	35.00	55.00	100	—
1920	4,282,000	—	BV	35.00	50.00	—
1944	10,000	BV	35.00	50.00	70.00	—
1945	Est. 140,000	—	—	—	BV+20%	—
1946	168,000	BV	35.00	50.00	100	—
1947	25,000	BV	35.00	50.00	75.00	—
1948 No specimens known	45,000	—	—	—	—	—
Note: During 1951-1972 a total of 4,590,493 pieces were restruck, most likely dated 1945. In 1996 matte restrikes were produced						

KM# 463 2-1/2 PESOS
2.0833 g., 0.9000 Gold .0602 oz. AGW, 15.5 mm. **Obv:** National arms **Rev:** Miguel Hidalgo y Costilla **Note:** Mint mark Mo.

Date	Mintage	F	VF	XF	Unc	BU
1918	1,704,000	—	BV	45.00	80.00	—
1919	984,000	—	BV	45.00	80.00	—
1920/10	607,000	—	BV	55.00	130	—
1920	Inc. above	—	BV	45.00	65.00	—
1944	20,000	—	BV	45.00	60.00	—
1945	Est. 180,000	—	—	—	BV+18%	—
1946	163,000	—	BV	45.00	60.00	—
1947	24,000	200	265	325	500	—
1948	63,000	—	BV	45.00	70.00	—
Note: During 1951-1972 a total of 5,025,087 pieces were restruck, most likely dated 1945. In 1996 matte restrikes were produced						

KM# 464 5 PESOS
4.1666 g., 0.9000 Gold .1205 oz. AGW, 19 mm. **Obv:** National arms **Rev:** Miguel Hidalgo y Costilla **Note:** Mint mark Mo.

Date	Mintage	F	VF	XF	Unc	BU
1905	18,000	120	175	245	600	—
1906	4,638,000	—	—	BV	90.00	—
1907/6	—	—	—	—	—	—
1907	1,088,000	—	—	BV	95.00	—
1910	100,000	—	—	BV	150	—

GOLD RUSH

Date	Mintage	F	VF	XF	Unc	BU
1918/7	609,000	—	—	BV	200	—
1918	Inc. above	—	—	BV	100	—
1919	506,000	—	—	BV	100	—
1920	2,385,000	—	—	BV	100	—
1955	Est. 48,000	—	—	—	BV+12 %	—
Note: During 1955-1972 a total of 1,767,645 pieces were restruck, most likely dated 1955. In 1996 matte restrikes were produced						

KM# 473 10 PESOS
8.3333 g., 0.9000 Gold .2411 oz. AGW, 22.5 mm.   **Obv:** National arms **Rev:** Miguel Hidalgo y Costilla **Note:** Mint mark Mo.

Date	Mintage	F	VF	XF	Unc	BU
1905	39,000	—	BV	170	225	—
1906	2,949,000	—	BV	165	185	—
1907	1,589,000	—	BV	165	185	—
1908	890,000	—	BV	165	185	—
1910	451,000	—	BV	165	185	—
1916	26,000	—	BV	175	350	—
1917	1,967,000	—	BV	165	185	—
1919	266,000	—	BV	165	200	—
1920	12,000	—	BV	425	700	—
1959	Est. 50,000	—	—	—	BV+7%	—
Note: *During 1961-1972 a total of 954,983 pieces were restruck, most likely dated 1959. In 1996 matte restrikes were produced						

KM# 478 20 PESOS
16.6666 g., 0.9000 Gold .4823 oz. AGW, 27.5 mm.   **Obv:** National arms, eagle left **Rev:** Gear-like design within upper circle above value **Note:** Mint mark Mo.

Date	Mintage	F	VF	XF	Unc	BU
1917	852,000	—	—	BV	345	—
1918	2,831,000	—	—	BV	345	—
1919	1,094,000	—	—	BV	345	—
1920/10	462,000	—	—	BV	345	—
1920	Inc. above	—	—	BV	345	—
1921/11	922,000	—	—	BV	345	—
1921/10	—	—	—	—	—	—
1921	Inc. above	—	—	BV	345	—
1959	Est. 13,000	—	—	—	—	—
Note: During 1960-1971 a total of 1,158,414 pieces were restruck, most likely dated 1959. In 1996 matte restrikes were produced						

KM# 481 50 PESOS
41.6666 g., 0.9000 Gold 1.2057 oz. AGW, 37 mm.   **Subject:** Centennial of Independence **Obv:** National arms **Rev:** Winged Victory **Edge:** Reeded **Designer:** Emilio del Moral **Note:** During 1949-1972 a total of 3,975,654 pieces were restruck, most likely dated 1947. In 1996 matte restrikes were produced. Mint mark Mo.

Date	Mintage	F	VF	XF	Unc	BU
1921	180,000	—	BV	875	950	1,000

KM# 481

Date	Mintage	F	VF	XF	Unc	BU
1922	463,000	—	—	BV	825	875
1923	432,000	—	—	BV	825	875
1924	439,000	—	—	BV	825	875
1925	716,000	—	—	BV	825	875
1926	600,000	—	—	BV	825	875
1927	606,000	—	—	BV	825	875
1928	538,000	—	—	BV	825	875
1929	458,000	—	—	BV	825	875
1930	372,000	—	—	BV	825	875
1931	137,000	—	—	BV	845	900
1944	593,000	—	—	BV	820	850
1945	1,012,000	—	—	BV	820	850
1946	1,588,000	—	—	BV	820	850
1947	309,000	—	—	—	BV+3%	—
1947 Specimen	—	—	—	—	—	—
Note: Value, $6,500						

KM# 482 50 PESOS
41.6666 g., 0.9000 Gold 1.2057 oz. AGW, 39 mm. **Obv:** National arms **Rev:** Winged Victory

Date	Mintage	F	VF	XF	Unc	BU
1943	89,000	—	—	—	BV	845

PERU

Spain established Lima, Peru, as the capital and headquarters of its administration of its South American territories in 1544. A mint was also established at Lima, which produced colonial coinage until republican coinage was begun in 1826. The gold republican coinage continued the colonial denominations of half escudo, escudo, 2 escudos, 4 escudos, and 8 escudos. The reverse design of the escudo and higher denominations shows Liberty holding a pole and shield.

KM # 192 5 SOLES
8.0645 g., 0.9000 Gold .2334 oz. AGW **Note:** Mint mark: LIMA

Date	Mintage	F	VF	XF	Unc	BU
1863LIMA YB	—	125	150	225	375	—

KM # 193 10 SOLES
16.1290 g., 0.9000 Gold .4667 oz. AGW **Note:** Mint mark: LIMA

Date	Mintage	F	VF	XF	Unc	BU
1863LIMA YB	—	225	250	300	500	—

KM # 194 20 SOLES
32.2581 g., 0.9000 Gold .9334 oz. AGW **Note:** Mint mark: LIMA

Date	Mintage	F	VF	XF	Unc	BU
1863LIMA YB	—	450	475	500	650	—

KM # 235 5 SOLES
2.3404 g., 0.9000 Gold .0677 oz. AGW **Note:** Struck at Lima.

Date	Mintage	F	VF	XF	Unc	BU
1956	4,510	—	—	—	50.00	—
1957	2,146	—	—	—	50.00	—
1959	1,536	—	—	—	60.00	—
1960	8,133	—	—	—	50.00	—
1961	1,154	—	—	—	60.00	—
1962	1,550	—	—	—	60.00	—
1963	3,945	—	—	—	50.00	—
1964	2,063	—	—	—	55.00	—
1965	14,000	—	—	—	50.00	—
1966	4,738	—	—	—	50.00	—
1967	3,651	—	—	—	50.00	—
1969	127	—	—	—	175	—

KM # 236 10 SOLES
4.6070 g., 0.9000 Gold .1354 oz. AGW **Note:** Struck at Lima.

Date	Mintage	F	VF	XF	Unc	BU
1956	5,410	—	—	BV	75.00	—
1957	1,300	—	—	BV	85.00	—
1959	1,103	—	—	BV	85.00	—
1960	7,178	—	—	BV	75.00	—
1961	1,634	—	—	BV	85.00	—
1962	1,676	—	—	BV	85.00	—
1963	3,372	—	—	BV	75.00	—
1964	1,554	—	—	BV	85.00	—
1965	14,000	—	—	BV	70.00	—
1966	2,601	—	—	BV	75.00	—
1967	3,002	—	—	BV	75.00	—
1968	100	—	BV	100	200	—
1969	100	—	BV	100	200	—

KM # 229 20 SOLES
9.3614 g., 0.9000 Gold .2709 oz. AGW **Note:** Struck at Lima.

Date	Mintage	F	VF	XF	Unc	BU
1950	1,800	—	—	BV	200	—
1951	9,264	—	—	BV	150	225
1952	424	—	—	BV	225	—
1953	1,435	—	—	BV	200	—
1954	1,732	—	—	BV	200	—
1955	1,971	—	—	BV	200	—
1956	1,201	—	—	BV	200	—

Date	Mintage	F	VF	XF	Unc	BU
1957	11,000	—	—	BV	145	175
1958	11,000	—	—	BV	145	175
1959	12,000	—	—	BV	145	175
1960	7,753	—	—	BV	145	175
1961	1,825	—	—	BV	200	—
1962	2,282	—	—	BV	175	—
1963	3,892	—	—	BV	165	—
1964	1,302	—	—	BV	200	—
1965	12,000	—	—	BV	145	175
1966	4,001	—	—	BV	145	175
1967	5,003	—	—	BV	145	175
1968	640	—	—	BV	200	—
1969	640	—	—	BV	200	—

What does "BV" mean?
"BV" means the coin's value in a particular grade is its bullion value, or the value of its gold content.

KM # 219 50 SOLES
33.4363 g., 0.9000 Gold .9675 oz. AGW

Date	Mintage	F	VF	XF	Unc	BU
1930	5,584	475	625	950	1,600	—
1931	5,538	475	625	950	1,500	—
1967	10,000	—	—	—	500	—
1968	300	—	—	—	650	—
1969	403	—	—	—	650	—

KM # 230 50 SOLES
23.4056 g., 0.9000 Gold .6772 oz. AGW   **Note:** Struck at Lima; similar to KM#229.

Date	Mintage	F	VF	XF	Unc	BU
1950	1,927	—	—	BV	350	—
1951	5,292	—	—	BV	350	450
1952	1,201	—	—	BV	450	—
1953	1,464	—	—	BV	400	—
1954	1,839	—	—	BV	375	—
1955	1,898	—	—	BV	375	—
1956	11,000	—	—	BV	325	425
1957	11,000	—	—	BV	325	425
1958	11,000	—	—	BV	325	425
1959	5,734	—	—	BV	325	425
1960	2,139	—	—	BV	365	—
1961	1,110	—	—	BV	450	—
1962	3,319	—	—	BV	350	—
1963	3,089	—	—	BV	350	—
1964/3	2,425	—	—	BV	350	—
1964	Inc. above	—	—	BV	360	—
1965	23,000	—	—	BV	325	425
1966	3,409	—	—	BV	350	450

KM # 230

GOLD RUSH

Date	Mintage	F	VF	XF	Unc	BU
1967	5,805	—	—	BV	350	450
1968	443	—	—	BV	450	—
1969	443	—	—	BV	450	—
1970	553	—	—	BV	450	—

KM # 231 100 SOLES
46.8071 g., 0.9000 Gold 1.3544 oz. AGW **Note:** Struck at Lima.

Date	Mintage	F	VF	XF	Unc	BU
1950	1,176	—	—	BV	700	800
1951	8,241	—	—	BV	650	750
1952	126	—	—	2,000	3,000	3,500
1953	498	—	—	BV	750	850
1954	1,808	—	—	BV	650	750
1955	901	—	—	BV	750	850
1956	1,159	—	—	BV	650	750
1957	550	—	—	BV	750	850
1958	101	—	—	3,000	4,000	4,500
1959	4,710	—	—	BV	625	725
1960	2,207	—	—	BV	625	725
1961	6,982	—	—	BV	600	700
1962	9,678	—	—	BV	600	700
1963	7,342	—	—	BV	600	700
1964	11,000	—	—	BV	600	700
1965	23,000	—	—	BV	600	—
1966	3,409	—	—	BV	625	725
1967	6,431	—	—	BV	625	725
1968	540	—	—	BV	750	850
1969	540	—	—	BV	750	850
1970	425	—	—	BV	750	850

RUSSIA

By the mid-19th century, Russia was the world's largest gold producer, and that status is reflected in its prolific gold coinage of the era. Of particular note are the 5-rouble coins of Nicholas I, who ruled from 1825 to 1855. The high mintage of 5-rouble coins continued under Alexander II (1855-1881), Alexander III (1881-1894), and Nicholas II (1894-1917).

C# 174 5 ROUBLES
6.5440 g., 0.9170 Gold .1929 oz. AGW **Ruler:** Nicholas I **Obv:** Crowned double imperial eagle **Rev:** Crown above inscription within wreath

Date	Mintage	F	VF	XF	Unc	BU
1826ПД	212,000	150	200	650	1,750	—

Date	Mintage	F	VF	XF	Unc	BU
1827ПД	—	300	500	2,000	3,500	—
1828ПД	604,000	150	200	650	1,750	3,000
1829ПД	733,000	150	200	650	1,750	3,000
1830ПД	490,000	150	200	650	1,750	3,000
1831ПД	846,000	150	200	650	1,750	3,000

C# 176 5 ROUBLES
6.5440 g., 0.9170 Gold .1929 oz. AGW   **Ruler:** Nicholas I **Subject:** Discovery of Gold at Kolyvan Mines **Obv:** Crowned double imperial eagle **Rev:** Value, text and date within circle

Date	Mintage	F	VF	XF	Unc	BU
1832ПД	1,000	1,200	2,500	5,000	7,500	—
1832ПД Proof	—	Value: 10,000				

C# 175.1 5 ROUBLES
6.5440 g., 0.9170 Gold .1929 oz. AGW   **Ruler:** Nicholas I **Obv:** Crowned double imperial eagle **Rev:** Value, text and date within circle

Date	Mintage	F	VF	XF	Unc	BU
1832ПД	481,000	175	250	325	600	1,200
1833ПД	829,000	175	250	325	600	1,200
1834ПД	1,346,000	150	200	275	500	1,000
1835ПД	1,440,000	150	200	275	500	1,000
1835П Rare	Inc. above	—	—	—	—	—
1835 Д Rare	Inc. above	—	—	—	—	—
Note: Without mintmark						
1836ПД	953,000	175	250	325	600	1,200
1837ПД	48,000	250	450	950	1,750	3,000
1838ПД	302,000	175	250	325	650	1,250
1839 АЧ	1,609,000	150	200	275	475	850
1840 АЧ	1,277,000	150	200	275	475	850
1841 АЧ	1,668,000	150	180	225	450	650
1842 АЧ	2,180,000	150	200	275	475	850
1843 АЧ	1,852,000	150	200	275	475	850
1844 КБ	2,365,000	150	200	275	475	850
1845 КБ	2,842,000	150	200	275	475	850
1846 КБ	3,442,000	150	200	275	475	850
Common date Proof	—	Value: 5,000				

C# 175.2 5 ROUBLES
6.5440 g., 0.9170 Gold .1929 oz. AGW   **Ruler:** Nicholas I **Obv:** Crowned double imperial eagle **Rev:** Value, text and date within circle

Date	Mintage	F	VF	XF	Unc	BU
1842MW	695	1,500	2,000	5,000	10,000	—

Date	Mintage	F	VF	XF	Unc	BU
1846MW	62	2,000	3,000	6,000	14,000	—
1848MW	485	1,500	2,000	5,000	10,000	—
1849MW	133	1,500	2,000	5,000	10,000	—
Common date Proof	—	Value: 10,000				

C# 175.3 5 ROUBLES
6.5440 g., 0.9170 Gold .1929 oz. AGW **Ruler:** Nicholas I **Obv:** Crowned double imperial eagle **Rev:** Value, text and date within circle **Note:** Different eagle.

Date	Mintage	F	VF	XF	Unc	BU
1846	—	—	—	—	—	—
1846СПБ АГ	—	150	200	275	475	850
Note: Mintage included in C#175.1						
1847СПБ АГ	3,900,000	150	200	300	550	950
1848СПБ АГ	2,900,000	145	185	275	475	850
1849СПБ АГ	3,100,000	145	185	275	475	850
1850СПБ АГ	3,900,000	145	185	275	475	850
1851СПБ АГ	3,400,000	145	185	275	475	850
1852СПБ АГ	3,900,000	145	185	275	475	850
1853СПБ АГ	3,900,000	145	185	275	475	850
1854СПБ АГ	3,900,000	145	185	275	475	850
Common date Proof	—	Value: 5,000				

Y# A26 5 ROUBLES
6.5440 g., 0.9170 Gold .1929 oz. AGW **Ruler:** Alexander II **Obv:** Crowned double imperial eagle **Rev:** Value, text and date within circle

Date	Mintage	F	VF	XF	Unc	BU
1855СПБ АГ	3,400,000	150	200	300	525	900
1856СПБ АГ	3,800,000	150	200	300	525	900
1857СПБ АГ	4,500,000	150	200	300	525	900
1858СПБ АГ	3,500,000	150	200	300	525	900
1858СПБ ПУ	—	150	200	300	525	900
Common date Proof	—	Value: 4,500				

Y# B26 5 ROUBLES
6.5440 g., 0.9170 Gold .1929 oz. AGW **Obv:** Crowned double imperial eagle, ribbons on crown **Rev:** Value, text and date within circle

Date	Mintage	F	VF	XF	Unc	BU
1859СПБ ПФ	3,900,000	145	185	275	475	850
1860СПБ ПФ	3,600,000	145	185	275	475	850
1861СПБ ПФ	3,500,000	145	185	275	475	850
1862СПБ ПФ	6,354,000	145	185	275	475	850
1863СПБ МИ	7,200,000	145	185	275	475	850

Date	Mintage	F	VF	XF	Unc	BU
1864СПБ АС	3,900,000	145	185	275	475	850
1865СПБ АС	3,902,000	145	185	275	475	850
1865СПБ СШ	Inc. above	145	185	275	475	850
1866СПБ СШ	3,900,000	145	185	275	475	850
1866СПБ НІ	Inc. above	145	185	275	475	850
1867СПБ НІ	3,494,000	145	185	275	475	850
1868СПБ НІ	3,400,000	145	185	275	475	850
1869СПБ НІ	3,900,000	145	185	275	475	850
1870СПБ НІ	5,000,000	145	185	275	475	850
1871СПБ НІІ	800,000	145	185	275	475	850
1872СПБ НІ	2,400,000	145	185	275	475	850
1873СПБ НІ	3,000,000	145	185	275	475	850
1874СПБ НІ	4,800,000	145	185	275	475	850
1875СПБ НІ	4,000,000	145	185	275	475	850
1876СПБ НІ	6,000,000	145	185	275	475	850
1877СПБ НІ	6,600,000	145	185	275	475	850
1877СПБ НФ	Inc. above	150	200	300	500	900
1878СПБ НФ	6,800,000	145	185	275	475	850
1879СПБ НФ	7,225,000	145	185	275	475	850
1880СПБ НФ	6,200,000	145	185	275	475	850
1881СПБ НФ	5,500,000	145	185	275	475	850
1882СПБ НФ	4,547,000	145	185	275	475	850
1883СПБ ДС	5,632,000	145	185	275	475	850
1883СПБ АГ	Inc. above	145	185	275	475	850
1884СПБ АГ	4,801,000	145	185	275	475	850
1885СПБ АГ	5,433,000	145	185	275	475	850
Common date Proof	—	Value: 4,500				

Y# 42 5 ROUBLES

6.4516 g., 0.9000 Gold .1867 oz. AGW   **Ruler:** Alexander III **Obv:** Head right **Rev:** Crowned double imperial eagle, ribbons on crown **Note:** Without mint mark, moneyer's initials on edge. Edge varieties exist.

Date	Mintage	F	VF	XF	Unc	BU
1886 АГ	351,000	165	225	325	550	950
1887 АГ	3,261,000	150	200	300	475	850
1888 АГ	5,257,000	150	200	300	475	850
1889 АГ	4,200,000	150	200	300	475	850
1890 АГ	5,600,000	150	200	300	475	850
1891 АГ	541,000	150	200	300	475	850
1892 АГ	128,000	175	250	350	600	1,000
1893 АГ	598,000	150	200	300	475	850
1894 АГ	598,000	150	200	300	475	850
Common date Proof	—	Value: 3,250				

Y# A61 5 ROUBLES
6.4516 g., 0.9000 Gold .1867 oz. AGW **Ruler:** Nicholas II **Obv:** Head left **Rev:** Crowned double imperial eagle, ribbons on crown, within circle flanked by stars **Note:** Without mint mark, moneyer's initials on edge.

Date	Mintage	F	VF	XF	Unc	BU
1895 АГ	36	—	9,000	20,000	35,000	—
1896 АГ	33	—	9,000	20,000	35,000	—

Y# 62 5 ROUBLES
4.3013 g., 0.9000 Gold .1244 oz. AGW **Ruler:** Nicholas II **Obv:** Head left **Rev:** Crowned double-headed imperial eagle, ribbons on crown **Note:** Struck at St. Petersburg without mint mark.

Date	Mintage	F	VF	XF	Unc	BU
1897 АГ	5,372,000	—	BV	90.00	110	220
1897 АГ Proof	—	Value: 3,500				
1898 АГ	52,378,000	—	BV	90.00	110	220
1899 ЗБ	20,400,000	—	BV	90.00	110	220
1899 ФЗ	Inc. above	—	BV	90.00	110	220
1900 ФЗ	31,000	—	BV	100	120	250
1901 ФЗ	7,500,000	—	—	BV	95.00	200
1901 АР	Inc. above	—	BV	90.00	110	220
1902 АР	6,240,000	—	—	BV	95.00	200
1903 АР	5,148,000	—	—	BV	95.00	200
1904 АР	2,016,000	—	—	BV	95.00	200
1906 ЭБ	10	—	—	7,000	10,000	—
1907 ЭБ	109	—	—	4,000	7,500	—
1909 ЭБ	—	—	BV	90.00	110	220
1910 ЭБ	200,000	—	BV	90.00	110	220
1911 ЭБ	100,000	BV	100	200	400	650
1901-11 Common date proof	—	Value: 2,500				

Y# 62

Y# A42 10 ROUBLES
12.9039 g., 0.9000 Gold .3734 oz. AGW **Ruler:** Alexander III **Obv:** Head right **Rev:** Crowned double imperial eagle, ribbons on crown **Note:** Without mint mark, moneyer's initials on edge.

Date	Mintage	F	VF	XF	Unc	BU
1886 АГ	57,000	400	750	1,350	3,000	—
1887 АГ	475,000	400	750	1,250	2,850	—
1888 АГ	23,000	400	750	1,350	3,000	—
1889 АГ	343,000	400	650	1,250	2,850	—
1890 АГ	15,000	400	750	1,350	3,500	—
1891 АГ	3,010	450	950	1,500	3,750	—
1892 АГ	8,006	450	950	1,500	4,500	—
1893 АГ Rare	1,008	—	—	—	—	—
Note: UBS Sale #67 9-06, XF realized $13,280						

Date	Mintage	F	VF	XF	Unc	BU
1894 AГ	1,007	600	1,000	2,250	5,500	—
Common date Proof	—	Value: 4,500				

Y# A63 10 ROUBLES

12.9039 g., 0.9000 Gold .3734 oz. AGW **Ruler:** Nicholas II **Obv:** Head left **Rev:** Crowned double imperial eagle, ribbons on crown, within circle flanked by stars **Rev. Legend:** ИМПЕРIАЛЪ (IMPERIAL) **Note:** Moneyer's initials on edge.

Date	Mintage	F	VF	XF	Unc	BU
1895 AГ	125	—	15,000	25,000	45,000	—
1895 AГ	125	—	15,000	25,000	45,000	—
1895 AГ	125	—	15,000	25,000	45,000	—
1896 AГ	125	—	15,000	25,000	45,000	—
1897 AГ	125	—	15,000	25,000	45,000	—

Y# 64 10 ROUBLES

8.6026 g., 0.9000 Gold .2489 oz. AGW **Ruler:** Nicholas II **Obv:** Head left **Rev:** Crowned double-headed imperial eagle, ribbons on crown **Note:** Without mint mark. Moneyer's initials on edge.

Date	Mintage	F	VF	XF	Unc	BU
1898 AГ	200,000	—	—	BV	190	375
1899 AГ	27,600,000	—	—	BV	175	360
1899 ФЗ	Inc. above	—	—	BV	175	360
1899 ЗБ	Inc. above	—	—	BV	190	375
1900 ФЗ	6,021,000	—	—	BV	175	360
1901 ФЗ	2,377,000	—	—	BV	190	360
1901 AP	Inc. above	—	—	BV	200	365
1902 AP	2,019,000	—	—	BV	190	360
1903 AP	2,817,000	—	—	BV	190	360
1904 AP	1,025,000	—	—	BV	190	360
1906 ЭБ Proof	10	Value: 15,000				
1909 ЭБ	50,000	—	BV	175	250	450
1910 ЭБ	100,000	—	BV	175	250	450
1911 ЭБ	50,000	—	BV	175	250	450
1901-11 Common date proof	—	Value: 4,500				

SPAIN

Spain's gold-coin heritage is long, rich, and colorful. Spain was Europe's most powerful country in the 16th century and played a leading role in exploring and colonizing the New World. Gold shipped to the mother country from the colonies added to the wealth it already held through the natural deposits on the Iberian Peninsula. Spain's power began to fade by the 17th century, but it held on to many of its colonies and their natural wealth into the 19th century.

KM# 630 2 ESCUDOS
1.6774 g., 0.9000 Gold .0485 oz. AGW **Ruler:** Isabel II **Obv:**
Draped laureate bust left **Obv. Legend:** ISABEL 2... **Rev:**
Crowned mantled arms **Rev. Legend:** REYNA DE LAS ESPANAS
Note: Mint mark: 6-pointed star.

Date	Mintage	F	VF	XF	Unc	BU
1865	—	125	180	275	375	—
1868 (68)	—	350	800	1,600	2,200	—

KM# 631.1 4 ESCUDOS
3.3548 g., 0.9000 Gold .0971 oz. AGW **Ruler:** Isabel II **Obv:**
Draped laureate bust left **Obv. Legend:** ISABEL 2... **Rev:**
Crowned mantled arms **Rev. Legend:** REYNA DE LAS ESPANAS
Note: Mint mark: 6-pointed star.

Date	Mintage	F	VF	XF	Unc	BU
1865	—	90.00	120	150	180	—
1866	—	90.00	120	150	180	—
1867	—	90.00	120	150	180	—
1868 (68)	—	90.00	140	175	210	—

KM# 631.2 4 ESCUDOS
3.3548 g., 0.9000 Gold .0971 oz. AGW **Ruler:** Isabel II **Obv:**
Draped laureate bust left **Rev:** Crowned mantled arms **Note:**
Mint mark: 7-pointed star.

Date	Mintage	F	VF	XF	Unc	BU
1865	—	275	550	950	1,300	—
1866	—	200	400	700	1,000	—

KM# 636.1 10 ESCUDOS
8.3870 g., 0.9000 Gold .2427 oz. AGW **Ruler:** Isabel II **Obv:**
Draped laureate bust left **Obv. Legend:** ISABEL 2... **Rev:**
Crowned mantled arms **Rev. Legend:** REYNA DE LAS ESPANAS
Note: Mint mark: 6-pointed star.

Date	Mintage	F	VF	XF	Unc	BU
1865	—	200	240	300	375	—
1866	—	200	300	450	600	—
1867	—	180	210	250	280	—
1868 (68)	—	180	210	240	270	—

KM# 636.2 10 ESCUDOS
8.3870 g., 0.9000 Gold .2427 oz. AGW **Ruler:** Isabel II **Obv:**
Draped laureate bust left **Rev:** Crowned mantled arms **Note:**
Mint mark: 7-pointed star.

Date	Mintage	F	VF	XF	Unc	BU
1866	—	1,200	2,500	4,500	6,500	—

KM# 636.3 10 ESCUDOS
8.3870 g., 0.9000 Gold .2427 oz. AGW **Ruler:** Isabel II **Obv:** Draped laureate bust left **Obv. Legend:** ISABEL 2... **Rev:** Crowned mantled arms **Rev. Legend:** REYNA DE LAS ESPANAS **Note:** Mint mark: 6-pointed star.

Date	Mintage	F	VF	XF	Unc	BU
1868 (73)	—	180	210	240	270	—

KM# 677 10 PESETAS
3.2258 g., 0.9000 Gold .0933 oz. AGW **Ruler:** Alfonso XII **Obv:** Young head right **Obv. Legend:** ALFONSO XII... **Rev:** Crowned mantled arms **Rev. Legend:** REY CONST... **Note:** Mint mark: 6-pointed star.

Date	Mintage	F	VF	XF	Unc	BU
1878 (78) EM-M	91,000	150	225	300	400	—
1879 (79) EM-M	33,000	700	1,250	1,800	2,500	—
1878 (61) DE-M	496	—	—	—	1,000	—
1878 (62) DE-M	18,000	—	—	—	150	—
Note: The above 2 coins dated (61) and (62) were restruck by the Spanish Mint from original dies in 1961 and 1962 and are considered official restrike issues

KM# 693 20 PESETAS
6.4516 g., 0.9000 Gold .1867 oz. AGW **Ruler:** Alfonso XIII **Obv:** Toddler's head right **Obv. Legend:** ALFONSO XIII... **Rev:** Crowned mantled arms **Rev. Legend:** REY CONST... **Note:** Mint mark: 6-pointed star.

Date	Mintage	F	VF	XF	Unc	BU
1889 (89) MP-M	875,000	—	235	275	375	—
1890 (90) MP-M	2,344,000	—	195	225	260	—
1887 (61) PG-V	800	—	—	450	750	—
1887 (62) PG-V	11,000	—	—	125	175	—
Note: The above 2 coins dated (61) and (62) were restruck by the Spanish Mint from original dies in 1961 and 1962 and are considered official restrike issues

KM# 701 20 PESETAS
6.4516 g., 0.9000 Gold .1867 oz. AGW **Ruler:** Alfonso XIII **Obv:** Child's head right **Obv. Legend:** ALFONSO XIII... **Rev:** Crowned mantled arms **Rev. Legend:** REY CONST... **Note:** Mint mark: 6-pointed star.

Date	Mintage	F	VF	XF	Unc	BU
1892 (92) PG-M	2,430,000	850	1,250	2,250	3,000	—

KM# 709 20 PESETAS
6.4516 g., 0.9000 Gold .1867 oz. AGW **Ruler:** Alfonso XIII **Obv:** Child's head right **Obv. Legend:** ALFONSO XIII POR... **Rev:** Crowned mantled arms **Rev. Legend:** REY CONST... **Note:** Mint mark: 6-pointed star.

Date	Mintage	F	VF	XF	Unc	BU
1899 (99) SM-V	2,086,000	—	225	300	400	—
1896 (61) PG-V	900	—	—	400	500	—

Date	Mintage	F	VF	XF	Unc	BU
1896 (62) PG-V	12,000	—	—	135	165	—

Note: The above 2 coins dated (61) and (62) were restruck by the Spanish Mint from original dies in 1961 and 1962 and are considered official restrike issues

KM# 724 20 PESETAS
6.4516 g., 0.9000 Gold .1867 oz. AGW **Obv:** Head right **Rev:** Crowned and mantled shield **Note:** Mint mark: 6-pointed star.

Date	Mintage	F	VF	XF	Unc	BU
1904 (04) SM-V	3,814	850	1,650	2,250	3,000	—

KM# 667 25 PESETAS
8.0645 g., 0.9000 Gold .2333 oz. AGW **Ruler:** Amadeao I **Obv:** Head right **Obv. Legend:** AMADEO I... **Rev:** Crowned mantled arms **Note:** Mint mark: 6-pointed star.

Date	Mintage	F	VF	XF	Unc	BU
1871 (75) SD-M Rare	25	—	—	—	—	—

KM# 673 25 PESETAS
8.0645 g., 0.9000 Gold .2333 oz. AGW **Ruler:** Alfonso XII **Obv:** Young head right **Obv. Legend:** ALFONSO XII... **Rev:** Crowned mantled arms **Rev. Legend:** REY CONST.. **Note:** Mint mark: 6-pointed star.

Date	Mintage	F	VF	XF	Unc	BU
1876 (76) DE-M	1,281,000	—	180	200	225	—
1877 (77) DE-M	10,048,000	—	175	190	220	—
1878 (78) DE-M	5,192,000	—	175	190	220	—
1878 (78) EM-M	3,000,000	—	175	190	220	—
1879 (79) EM-M	3,478,000	—	175	190	220	—
1880 (80) MS-M	6,863,000	—	175	190	220	—
1876 (61) DE-M	300	—	—	1,500	2,000	—
1876 (62) DE-M	6,000	—	—	250	350	—

Note: For above 2 coins dated (61) and (62) see note after 10 Pesetas, KM#677

KM# 673

KM# 687 25 PESETAS
8.0645 g., 0.9000 Gold .2333 oz. AGW **Ruler:** Alfonso XII **Obv:** Head right **Obv. Legend:** ALFONSO XII... **Rev:** Crowned mantled arms **Rev. Legend:** REY CONST... **Note:** Mint mark: 6-pointed star.

Date	Mintage	F	VF	XF	Unc	BU
1881 (81) MS-M	4,366,000	—	175	200	225	—
1882 (82) MS-M	414,000	—	400	600	700	—
1883 (83) MS-M	669,000	—	400	500	600	—
1884 (84) MS-M	1,033,000	—	225	300	400	—
1885 (85) MS-M	503,000	—	1,000	1,500	1,800	—
1885 (86) MS-M	491,000	—	3,400	4,500	10,000	—

SWITZERLAND

The contemporary Swiss confederation was a latecomer to gold coinage, but it produced 10-franc and 20-franc pieces of significant mintage in the late 19th and early 20th centuries. The result is affordable and desirable gold pieces for collectors and investors today.

KM# 36 10 FRANCS
3.2258 g., 0.9000 Gold .0933 oz. AGW **Obv:** Young bust left **Rev:** Radiant cross above date and sprigs **Designer:** Fritz Ulysse Landry

Date	Mintage	F	VF	XF	Unc	BU
1911B	100,000	75.00	150	250	350	500
1912B	200,000	—	BV	75.00	125	175
1913B	600,000	—	BV	70.00	95.00	150
1914B	200,000	—	BV	75.00	115	160
1915B	400,000	—	BV	70.00	100	125
1916B	130,000	—	BV	75.00	115	160
1922B	1,020,000	—	—	BV	70.00	95.00

KM# 31.1 20 FRANCS
6.4516 g., 0.9000 Gold .1867 oz. AGW **Obv:** Crowned head left **Obv. Legend:** CONFOEDERATIO HELVETICA **Rev:** Shield divides value, star above, date below, all within wreath **Edge:** Reeded

Date	Mintage	F	VF	XF	Unc	BU
1883	250,000	—	BV	125	160	210

KM# 31.3 20 FRANCS
6.4516 g., 0.9000 Gold .1867 oz. AGW **Obv:** Crowned head left **Obv. Legend:** CONFOEDERATIO HELVETICA **Rev:** Shield divides value, star above, date below, all within wreath **Edge:** DOMINUS XXX PROVIDEBIT XXXXXXXXXX

Date	Mintage	F	VF	XF	Unc	BU
1886	250,000	—	BV	125	160	210
1887B	176	—	—	18,000	27,500	38,500
1888B	4,224	—	3,000	6,000	9,000	12,500
1889B	100,000	BV	135	170	200	300
1890B	125,000	—	BV	125	160	250
1891B	100,000	BV	125	150	175	250
1892B	100,000	BV	125	150	175	250
1893B	100,000	BV	125	150	175	250
1893B	25	—	—	—	—	30,000
Note: Struck of bright Valaisan gold from Gondo with a small cross punched in the center of the Swiss cross						
1894B	121,000	—	BV	135	170	250
1895B	200,000	—	BV	130	165	250
1895B	19	—	—	—	—	30,000
Note: Struck of bright Valaisan gold from Gondo with a small cross punched in the center of the Swiss cross						
1896B	400,000	—	BV	125	160	225

GOLD RUSH

KM# 35.1 20 FRANCS
6.4516 g., 0.9000 Gold .1867 oz. AGW **Obv:** Young head left
Obv. Legend: HELVETIA **Rev:** Shield within oak branches divides
value **Designer:** Fritz Ulysse Landry

Date	Mintage	F	VF	XF	Unc	BU
1897B	400,000	—	BV	125	150	210
1897B Rare	29	—	—	—	—	—
Note: Struck of bright Valaisan gold from Gondo with a small cross punched in the center of the Swiss cross						
1898B	400,000	—	BV	125	150	210
1899B	300,000	—	BV	125	150	210
1900B	400,000	—	BV	125	150	210
1901B	500,000	—	—	BV	140	175
1902B	600,000	—	—	BV	140	175
1903B	200,000	—	—	BV	145	190
1904B	100,000	—	BV	150	200	225
1905B	100,000	—	BV	150	200	225
1906B	100,000	—	BV	150	200	225
1907B	150,000	—	—	BV	140	185
1908B	355,000	—	—	—	135	175
1909B	400,000	—	—	—	135	175
1910B	375,000	—	—	—	135	175
1911B	350,000	—	—	—	135	175
1912B	450,000	—	—	—	135	175
1913B	700,000	—	—	—	135	175
1914B	700,000	—	—	—	135	175
1915B	750,000	—	—	—	135	175
1916B	300,000	—	—	—	135	175
1922B	2,783,678	—	—	—	BV	135
1925B	400,000	—	—	—	135	150
1926B	50,000	BV	125	150	165	210
1927B	5,015,000	—	—	—	BV	150
1930B	3,371,764	—	—	—	BV	150
1935B	175,000	—	—	BV	150	185
1935L-B	20,008,813	—	—	—	BV	135
Note: The 1935L-B issue was struck in 1945, 1946 and 1947						

KM# 35.2 20 FRANCS
6.4516 g., 0.9000 Gold .1867 oz. AGW **Obv:** Bust left **Rev:**
Shield within oak branches divides value **Edge Lettering:** AD
LEGEM ANNI MCMXXXI

Date	Mintage	F	VF	XF	Unc	BU
1947B	9,200,000	—	—	—	BV	145
1949B	10,000,000	—	—	—	BV	145

KM# 39 100 FRANCS
32.2581 g., 0.9000 Gold .9334 oz. AGW **Obv:** Young bust left
Rev: Radiant cross above value, date and sprigs **Designer:** Fritz
Ulysse Landry

Date	Mintage	F	VF	XF	Unc	BU
1925B	5,000	—	4,000	6,000	7,500	10,000

KM# 39

CHAPTER 6

WORLD GOLD COMMEMORATIVE

ountries no longer strike gold coins for circulation, but many produce gold commemorative coins today. Some of the coins emulate the designs of the country's classic older issues. The new commemoratives are non-circulating, legal-tender pieces sold at a premium above face value directly to the public by the issuing authority. Current and past issues can also be purchased on the secondary market from dealers. Collectors should be aware that oftentimes values for modern commemoratives on the secondary market drop from their original issue price after the coin has been on the market for several years.

Andorra, KM# 82

ANDORRA

KM# 82 50 DINERS
16.9650 g., 0.9160 Gold .4996 oz. AGW   **Obv:** Crowned arms to left of five line inscription, value below, date at bottom **Rev:** Musician Pau Casals

Date	Mintage	F	VF	XF	Unc	BU
1993 Proof	5,000			Value: 345		

AUSTRALIA

KM# 11 100 POUNDS
31.2100 g., 0.9990 Gold 1.0025 oz. AGW   **Ruler:** Elizabeth II **Subject:** Normandy Invasion **Obv:** Crowned bust, right, date below **Obv. Designer:** Raphael Maklouf **Rev:** Normandy beach landing scene

Date	Mintage	F	VF	XF	Unc	BU
1994 Proof	Est. 500			Value: 825		

KM# 73 200 DOLLARS
10.0000 g., 0.9170 Gold .2948 oz. AGW   **Ruler:** Elizabeth II **Subject:** Wedding of Prince Charles and Lady Diana **Obv:** Young bust right **Obv. Designer:** Arnold Machin **Rev:** Conjoined heads of Prince Charles and Lady Diana left **Rev. Designer:** Stuart Devlin

Date	Mintage	F	VF	XF	Unc	BU
1981	77,890	—	—	—	200	—

KM# 135 200 DOLLARS
10.0000 g., 0.9170 Gold .2948 oz. AGW   **Ruler:** Elizabeth II **Subject:** Pride of Australia **Obv:** Crowned head right **Obv. Designer:** Raphael Maklouf **Rev:** Platypus above value **Rev. Designer:** Horst Hahne

Date	Mintage	F	VF	XF	Unc	BU
1990	8,340	—	—	—	200	—
1990 Proof	14,616			Value: 220		

KM# 220 200 DOLLARS
16.8200 g., 0.9170 Gold .4958 oz. AGW **Ruler:** Elizabeth II
Series: Olympic Centenary - 1896-1996 **Obv:** Crowned head
right **Obv. Designer:** Raphael Maklouf **Rev:** Gymnast in flight,
Olympic logo top right **Edge Lettering:** CITIUS ALTIUS FORTIUS

Date	Mintage	F	VF	XF	Unc	BU
1993 Proof	60,000			Value: 350		

AUSTRIA

KM# 3006 500 SCHILLING
8.1130 g., 0.9860 Gold .2578 oz. AGW   **Subject:** 150th Anniversary
- Vienna Philharmonic **Obv:** Vienna Philharmonic Hall, date below,
value at bottom **Rev:** Orchestra instruments, five violins facing

Date	Mintage	F	VF	XF	Unc	BU
1992 Proof	43,000			Value: 185		

KM# 3008 1000 SCHILLING
16.2250 g., 0.9860 Gold .5155 oz. AGW   **Obv:** City building,
value below, date upper right **Rev:** 1/2-length figure of Johann
Strauss playing violin looking forward

Date	Mintage	F	VF	XF	Unc	BU
1992 Proof	42,000			Value: 345		

Austria, KM# 3008

KM# 3037 1000 SCHILLING
16.2250 g., 0.9860 Gold .5155 oz. AGW   **Subject:** Millennium of the
Name Osterreich **Obv:** Land grant within circle, dates at bottom,
value below circle **Rev:** Seated, crowned figure of Otto III, facing

Date	Mintage	F	VF	XF	Unc	BU
ND(1996) Proof	50,000			Value: 340		

BAHAMAS

KM# 71 100 DOLLARS
18.0145 g., 0.5000 Gold .2896 oz. AGW, 33 mm. **Ruler:**
Elizabeth II **Subject:** 1st Anniversary of Independence **Obv:**
National arms, date below **Rev:** Two flamingos, value at
bottom, date at right **Designer:** Arnold Machin

Date	Mintage	F	VF	XF	Unc	BU
1974	4,486	—	—	—	190	—
1974 Proof	4,153			Value: 200		

KM# 121 250 DOLLARS
47.5400 g., 0.9170 Gold 1.4017 oz. AGW **Ruler:** Elizabeth II
Obv: Bust of Queen Elizabeth II right **Obv. Designer:** Raphael
Maklouf **Rev:** Queen Isabella receiving Columbus, date at
bottom, value at top

Date	Mintage	F	VF	XF	Unc	BU
1987 Proof	100			Value: 1,000		

GOLD RUSH

BELIZE

KM# 58 100 DOLLARS
6.2100 g., 0.5000 Gold .0998 oz. AGW   **Obv:** National arms,
denomination below **Rev:** Queen angelfish, left, date below

Date	Mintage	F	VF	XF	Unc	BU
1979FM (U)	400	—	—	—	125	—
1979FM (P)	4,465	Value: 90.00				

BERMUDA

KM# 118 15 DOLLARS
15.9700 g., 0.9990 Gold .5129 oz. AGW, 28.4 mm.   **Ruler:**
Elizabeth II **Subject:** Tall Ships **Obv:** Head with tiara right **Obv.
Designer:** Ian Rank-Broadley **Rev:** Three-masted sailing ship
Edge: Reeded

Date	Mintage	F	VF	XF	Unc	BU
2000 Proof	1,500	Value: 385				

BOSNIA & HERZ

KM# 22 10,000 DINARA
6.2200 g., 0.9990 Gold .1998 oz. AGW   **Series:** Preserve Planet
Earth **Obv:** National arms above bridge, date below **Rev:**
Eohippu, right, denomination below

Date	Mintage	F	VF	XF	Unc	BU
1994 Proof	Est. 5,000	Value: 185				

BRAZIL

KM# 655 20 REAIS
8.0000 g., 0.9000 Gold .2315 oz. AGW, 22 mm.   **Subject:** 500
Years - Discovery of Brazil **Obv:** Partial compass face and
feathers at right, anniversary dates at left **Rev:** Ornamented
map, denomination at left **Edge:** Reeded

Date	Mintage	F	VF	XF	Unc	BU
ND(2000) Proof	—	Value: 245				

Brazil, KM# 655

BRITISH VIGIN ISLANDS

KM# 121 500 DOLLARS
19.8126 g., 0.5000 Gold .3185 oz. AGW   **Ruler:** Elizabeth II
Subject: Discovery of America **Obv:** Crowned head right **Rev:**
Christopher Columbus 3/4 facing

Date	Mintage	F	VF	XF	Unc	BU
ND(1991)FM (P)	—	Value: 500				

BULGARIA

KM# 72 20 LEVA
16.8889 g., 0.9000 Gold .4887 oz. AGW **Subject:** 20th Anniversary - Peoples Republic **Obv:** Flag above denomination, dates at bottom **Rev:** Head of Georgi Dimitrov, left, two dates below

Date	Mintage	F	VF	XF	Unc	BU
ND(1964) Proof	5,000			Value: 335		

CANADA

Canada, KM# 142

KM# 131 100 DOLLARS
Weight: 16.9655 g. **Composition:** 0.9170 Gold 0.5000 oz. AGW **Ruler:** Elizabeth II **Subject:** National anthem **Obverse:** Young bust right, denomination at left, date above right **Reverse:** Music score on map **Rev. Designer:** Roger Savage

Date	Mintage	MS-63	Proof
1981 Proof	102,000	—	340

KM# 142 100 DOLLARS
Weight: 16.9655 g. **Composition:** 0.9170 Gold 0.5000 oz. AGW **Ruler:** Elizabeth II **Subject:** Jacques Cartier **Obverse:** Young bust right **Reverse:** Cartier head on right facing left, ship on left, date lower right, denomination above **Rev. Designer:** Carola Tietz

Date	Mintage	MS-63	Proof
ND(1984) Proof	67,662	—	340

KM# 144 100 DOLLARS
Weight: 16.9655 g. **Composition:** 0.9170 Gold 0.5000 oz. AGW **Ruler:** Elizabeth II **Subject:** National Parks **Obverse:** Young bust right **Reverse:** Bighorn sheep, denomination divides dates below **Rev. Designer:** Hector Greville

Date	Mintage	MS-63	Proof
ND(1985) Proof	61,332	—	340

KM# 158 100 DOLLARS
Weight: 13.3375 g. **Composition:** 0.5830 Gold 0.2500 oz. AGW **Ruler:** Elizabeth II Subject: 1988 Calgary Olympics **Obverse:** Young bust right, maple leaf below, date at right **Reverse:** Torch and logo, denomination below **Rev. Designer:** Friedrich Peter **Edge:** Lettered in English and French

Date	Mintage	MS-63	Proof
1987 Proof	142,750	—	175
Note: lettered edge			
1987 Proof	Inc. above	—	350
Note: plain edge			

CAYMAN ISLANDS

KM# 13 100 DOLLARS
22.6801 g., 0.5000 Gold .3646 oz. AGW **Ruler:** Elizabeth II **Obv:** Young bust right **Rev:** Sovereign Queens of England in circle **Rev. Designer:** Michael Rizzello

Date	Mintage	F	VF	XF	Unc	BU
1975	8,053	—	—	—	245	—
1975 Proof	4,950			Value: 250		
1976	2,028	—	—	—	245	—
1976 Proof	3,560			Value: 250		
1977	—	—	—	—	245	—
1977 Proof	2,845			Value: 250		

CHILE

KM# 186 200 PESOS
40.6794 g., 0.9000 Gold 1.1771 oz. AGW **Subject:** 150th Anniversary of San Martin's passage through Andes Mountains, from a painting by Vila Prades **Obv:** Coat of arms, date at left, denomination below **Rev:** Riders passing through mountains, two dates below

Date	Mintage	F	VF	XF	Unc	BU
1968 Proof	965			Value: 800		

Chile, KM# 186

CHINA, PEOPLE'S REPUBLIC

Y# 414 50 YUAN
15.5517 g., 0.9990 Gold .5000 oz. AGW **Subject:** Chairman Mao **Rev:** Bust, 3/4 left, denomination at left

Date	Mintage	F	VF	XF	Unc	BU
1993 Proof	5,000			Value: 425		
1993(s) Proof	2,500			Value: 545		

Y# 445 50 YUAN
15.5517 g., 0.9990 Gold .5000 oz. AGW **Subject:** Taiwan Temples **Obv:** Great Wall, date below **Rev:** Buddha statue, denomination below

Date	Mintage	F	VF	XF	Unc	BU
1993 Proof	1,000			Value: 370		

Y# 451 100 YUAN
31.1030 g., 0.9990 Gold 1.0000 oz. AGW **Subject:** Year of the Pig **Obv:** National emblem, date below **Rev:** Pig, denomination at right

Date	Mintage	F	VF	XF	Unc	BU
1995 Proof	1,800			BV+15%		

Colombia, KM# 269

Y# 47 400 YUAN
13.3600 g., 0.9170 Gold .3939 oz. AGW **Subject:** 70th Anniversary of 1911 Revolution **Obv:** Bust of Sun-Yat-sen, facing, two dates below **Rev:** Nationalist troops attacking, denomination and date below

Date	Mintage	F	VF	XF	Unc	BU
1981 Proof	1,338			Value: 1,100		

COLOMBIA

KM# 269 30,000 PESOS
34.5800 g., 0.9000 Gold 1.0007 oz. AGW **Subject:** Death of Bolivar **Obv:** Funeral scene, dates below **Rev:** Cornucopias flank symbol at center, denomination below

Date	Mintage	F	VF	XF	Unc	BU
1980 Proof	500			Value: 725		

COOK ISLANDS

KM# 204 50 DOLLARS
7.7760 g., 0.5833 Gold .1458 oz. AGW **Ruler:** Elizabeth II **Subject:** 500 Years of America **Obv:** Crowned head right, date below **Rev:** Bust of John Cabot at left, ship at right, denomination below

Date	Mintage	F	VF	XF	Unc	BU
1992 Proof	5,000			Value: 95.00		

KM# 19 100 DOLLARS
9.6000 g., 0.9000 Gold .2778 oz. AGW, 26 mm.
Ruler: Elizabeth II **Subject:** Queen's Silver Jubilee **Obv:** Young bust right, date below **Rev:** Crowned EIIR monogram **Rev. Designer:** James Berry

Date	Mintage	F	VF	XF	Unc	BU
1977FM (M)	50	—	—	—	285	—
1977FM (P)	562	—	—	—	185	—
1977FM Proof	9,364			Value: 180		

CZECH REPUBLIC

X# 8 5 DUCAT
17.5000 g., 0.9860 Gold .5548 oz. AGW, 35.3 mm.
Obv: Crowned Bohemian lion rampant left **Rev:** Karlstein Castle **Edge:** Reeded **Note:** Prev. KM#M8.

Date	Mintage	F	VF	XF	Unc	BU
1996 Proof	—			Value: 830		

KM# 19 300 DOLLARS
19.2000 g., 0.9000 Gold .5556 oz. AGW   **Subject:** Visit of Pope
John Paul II **Obv:** Young bust right **Obv. Designer:** Arnold
Machin **Rev:** Head with beanie left, denomination below

Date	Mintage	F	VF	XF	Unc	BU
ND(1979)CHI	5,000	—	—	—	375	—
ND(1979)CHI	300	—	—	—	550	—

EGYPT

KM# 550 100 POUNDS
17.1500 g., 0.9000 Gold .4963 oz. AGW   **Obv:** Denomination,
dates and text **Rev:** Bust of Queen Nefertiti right **Rev. Designer:**
Dominic Angelini

Date	Mintage	F	VF	XF	Unc
AH1404-1983 Proof	16,000	Value: 725			

FALKLAND ISLANDS

KM# 81b.1 50 PENCE
39.9400 g., 0.9166 Gold 1.177 oz. AGW, 38.6 mm.
Ruler: Elizabeth II **Subject:** Queen's Golden Jubilee
Obv: Crowned bust right, denomination below **Rev:** Coronation
Throne below multicolored bunting **Edge:** Reeded

Date	Mintage	F	VF	XF	Unc	BU
2002 Proof	150	Value: 925				

FRANCE

KM# 973 500 FRANCS
17.0000 g., 0.9200 Gold .5029 oz. AGW   **Series:** 1992 Olympics
Obv: Alpine skiing **Obv. Designer:** Guy Brun **Rev:** Cross on flame,
date and denomination, Olympic logo below **Note:** Without
mint mark.

Date	Mintage	F	VF	XF	Unc	BU
1989 Proof	19,000	Value: 350				

KM# 1027 500 FRANCS
155.5175 g., 0.9990 Gold 5.0000 oz. AGW   **Series:** Bicentennial
of the Louvre **Obv:** Mona Lisa **Rev:** Patterned pyramids front
building

Date	Mintage	F	VF	XF	Unc	BU
1993 Proof	99	Value: 3,750				
1994 Proof	99	Value: 3,800				

France, KM# 1027

Germany, KM# 235

KM# 1003 500 FRANCS - 70 ECUS
17.0000 g., 0.9200 Gold .5029 oz. AGW   **Subject:** Descartes **Obv:** Finger pointing to page with stars **Rev:** Head 3/4 facing

Date	Mintage	F	VF	XF	Unc	BU
1991 Proof	3,000			Value: 425		

GERMANY, FEDERAL REPUBLIC

KM# 235 100 EURO
15.5500 g., 0.9999 Gold 0.4999 oz. AGW, 28 mm.   **Obv:** Stylized eagle, denomination below **Rev:** Bamberg city view **Edge:** Reeded

Date	Mintage	F	VF	XF	Unc	BU
2004A Proof	80,000			Value: 350		
2004D Proof	80,000			Value: 350		
2004F Proof	80,000			Value: 350		
2004G Proof	80,000			Value: 350		
2004J Proof	80,000			Value: 350		

GIBRALTAR

KM# 771b 5 POUNDS
39.8300 g., 0.9170 Gold 1.1743 oz. AGW, 36 mm.   **Ruler:** Elizabeth II **Obv:** Head with tiara right **Rev:** Millennium 2000

Date	Mintage	F	VF	XF	Unc	BU
1998 Proof	850			Value: 875		

GREAT BRITAIN

KM# 943 SOVEREIGN
7.9881 g., 0.9170 Gold .2354 oz. AGW   **Ruler:** Elizabeth II **Obv:** Crowned head right **Obv. Designer:** Raphael Maklouf **Rev:** St. George slaying the dragon

Date	Mintage	F	VF	XF	Unc	BU
1985 Proof	17,000			Value: 225		
1986 Proof	25,000			Value: 225		
1987 Proof	22,000			Value: 225		
1988 Proof	Est. 25,000			Value: 225		
1990 Proof	Est. 20,000			Value: 225		
1991 Proof	Est. 9,000			Value: 250		
1992 Proof	7,500			Value: 250		
1993 Proof	7,500			Value: 250		
1994 Proof	Est. 7,500			Value: 250		
1995 Proof	7,500			Value: 250		
1996 Proof	7,500			Value: 250		
1997 Proof	7,500			Value: 250		

KM# 1027 2 POUNDS
15.9700 g., 0.9167 Gold 0.4707 oz. AGW, 28.4 mm. **Ruler:**
Elizabeth II **Subject:** Queen Elizabeth II's Golden Jubilee **Obv:**
Head with tiara right **Obv. Designer:** Ian Rank- Broadley **Rev:**
Crowned arms within wreath, date below **Edge:** Reeded **Note:**
In proof sets only.

Date	Mintage	F	VF	XF	Unc	BU
2002	8,000			Value: 435		

KM# 974b 5 POUNDS
39.9400 g., 0.9170 Gold 1.1775 oz. AGW, 38.61 mm. **Ruler:**
Elizabeth II **Subject:** 70th Birthday of Queen Elizabeth II **Obv:**
Crowned head right **Rev:** Five banners above Windsor Castle
Rev. Designer: Avril Vaughan

Date	Mintage	F	VF	XF	Unc	BU
ND(1996) Proof	Est. 2,750			Value: 900		

HONG KONG

KM# 40 1,000 DOLLARS
15.9700 g., 0.9170 Gold .4708 oz. AGW **Ruler:** Elizabeth II
Subject: Year of the Dragon **Obv:** Young bust right **Rev:** Dragon
left **Rev. Designer:** Elizabeth Haddon-Care

Date	Mintage	F	VF	XF	Unc	BU
1976	20,000	—	—	—	465	500
1976 Proof	6,911			Value: 1,000		

Hong Kong, KM# 40

INDONESIA

KM# 41 100,000 RUPIAH
33.4370 g., 0.9000 Gold .9676 oz. AGW **Series:** Conservation
Obv: National emblem **Rev:** Komodo dragon lizard (varanus
komodensis) **Rev. Designer:** Leslie Durbin

Date	Mintage	F	VF	XF	Unc	BU
1974	5,333	—	—	—	675	—
1974 Proof	1,369			Value: 725		

ISLE OF MAN

KM# 912b 5 POUNDS
39.8300 g., 0.9167 Gold 1.1740 oz. AGW, 36.5 mm. **Ruler:**
Elizabeth II **Subject:** 50th Birthday - Prince Charles **Obv:** Head
with tiara right **Obv. Designer:** Ian Rank-Broadley **Rev:** Portrait
of Prince Charles

Date	Mintage	F	VF	XF	Unc	BU
1998 Proof	Est. 850			Value: 885		

KM# 334 CROWN
31.1000 g., 0.9990 Gold 1.0000 oz. AGW **Ruler:** Elizabeth II
Obv: Crowned bust right **Obv. Designer:** Raphael Maklouf **Rev:**
Seated Siamese cat

Date	Mintage	F	VF	XF	Unc	BU
1992 Proof	—		Value: 725			
1992	—	—	—	—	675	700

ISRAEL

KM# 52 100 LIROT
25.0000 g., 0.8000 Gold .6430 oz. AGW, 33 mm. **Subject:** 20th
Anniversary - Jerusalem Reunification **Obv:** Building pillars, text and
value **Rev:** Menorah flanked by sprigs to upper left of city view

Date	Mintage	F	VF	XF	Unc	BU
JE5728-1968(b) Proof	12,490		Value: 450			

KM# 341 10 NEW SHEQALIM
16.9600 g., 0.9170 Gold .5000 oz. AGW, 30 mm. **Series:** Biblical
Obv: Value **Rev:** Joseph standing before sheaves of wheat into
his brothers **Edge:** Reeded

Date	Mintage	F	VF	XF	Unc	BU
JE5760-2000(u) Proof	700		Value: 695			

JAMAICA

Jamaica, KM# 78

KM# 78 250 DOLLARS
43.2200 g., 0.9000 Gold 1.2507 oz. AGW **Ruler:** Elizabeth II
Subject: 25th Anniversary of Coronation **Obv:** Arms with supporters
Rev: Queen seated on throne with crown, sceptre and orb

Date	Mintage	F	VF	XF	Unc	BU
ND(1978) Proof	3,005		Value: 875			

JAPAN

Y# 121 10,000 YEN
15.6000 g., 1.0000 Gold .5022 oz. AGW **Ruler:** Akihito (Heisei)
Series: 1998 Nagano Winter Olympics **Obv:** Figure skater **Rev:**
Value, dates, and gentian plant

Date	Mintage	F	VF	XF	Unc	BU
Yr.9(1997) Proof	55,000		Value: 675			

JORDAN

KM# 27 25 DINARS
69.1100 g., 0.9000 Gold 1.9999 oz. AGW, 48 mm. **Ruler:**
Hussein Ibn Talal **Obv:** Head right with crowned mantled arms
above **Rev:** Dome of the Rock, Jerusalem, above value **Edge:** Milled

Date	Mintage	F	VF	XF	Unc	BU
AH1389//1969 Proof	1,000		Value: 1,400			

GOLD RUSH

KENYA

KM# 8 250 SHILLINGS
19.0000 g., 0.9170 Gold .5602 oz. AGW **Subject:** 75th Anniversary - Birth of President Jomo Kenyatta **Obv:** Rooster with axe above value and date **Rev:** Bust left **Designer:** Norman Sillman

Date	Mintage	F	VF	XF	Unc	BU
1966	—	—	—	—	400	420
1966 Proof	1,000	Value: 445				

Kenya, KM# 8

KOREA, SOUTH

KM# 64 25,000 WON
16.8100 g., 0.9250 Gold .5000 oz. AGW, 27 mm. **Series:** 1988 Olympics **Obv:** Arms above floral spray **Rev:** Fan dancing

Date	Mintage	F	VF	XF	Unc	BU
1987	42,500	—	—	—	340	350
1987 Proof	117,500	Value: 360				

LATVIA

KM# 20 100 LATU
13.3380 g., 0.8330 Gold .2501 oz. AGW **Subject:** 75th Anniversary - Declaration of Independence **Obv:** Arms with supporters **Rev:** Artistic lined design above value and dates

Date	Mintage	F	VF	XF	Unc	BU
ND(1993) Proof	5,000	Value: 250				

LATVIA

KM# 36 100 DOLLARS
10.9300 g., 0.9000 Gold .3163 oz. AGW **Subject:** 130th Anniversary of the Republic **Obv:** Bust 3/4 left Rev: National arms

Date	Mintage	F	VF	XF	Unc	BU
1977FM (U)	787	—	--	—	235	—
1977FM (P)	4,250	Value: 220				

MACAO

KM# 69 1000 PATACAS
15.9760 g., 0.9170 Gold .4711 oz. AGW **Subject:** Year of the Dog **Obv:** Church facade flanked by stars above date **Rev:** Dog

Date	Mintage	F	VF	XF	Unc	BU
1994	Est. 500	—	—	—	345	—
1994 Proof	Est. 4,500	Value: 375				

MALAYSIA

KM# 21 500 RINGGIT
33.4370 g., 0.9000 Gold .9676 oz. AGW **Series:** Conservation
Obv: Arms with supporters **Rev:** Malayan Tapir

Date	Mintage	F	VF	XF	Unc	BU
1976	2,894	—	—	—	700	725
1976 Proof	508	Value: 1,700				

MAURITIUS

KM# 42 1000 RUPEES
33.4370 g., 0.9000 Gold .9676 oz. AGW **Series:** Conservation
Subject: Mauritius flycatcher **Obv:** Young bust right **Rev:** Bird on
nest in branch **Rev. Designer:** Christopher Ironside

Date	Mintage	F	VF	XF	Unc	BU
1975	1,966	—	—	—	675	—
1975 Proof	716	Value: 750				

NEW ZEALAND

KM# 144 10 DOLLARS
39.9400 g., 0.9166 Gold 1.177 oz. AGW, 38.61 mm. **Ruler:**
Elizabeth II **Subject:** Lord of the Rings **Obv:** Head with tiara
right Obv. **Designer:** Ian Rank-Broadley **Rev:** Inscribed ring
around value **Rev. Designer:** Matthew Bonaccorsi Edge: Reeded

Date	Mintage	F	VF	XF	Unc	BU
2003 Proof	—	Value: 1,000				

NICARAGUA

KM# 41 2000 CORDOBAS
19.2000 g., 0.9000 Gold .5556 oz. AGW **Subject:** U.S.
Bicentennial **Obv:** National emblem **Rev:** Betsy Ross sewing flag
on left, astronaut placing flag on moon on right

Date	Mintage	F	VF	XF	Unc	BU
1975	320	—	—	—	525	550
1975 Proof	100	Value: 850				

Nicaragua, KM# 41

NORWAY

KM# 467 1500 KRONER
16.9600 g., 0.9170 Gold .4994 oz. AGW **Ruler:** Olav V Subject:
Year 2000 **Obv:** Head right **Rev:** Tree and roots

Date	Mintage	VG	F	VF	XF	BU
2000 Proof	7,500	Value: 425				

OMAN

KM# 102 OMANI RIAL
37.8000 g., 0.9160 Gold 1.1132 oz. AGW **Subject:** 26th National Day Anniversary - Sultanah **Obv:** National arms **Rev:** Sailing ship - Sultanah within circle

Date	Mintage	F	VF	XF	Unc	BU
1996 Proof	—		Value: 825			

KM# 63 75 OMANI RIALS
33.4370 g., 0.9000 Gold .9676 oz. AGW **Subject:** Conservation **Obv:** National arms above date **Rev:** Arabian Tahr

Date	Mintage	F	VF	XF	Unc	BU
AH1397 (1976)	825	—	—	—	675	725
AH1397 (1976) Proof	325		Value: 925			

PANAMA

KM# 67 100 BALBOAS
7.1300 g., 0.5000 Gold .1146 oz. AGW **Subject:** Panama Canal Centennial **Obv:** National coat of arms **Rev:** Bust 1/4 left

Date	Mintage	F	VF	XF	Unc	BU
ND (1980)FM (U)	77	—	—	—	700	—
ND (1980)FM (P)	2,468		Value: 135			
ND(1980)FM (P) FDC	Inc. above		Value: 150			

PHILIPPINES

KM# 220 5000 PISO
68.7400 g., 0.9000 Gold 1.9893 oz. AGW **Subject:** 5th Anniversary of the New Society **Obv:** Design within beaded circle **Rev:** Conjoined busts of Ferdindand and Imelda Marcos right

Date	Mintage	F	VF	XF	Unc	BU
ND(1977)FM (U)	100	—	—	—	1,650	—
ND(1977)FM (P)	3,832		Value: 1,400			

Philippines, KM# 220

POLAND

Y# 140 10,000 ZLOTYCH
34.5000 g., 0.9000 Gold .9984 oz. AGW **Subject:** Visit of Pope John Paul II **Obv:** Imperial eagle above value **Rev:** Half-figure of Pope 1/4 left

Date	Mintage	F	VF	XF	Unc	BU
1982CHI	200	—	—	—	1,850	—
1982CHI Proof	700		Value: 1,950			
1985CHI Proof, rare	1	—	—	—	—	—
1986CHI Rare	Est. 6	—	—	—	—	—
1986CHI Proof, rare	Est. 13	—	—	—	—	—

Y# 397 200 ZLOTYCH
23.3200 g., 0.9000 Gold .6748 oz. AGW **Subject:** Solidarity **Obv:** Crowned eagle with wings open **Rev:** Multicolor Solidarity logo, map and two children **Edge:** Plain

Date	Mintage	F	VF	XF	Unc	BU
2000 Proof	2,500		Value: 550			

PORTUGAL

KM# 660b 200 ESCUDOS
27.2000 g., 0.9170 Gold .8000 oz. AGW **Subject:** New World - America **Obv:** Shield within design **Rev:** Head 1/4 left and ships

Date	Mintage	F	VF	XF	Unc	BU
ND(1992) Proof	6,000		Value: 585			

KM# 710b 200 ESCUDOS
27.2000 g., 0.9167 Gold .8017 oz. AGW **Subject:** Discovery of Africa **Obv:** Shield, ship, and palm tree **Rev:** Ship, map, and hunter

Date	Mintage	F	VF	XF	Unc	BU
1998 Proof	5,000		Value: 565			

KM# 758b 8 EURO
31.1000 g., 0.9166 Gold 0.9165 oz. AGW, 36 mm. **Subject:** Euro 2004 Soccer **Obv:** National arms **Rev:** Symbolic explosion of a goal **Edge:** Reeded

Date	Mintage	F	VF	XF	Unc	BU
2004INCM Proof	10,000		Value: 650			

Portugal, KM# 758b

ROMANIA

KM# 155 5000 LEI
31.1030 g., 0.9990 Gold .9990 oz. AGW, 35 mm. **Subject:** Michael the Brave's Unification of Romania in 1600 **Obv:** Shield and old seal within circle **Rev:** Bust with headdress and church **Edge:** Plain

Date	Mintage	F	VF	XF	Unc	BU
2000 Proof	Est. 1,500		Value: 825			

RUSSIA

Y# 354 50 ROUBLES
8.6397 g., 0.9000 Gold .2500 oz. AGW **Obv:** Double-headed eagle **Rev:** Moscow's Pashkov Palace

Date	Mintage	F	VF	XF	Unc	BU
1992 Proof	7,500		Value: 215			

GOLD RUSH

Y# 537 50 ROUBLES
7.7759 g., 0.9990 Gold .2500 oz. AGW **Series:** Wildlife **Obv:**
Double-headed eagle **Rev:** Tiger head

Date	Mintage	F	VF	XF	Unc	BU
1996 Proof	1,500		Value: 225			

Y# 555 50 ROUBLES
8.6397 g., 0.9000 Gold .2500 oz. AGW **Subject:** 850th
Anniversary - Moscow **Obv:** Double-headed eagle **Rev:** Shield
flanked by designs

Date	Mintage	F	VF	XF	Unc	BU
1997 Proof	10,000		Value: 210			

Y# 685 100 ROUBLES
17.4500 g., 0.9000 Gold .5049 oz. AGW, 30 mm. **Subject:**
Siberian Exploration **Obv:** Double-headed eagle within beaded
circle **Rev:** Head and silhouette left, sailboat and other designs
Edge: Reeded

Date	Mintage	F	VF	XF	Unc	BU
2001 Proof	1,000		Value: 425			

SAINT HELENA & ASCENSION

KM# 10 50 POUNDS
32.2600 g., 0.9990 Platinum 1.0051 oz. APW **Ruler:**
Queen Elizabeth II **Subject:** 165th Anniversary of Napoleon's
Death **Obv:** Crowned bust right **Rev:** Sailing ship at right and 1/2
figure at left looking right **Note:** Similar to KM#9.

Date	Mintage	F	VF	XF	Unc	BU
1986 Proof	5,000		Value: 1,350			

SAMOA

KM# 81 100 TALA
7.5000 g., 0.9170 Gold .2211 oz. AGW **Series:** Save the Children
Obv: National arms **Rev:** Children playing

Date	Mintage	F	VF	XF	Unc	BU
1990 Proof	3,000		Value: 155			

Samoa, KM# 81

SAN MARINO

KM# 260 5 SCUDI
16.9500 g., 0.9170 Gold .5 oz. AGW **Subject:** Founding of the
Republic **Obv:** Doves in front of smoking towers **Rev:** Three
kneeling figures to right of standing figure **Designer:** Bino Bini

Date	Mintage	F	VF	XF	Unc	BU
1990R Proof	6,500		Value: 350			

Slovakia, KM# 79

SINGAPORE

KM# 152 50 DOLLARS
31.1035 g., 0.9999 Gold 1.0000 oz. AGW   **Subject:** 50th Anniversary - Singapore Airlines **Obv:** Arms with supporters **Rev:** Airplane in front of numeral 50

Date	Mintage	F	VF	XF	Unc	BU
1997 Proof	1,800		Value: 1,100			

SLOVAKIA

KM# 79 10,000 KORUN
24.8828 g., Bi-Metallic .999 Gold 12.4414g 23mm round center in .999 Palladium 12.4414g 40mm pentagon, 40 mm. **Subject:** Slovakian entry into the European Union **Obv:** National arms above date in center **Rev:** European map with entry date **Edge:** Plain

Date	Mintage	F	VF	XF	Unc	BU
2004 Proof	7,200		Value: 800			

SLOVENIA

KM# 49 20,000 TOLARJEV
7.0000 g., 0.9000 Gold 0.2025 oz. AGW, 24 mm. **Subject:** 35th Chess Olympiad **Obv:** Rearing horse and reflection **Rev:** Chess pieces in starting positions and reflection **Edge:** Reeded

Date	Mintage	F	VF	XF	Unc	BU
2002 Proof	500		Value: 300			

SOUTH AFRICA

KM# 290 25 RAND
31.1035 g., 0.9999 Gold 0.9999 oz. AGW, 32.7 mm. **Subject:** 10th Anniversary of South African Democracy **Obv:** Protea flower **Rev:** Two images of Nelson Mandela **Edge:** Reeded

Date	Mintage	F	VF	XF	Unc	BU
2004 Proof	5,000		Value: 700			

KM# 130 PROTEA
33.9300 g., 0.9170 Gold 1.0000 oz. AGW **Subject:** The Great Trek **Obv:** Protea flower **Rev:** Wheel and arrow design

Date	Mintage	F	VF	XF	Unc	BU
1988 Proof	2,956		Value: 735			

SPAIN

KM# 845 80,000 PESETAS
27.0000 g., 0.9990 Gold .8682 oz. AGW   **Ruler:** Juan Carlos I **Subject:** Discovery of America **Obv:** Crowned busts of Juan Carlos and Sofia facing each other within beaded circle **Rev:**

Crowned busts of Ferdinand and Isabella facing each other within beaded circle

Date	Mintage	F	VF	XF	Unc	BU
1989	6,000	—	—	—	—	640
1989 Proof	7,000	Value: 640				

SUDAN

KM# 72 100 POUNDS
33.4370 g., 0.9000 Gold .9676 oz. AGW **Subject:** Conservation
Obv: Eagle divides dates **Rev:** Scimitar-horned oryx

Date	Mintage	F	VF	XF	Unc
AH1396-1976	872	—	—	—	700
AH1396-1976 Proof	251	Value: 750			

TANZANIA

KM# 31 2500 SHILINGI
46.8500 g., 0.9170 Gold 1.3808 oz. AGW 25 Years of Independence **Obv:** President J.K. Nyerere 1/4 left within circle Obv. **Designer:** Philip Nathan **Rev:** National arms

Date	Mintage	F	VF	XF	Unc	BU
ND(1985) Proof	—	Value: 1,000				

Tanzania, KM# 31

THAILAND

Y# 122 5000 BAHT
30.0000 g., 0.9000 Gold .8681 oz. AGW **Ruler:** Rama IX Subject: 50th Birthday - King Rama IX **Obv:** Bust left **Rev:** Radiant crowned monogram

Date	Mintage	F	VF	XF	Unc	BU
BE2520 (1977)	6,400	—	—	—	620	650

TURKEY

KM# 1097 60,000,000 LIRA
15.0000 g., 0.9167 Gold .4921 oz. AGW **Subject:** 700th Anniversary - The Ottoman Empire **Obverse:** Value within wreath **Reverse:** Ottoman coat of arms **Edge:** Reeded Mint: Istanbul

Date	Mintage	F	VF	XF	Unc
1999 Proof	1,904	Value: 400			

YEMEN ARAB REPUBLIC

KM# 11a 50 RIYALS/RIALS
49.0000 g., 0.9000 Gold 1.4180 oz. AGW **Subject:** Qadhi Mohammed Mahmud Azzubairi Memorial **Obv:** National arms above dates and denomination

Date	Mintage	F	VF	XF	Unc	BU
1969 Proof	—	Value: 1,100				

CHAPTER 7

WORLD GOLD BULLION COINS

A number of countries strike and sell bullion coins in gold, silver, and platinum as a convenient way for private citizens to own precious metals. The coins usually are legal tender with a nominal face value, but they are bought and sold for their precious-metal content. Collector versions of current-year issues – proof coins and specially prepared uncirculated versions – can sometimes be purchased directly from the issuing authority. Current and past issues are bought and sold on the secondary market with their values tied to the current price for the precious metal they contain. Proof versions or scarce dates may command collectible premiums above their precious-metal values.

South Africa was the sole player in the bullion-coin market for a number of years. It introduced the Krugerrand, which contains one ounce of 0.917-fine gold, in 1967. Fractional versions of the Krugerrand – one-tenth ounce, quarter ounce, and half ounce – were introduced in 1980.

Other countries followed with their own versions of bullion coins. Among the most popular are Canada's Maple Leaf, China's Panda, Great Britain's Britannia, the Isle of Man's Angel, and the United States' American Eagle bullion series (see the U.S. section).

Bullion coins and some classic world gold coins, such as France's 20-franc coin, offer good liquidity for the investor in gold bullion and are widely traded for their precious-metal content.

CANADA

KM# 542 50 CENTS
Composition: 0.9999 Gold 0.0425 oz. AGW **Ruler:** Elizabeth II
Subject: Voyageurs **Obverse:** Head right

Date	Mintage	MS-63	Proof
2005 Proof	—	—	65.00

KM# 238 DOLLAR
Weight: 1.5551 g. Composition: 0.9999 Gold 0.05 oz. AGW
Ruler: Elizabeth II **Obverse:** Crowned head right, denomination and date below **Reverse:** Maple leaf flanked by 9999

Date	Mintage	MS-63	Proof
1993	37,080	BV+37%	—
1994	78,860	BV+37%	—
1995	85,920	BV+37%	—
1996	56,520	BV+37%	—
1997	59,720	BV+37%	—
1998	44,260	BV+37%	—
1999	—	BV+46%	—
Note: Maple leaf with oval			

KM# 365 DOLLAR
Weight: 1.5551 g. **Composition:** 0.9999 Gold 0.05 oz. AGW
Ruler: Elizabeth II **Obverse:** Crowned head right **Reverse:** Maple leaf hologram

Date	Mintage	MS-63	Proof
1999	500	90.00	—

KM# 438 DOLLAR
Weight: 1.5810 g. **Composition:** 0.9990 Gold 0.0508 oz. AGW
Ruler: Elizabeth II **Subject:** Holographic Maple Leaves **Obverse:** Crowned head right **Reverse:** Three maple leaves multicolor hologram **Edge:** Reeded. **Size:** 14.1 mm.

Date	Mintage	MS-63	Proof
2001 in sets only	600	75.00	—

KM# 256 2 DOLLARS
Weight: 2.0735 g. **Composition:** 0.9999 Gold 0.0666 oz. AGW
Ruler: Elizabeth II **Obverse:** Crowned head right, denomination and date below **Reverse:** Maple leaf flanked by 9999

Date	Mintage	MS-63	Proof
1994	5,493	85.00	—

KM# 135 5 DOLLARS
Weight: 3.1200 g. **Composition:** 0.9999 Gold .1000 oz. AGW
Ruler: Elizabeth II **Obverse:** Young bust right, date and denomination below **Obv. Designer:** Arnold Machin **Reverse:** Maple leaf flanked by 9999

Date	Mintage	MS-63	Proof
1982	246,000	BV+14%	—
1983	304,000	BV+14%	—
1984	262,000	BV+14%	—
1985	398,000	BV+14%	—
1986	529,516	BV+14%	—
1987	459,000	BV+14%	—
1988	506,500	BV+14%	—
1989	539,000	BV+14%	—
1989 Proof	16,992	—	80.00

KM# 188 5 DOLLARS
Weight: 3.1200 g. **Composition:** 0.9999 Gold 0.1000 oz. AGW
Ruler: Elizabeth II **Obverse:** Elizabeth II effigy **Obv. Designer:** Dora dePedery- Hunt **Reverse:** Maple leaf

Date	Mintage	MS-63	Proof
1990	476,000	BV+14%	—
1991	322,000	BV+14%	—
1992	384,000	BV+14%	—
1993	248,630	BV+14%	—
1994	313,150	BV+14%	—

Date	Mintage	MS-63	Proof
1995	294,890	BV+14%	—
1996	179,220	BV+14%	—
1997	188,540	BV+14%	—
1998	301,940	BV+14%	—
1999	—	BV+19%	—
Note: Maple leaf with oval "20 Years ANS" privy mark			

KM# 366 5 DOLLARS
Weight: 3.1200 g. **Composition:** 0.9999 Gold 0.1000 oz. AGW
Ruler: Elizabeth II **Reverse:** Maple leaf hologram

Date	Mintage	MS-63	Proof
1999	500	160	—

KM# 439 5 DOLLARS
Weight: 3.1310 g. **Composition:** 0.9999 Gold 0.1007 oz. AGW
Ruler: Elizabeth II **Subject:** Holographic Maple Leaves **Obverse:**
Crowned head right **Reverse:** Three maple leaves multicolor
hologram **Edge:** Reeded **Size:** 16 mm.

Date	Mintage	MS-63	Proof
2001 in sets only	600	150	—

KM# 136 10 DOLLARS
Weight: 7.7850 g. **Composition:** 0.9999 Gold 0.2500 oz.
AGW **Ruler:** Elizabeth II **Obverse:** Young bust right, date and
denomination below **Obv. Designer:** Arnold Machin **Reverse:**
Maple leaf flanked by 9999

Date	Mintage	MS-63	Proof
1982	184,000	BV+10%	—
1983	308,800	BV+10%	—
1984	242,400	BV+10%	—
1985	620,000	BV+10%	—
1986	915,200	BV+10%	—
1987	376,000	BV+10%	—
1988	436,000	BV+10%	—
1989	328,800	BV+10%	—
1989 Proof	6,998	—	185

KM# 189 10 DOLLARS
Weight: 7.7850 g. **Composition:** 0.9999 Gold 0.2500 oz. AGW
Ruler: Elizabeth II **Obverse:** Crowned head right, date and
denomination below **Obv. Designer:** Dora dePedery-Hunt
Reverse: Maple leaf flanked by 9999

Date	Mintage	MS-63	Proof
1990	253,600	BV+10%	—
1991	166,400	BV+10%	—
1992	179,600	BV+10%	—
1993	158,452	BV+10%	—

Date	Mintage	MS-63	Proof
1994	148,792	BV+10%	—
1995	127,596	BV+10%	—
1996	89,148	BV+10%	—
1997	98,104	BV+10%	—
1998	85,472	BV+10%	—
1999	—	BV+15%	—
Note: Maple leaf with oval "20 Years ANS" privy mark			

KM# 367 10 DOLLARS
Weight: 7.7850 g. **Composition:** 0.9999 Gold 0.2500 oz. AGW
Ruler: Elizabeth II **Reverse:** Maple leaf hologram

Date	Mintage	MS-63	Proof
1999	—	210	—

KM# 440 10 DOLLARS
Weight: 7.7970 g. **Composition:** 0.9999 Gold 0.2507 oz. AGW
Ruler: Elizabeth II **Subject:** Holographic Maples Leaves **Obverse:**
Crowned head right **Reverse:** Three maple leaves multicolor
hologram **Edge:** Reeded **Size:** 20 mm.

Date	Mintage	MS-63	Proof
2001	15,000	180	—

KM# 153 20 DOLLARS
Weight: 15.5515 g. **Composition:** 0.9999 Gold 0.5000 oz.
AGW **Ruler:** Elizabeth II **Obverse:** Young bust right, date and
denomination below **Obv. Designer:** Arnold Machin **Reverse:**
Maple leaf flanked by 9999 **Size:** 32 mm.

Date	Mintage	MS-63	Proof
1986	529,200	BV+7%	—
1987	332,800	BV+7%	—
1988	538,400	BV+7%	—
1989	259,200	BV+7%	—
1989 Proof	6,998	—	360

KM# 190 20 DOLLARS
Weight: 15.5515 g. **Composition:** 0.9999 Gold 0.5000 oz.
AGW **Ruler:** Elizabeth II **Obverse:** Crowned head right, date
and denomination below **Obv. Designer:** Dora dePedery-Hunt
Reverse: Maple leaf flanked by 9999

Date	Mintage	MS-63	Proof
1990	174,400	BV+7%	—
1991	96,200	BV+7%	—
1992	108,000	BV+7%	—
1993	99,492	BV+7%	—
1994	104,766	BV+7%	—
1995	103,162	BV+7%	—
1996	66,246	BV+7%	—

Date	Mintage	MS-63	Proof
1997	63,354	BV+7%	—
1998	65,366	BV+7%	—
1999	—	BV+12%	—
Note: Maple leaf with oval "20 Years ANS" privy mark			

KM# 368 20 DOLLARS
Weight: 15.5515 g. **Composition:** 0.9999 Gold 0.5000 oz. AGW
Ruler: Elizabeth II **Reverse:** Maple leaf hologram

Date	Mintage	MS-63	Proof
1999	500	700	—

KM# 441 20 DOLLARS
Weight: 15.5840 g. **Composition:** 0.9999 Gold 0.501 oz. AGW
Ruler: Elizabeth II **Subject:** Holographic Maples Leaves **Obverse:** Crowned head right **Reverse:** Three maple leaves multicolor hologram **Edge:** Reeded **Size:** 25 mm.

Date	Mintage	MS-63	Proof
2001 in sets only	600	675	—

KM# 125.1 50 DOLLARS
Weight: 31.1030 g. **Composition:** 0.9990 Gold 1.0000 oz. AGW
Ruler: Elizabeth II **Obverse:** Young bust right, denomination and date below **Reverse:** Maple leaf flanked by .999

Date	Mintage	MS-63	Proof
1979	1,000,000	BV+4%	—
1980	1,251,500	BV+4%	—
1981	863,000	BV+4%	—
1982	883,000	BV+4%	—

KM# 125.2 50 DOLLARS
Weight: 31.1030 g. **Composition:** 0.9999 Gold 1.0000 oz. AGW **Ruler:** Elizabeth II **Obverse:** Young bust right, date and denomination below **Reverse:** Maple leaf flanked by .9999

Date	Mintage	MS-63	Proof
1983	843,000	BV+4%	—
1984	1,067,500	BV+4%	—
1985	1,908,000	BV+4%	—
1986	779,115	BV+4%	—
1987	978,000	BV+4%	—
1988	826,500	BV+4%	—
1989	856,000	BV+4%	—
1989 Proof	17,781	—	685

KM# 191 50 DOLLARS
Weight: 31.1030 g. **Composition:** 0.9999 Gold 1.000 oz. AGW
Ruler: Elizabeth II **Obverse:** Crowned head right, date and
denomination below **Obv. Designer:** Dora dePedery-Hunt
Reverse: Maple leaf flanked by .9999

Date	Mintage	MS-63	Proof
1990	815,000	BV+4%	—
1991	290,000	BV+4%	—
1992	368,900	BV+4%	—
1993	321,413	BV+4%	—
1994	180,357	BV+4%	—
1995	208,729	BV+4%	—
1996	143,682	BV+4%	—
1997	478,211	BV+4%	—
1998	593,704	BV+4%	—
1999	—	BV+7%	—
Note: Maple leaf with oval "20 Years ANS" privy mark			

KM# 305 50 DOLLARS
Weight: 31.1030 g. **Composition:** 0.9999 Gold 1 oz. AGW **Ruler:**
Elizabeth II **Obverse:** Crowned head denomination below,
within circle, dates below **Reverse:** Mountie at gallop right,
within circle **Rev. Designer:** Ago Aarand **Shape:** 10-sided

Date	Mintage	MS-63	Proof
1997	12,913	685	—

KM# 369 50 DOLLARS
Weight: 31.1030 g. **Composition:** 0.9999 Gold 1.0000 oz. AGW
Ruler: Elizabeth II **Obverse:** Crowned head right, date and
denomination below **Reverse:** Maple leaf hologram flanked by
9999, with fireworks privy mark

Date	Mintage	MS-63	Proof
2000	500	1,400	—

KM# 364 50 DOLLARS
Weight: 31.1030 g. **Composition:** 0.9999 Gold 1.0000 oz. AGW
Ruler: Elizabeth II **Obverse:** Crowned head right, denomination
and date below **Reverse:** Maple leaf flanked by 9999, with
fireworks privy mark

Date	Mintage	MS-63	Proof
2000	—	785	—

KM# 442 50 DOLLARS
Weight: 31.1500 g. **Composition:** 0.9999 Gold 1.0014 oz. AGW
Ruler: Elizabeth II **Subject:** Holographic Maples Leaves **Obverse:**
Crowned head right **Reverse:** Three maple leaves multicolor
hologram **Edge:** Reeded **Size:** 30 mm.

Date	Mintage	MS-63	Proof
2001 in sets only	600	1,350	—

CHINA, PEOPLE'S REPUBLIC

X# MB12 1.5 GRAMS
1.5000 g., 0.9999 Gold 0.0482 oz. AGW   **Rev:** Yin-yang
Note: Struck by the Singapore Mint.

Date	Mintage	F	VF	XF	Unc	BU
1984SM Proof	1,500			Value: 40.00		

X# MB32 1/20 OUNCE
1.5551 g., 0.9990 Gold 0.0499 oz. AGW   **Subject:** Tokyo
International Coin Show - "Tong-Tong"

Date	Mintage	F	VF	XF	Unc	BU
1987 Proof	25,025			Value: 35.00		

X# MB8 1/10 OUNCE
3.1103 g., 0.9990 Gold .1000 oz. AGW   **Obv:** Temple of Heaven
Rev: Panda with bamboo shoot **Note:** Prev. Y#40.

Date	Mintage	F	VF	XF	Unc	BU
1982	75,000	—	—	—	—	90.00

X# MB41 1/10 OUNCE
3.1103 g., 0.9990 Gold 0.0999 oz. AGW   **Subject:** Tokyo
International Coin Show

Date	Mintage	F	VF	XF	Unc	BU
1989 Proof	30,000			Value: 85.00		

X# MB9 1/4 OUNCE
7.7758 g., 0.9990 Gold 0.2497 oz. AGW   **Obv:** Similar to 1
Ounce, Y#43 **Note:** Prev. Y#41.

Date	Mintage	F	VF	XF	Unc	BU
1982	40,000	—	—	—	—	185

Y# 41 1/4 OUNCE
7.7758 g., 0.9990 Gold .2500 oz. AGW   **Obv:** Temple of Heaven
Rev: Panda with bamboo shoot

Date	Mintage	F	VF	XF	Unc	BU
1982	40,000	—	—	—	—	175
1982	40,000	—	—	—	—	175

X# MB36 1/4 OUNCE
7.7758 g., 0.9990 Gold .2500 oz. AGW   **Subject:** Mazu

Date	Mintage	F	VF	XF	Unc	BU
1987	5,000	—	—	—	175	—
1987 Proof	2,000			Value: 190		

X# MB37 1/4 OUNCE
7.7758 g., 0.9990 Gold 0.2497 oz. AGW   **Subject:** Sakyamnni
Buddha

Date	Mintage	F	VF	XF	Unc	BU
1988	5,000	—	—	—	175	—
1988 Proof	2,000			Value: 190		

X# MB38 1/4 OUNCE
7.7758 g., 0.9990 Gold 0.2497 oz. AGW **Subject:** Badhisattva Avalokitesvara

Date	Mintage	F	VF	XF	Unc	BU
1988	5,000	—	—	—	175	—
1988 Proof	2,000			Value: 190		

X# MB47 1/4 OUNCE
7.7758 g., 0.9990 Gold 0.2497 oz. AGW **Subject:** Maitreya Buddha

Date	Mintage	F	VF	XF	Unc	BU
1989	5,000	—	—	—	175	—
1989 Proof	2,000			Value: 190		

X# MB49 1/4 OUNCE
7.7758 g., 0.9990 Gold 0.2497 oz. AGW **Subject:** General Guan Yu

Date	Mintage	F	VF	XF	Unc	BU
1989	5,000	—	—	—	175	—
1989 Proof	2,000			Value: 190		

X# MBA10 1/2 OUNCE
15.5517 g., 0.9990 Gold .5000 oz. AGW **Obv:** Temple of Heaven **Rev:** Panda with bamboo shoot

Date	Mintage	F	VF	XF	Unc	BU
1982	13,000	—	—	—	—	385

X# MB43 1/2 OUNCE
15.5517 g., 0.9990 Gold 0.4995 oz. AGW **Subject:** 2nd Hong Kong Coin Exposition - Great Wall

Date	Mintage	F	VF	XF	Unc	BU
1989 Proof	1,300			Value: 375		

X# MB44 1/2 OUNCE
15.5517 g., 0.9990 Gold 0.4995 oz. AGW **Subject:** Munich International Coin Exposition

Date	Mintage	F	VF	XF	Unc	BU
1989 Proof	1,500			Value: 375		

X# MB54 1/2 OUNCE
15.5517 g., 0.9990 Gold 0.4995 oz. AGW **Subject:** 18th New York International Numismatic Convention - Tang Horse

Date	Mintage	F	VF	XF	Unc	BU
1989 Proof	5,000			Value: 365		

X# MB60 1/2 OUNCE
15.5517 g., 0.9990 Gold 0.4995 oz. AGW **Subject:** Munich International Coin Exposition

Date	Mintage	F	VF	XF	Unc	BU
1990 Proof	1,500			Value: 375		

X# MBA11 OUNCE
31.1035 g., 0.9990 Gold 1.0000 oz. AGW   **Obv:** Temple of Heaven **Rev:** Panda with bamboo shoot

Date	Mintage	F	VF	XF	Unc	BU
1982	16,000	—	—	—	—	850

X# MB7 OUNCE
31.1035 g., 0.9990 Gold 0.999 oz. AGW   **Subject:** 1st San Francisco International Coin Expo

Date	Mintage	F	VF	XF	Unc	BU
1987 Proof	3,000	Value: 750				

X# MB14 OUNCE
31.1035 g., 0.9990 Gold 0.999 oz. AGW   **Subject:** 96th American Numismtic Association Convention - New Orleans

Date	Mintage	F	VF	XF	Unc	BU
1987 Proof	3,000	Value: 735				

X# MB16 OUNCE
31.1035 g., 0.9990 Gold 0.999 oz. AGW   **Subject:** Tokyo International Coin Show - "Tong-Tong"

Date	Mintage	F	VF	XF	Unc	BU
1987 Proof	5,000	Value: 725				

X# MB18 OUNCE
31.1035 g., 0.9990 Gold 0.999 oz. AGW   **Subject:** 16th New York International Numismatic Convention

Date	Mintage	F	VF	XF	Unc	BU
1987 Proof	2,000	Value: 735				

X# MB20 OUNCE
31.1035 g., 0.9990 Gold 0.999 oz. AGW   **Subject:** Basel International Coin Week

Date	Mintage	F	VF	XF	Unc	BU
1988 Proof	450	Value: 900				

X# MB21 OUNCE
31.1035 g., 0.9990 Gold 0.999 oz. AGW   **Note:** Error with "Pt." (platinum die).

Date	Mintage	F	VF	XF	Unc	BU
1988 Proof	550	Value: 850				

X# MB23 OUNCE
31.1035 g., 0.9990 Gold 0.999 oz. AGW   **Subject:** 2nd San Francisco International Coin Expo

Date	Mintage	F	VF	XF	Unc	BU
1988 Proof	1,500	Value: 735				

X# MB25 OUNCE
31.1035 g., 0.9990 Gold 0.999 oz. AGW **Subject:** Munich Coin Bourse

Date	Mintage	F	VF	XF	Unc	BU
1988 Proof	2,000			Value: 725		

X# MB27 OUNCE
31.1035 g., 0.9990 Gold 0.999 oz. AGW **Subject:** 1st Hong Kong Coin Exposition - China

Date	Mintage	F	VF	XF	Unc	BU
1988 Proof	800			Value: 750		

X# MB29 OUNCE
31.1035 g., 0.9990 Gold 0.999 oz. AGW **Subject:** 97th American Numismatic Association Convention - Cincinnati

Date	Mintage	F	VF	XF	Unc	BU
1988 Proof	1,000			Value: 750		

X# MB31 OUNCE
31.1035 g., 0.9990 Gold 0.999 oz. AGW **Subject:** American Numismatic Association Convention - New Orleans

Date	Mintage	F	VF	XF	Unc	BU
1988 Proof	3,000			Value: 725		

X# MB51 OUNCE
31.1035 g., 0.9990 Gold 0.999 oz. AGW **Subject:** 3rd San Francisco International Coin Expo

Date	Mintage	F	VF	XF	Unc	BU
1989 Proof	1,500			Value: 725		

X# MB33 5 OUNCES
155.5150 g., 0.9990 Gold 4.9949 oz. AGW, 69 mm.
Subject: Tokyo International Coin Show - "Tong-Tong"

Date	Mintage	F	VF	XF	Unc	BU
1987 Proof	1,500			Value: 3,500		

X# MB46 5 OUNCES
155.5150 g., 0.9990 Gold 4.9949 oz. AGW **Subject:** Bodhisattva Avalokitesvara

Date	Mintage	F	VF	XF	Unc	BU
1989 Proof	500			Value: 3,600		

X# MB50 5 OUNCES
155.5150 g., 0.9990 Gold 4.9949 oz. AGW **Subject:** General Guan Yu

Date	Mintage	F	VF	XF	Unc	BU
1989 Proof	500			Value: 3,600		

X# MB34 12 OUNCES (Troy Pound)
375.2360 g., 0.9990 Gold 12.052 oz. AGW, 79 mm.
Rev: Longevity

Date	Mintage	F	VF	XF	Unc	BU
ND(1988) Proof	200			Value: 8,500		

GREAT BRITAIN

KM# 950 10 POUNDS (1/10 Ounce - Britannia)
3.4120 g., 0.9170 Gold .1000 oz. AGW   **Ruler:** Elizabeth II **Obv:**
Crowned head right **Rev:** Britannia standing **Note:** Copper alloy.

Date	Mintage	F	VF	XF	Unc	BU
1987	—	—	—	—	BV+16%	—
1987 Proof	3,500			Value: 80.00		
1988	—	—	—	—	BV+16%	—
1988 Proof	2,694			Value: 80.00		
1989	—	—	—	—	BV+16%	—
1989 Proof	1,609			Value: 80.00		

KM# 950a 10 POUNDS (1/10 Ounce - Britannia)
3.4120 g., 0.9170 Gold .1000 oz. AGW   **Ruler:** Elizabeth II **Obv:**
Crowned head right **Rev:** Britannia standing **Note:** Silver alloy.

Date	Mintage	F	VF	XF	Unc	BU
1990 Proof	1,571			Value: 80.00		
1991 Proof	954			Value: 125		
1992 Proof	1,000			Value: 125		
1993 Proof	997			Value: 125		
1994 Proof	994			Value: 110		
1995 Proof	1,500			Value: 110		
1996 Proof	2,379			Value: 110		
1999 Proof	Est. 5,750			Value: 100		

KM# 950a

KM# 982 10 POUNDS (1/10 Ounce - Britannia)
3.4100 g., 0.9167 Gold .1005 oz. AGW   **Ruler:** Elizabeth II **Obv:**
Crowned head right **Rev:** Britannia in chariot

Date	Mintage	F	VF	XF	Unc	BU
1997 Proof	11,821			Value: 120		

KM# 1008 10 POUNDS (1/10 Ounce - Britannia)
3.4100 g., 0.9167 Gold .1005 oz. AGW   **Ruler:** Elizabeth II **Obv:**
Head with tiara right **Obv. Designer:** Ian Rank-Broadley **Rev:**
Britannia standing **Rev. Designer:** Philip Nathan **Edge:** Reeded

Date	Mintage	F	VF	XF	Unc	BU
1999 Proof	1,058			Value: 115		
2000 Proof	659			Value: 100		
2002 Proof	1,500			Value: 115		
2004	—	—	—	—	—	—
2004 Proof	—			Value: 200		

KM# 1020 10 POUNDS (1/10 Ounce - Britannia)
3.4100 g., 0.9167 Gold .1005 oz. AGW, 16.5 mm. **Ruler:**
Elizabeth II **Subject:** Britannia Bullion **Obv:** Head with tiara right
Obv. Designer: Ian Rank-Broadley **Rev:** Stylized "Britannia and
the Lion" **Rev. Designer:** Philip Nathan **Edge:** Reeded

Date	Mintage	F	VF	XF	Unc	BU
2001	1,100	—	—	—	BV+16%	—
2001 Proof	1,557	Value: 115				

KM# 1040 10 POUNDS (1/10 Ounce - Britannia)
3.4100 g., 0.9167 Gold 0.1005 oz. AGW, 16.5 mm. **Ruler:**
Elizabeth II **Obv:** Head with tiara right **Obv. Designer:** Ian
Rank-Broadley **Rev:** Britannia portrait behind wavy lines **Rev.
Designer:** Philip Nathan **Edge:** Reeded

Date	Mintage	F	VF	XF	Unc	BU
2003	—	—	—	—	BV+16%	—
2003 Proof	4,000	Value: 115				

KM# 1068 10 POUNDS (1/10 Ounce - Britannia)
3.4100 g., 0.9167 Gold 0.1005 oz. AGW, 16.5 mm. **Ruler:**
Elizabeth II **Obv:** Head with tiara right **Obv. Designer:** Ian Rank-
Broadley **Rev:** Seated Britannia **Rev. Designer:** Philip Nathan
Edge: Reeded

Date	Mintage	F	VF	XF	Unc	BU
2005 Proof	3,500	Value: 150				

KM# 951 25 POUNDS (1/4 Ounce - Britannia)
8.5130 g., 0.9170 Gold .2500 oz. AGW **Ruler:** Elizabeth II **Obv:**
Crowned head right **Rev:** Britannia standing **Note:** Copper alloy.

Date	Mintage	F	VF	XF	Unc	BU
1987	—	—	—	—	BV+10%	—
1987 Proof	3,500	Value: 185				
1988	—	—	—	—	BV+10%	—
1988 Proof	Est. 14,000	Value: 185				
1989	—	—	—	—	BV+10%	—
1989 Proof	Est. 4,000	Value: 185				

KM# 951a 25 POUNDS (1/4 Ounce - Britannia)
8.5130 g., 0.9170 Gold .2500 oz. AGW **Ruler:** Elizabeth II **Obv:**
Crowned head right **Rev:** Britannia standing **Note:** Silver alloy.

Date	Mintage	F	VF	XF	Unc	BU
1990 Proof	Est. 2,500	Value: 195				
1991 Proof	750	Value: 225				
1992 Proof	500	Value: 225				
1993 Proof	Est. 500	Value: 225				
1994 Proof	500	Value: 215				
1995 Proof	500	Value: 215				
1996 Proof	2,500	Value: 215				
1999 Proof	1,750	Value: 215				

KM# 983 25 POUNDS (1/4 Ounce - Britannia)
8.5100 g., 0.9167 Gold .2508 oz. AGW **Ruler:** Elizabeth II **Obv:**
Crowned head right **Rev:** Britannia in chariot

Date	Mintage	F	VF	XF	Unc	BU
1997 Proof	Est. 4,000			Value: 215		

KM# 1009 25 POUNDS (1/4 Ounce - Britannia)
8.5100 g., 0.9167 Gold .2508 oz. AGW **Ruler:** Elizabeth II **Obv:**
Head with tiara right **Obv. Designer:** Ian Rank-Broadley **Rev:**
Britannia standing **Rev. Designer:** Philip Nathan **Edge:** Reeded

Date	Mintage	F	VF	XF	Unc	BU
1999 Proof	1,000			Value: 220		
2000 Proof	Est. 500			Value: 200		
2002 Proof	750			Value: 225		
2004	—	—	—	—	—	—
2004 Proof	—			Value: 350		

KM# 1021 25 POUNDS (1/4 Ounce - Britannia)
8.5100 g., 0.9167 Gold .2508 oz. AGW, 22 mm. **Ruler:**
Elizabeth II **Subject:** Britannia Bullion **Obv:** Head with tiara right
Obv. Designer: Ian Rank-Broadley **Rev:** Stylized "Britannia and
the Lion" **Rev. Designer:** Philip Nathan **Edge:** Reeded

Date	Mintage	F	VF	XF	Unc	BU
2001	1,100	—	—	—	BV+35%	—
2001 Proof	1,500			Value: 225		

KM# 1041 25 POUNDS (1/4 Ounce - Britannia)
8.5100 g., 0.9167 Gold 0.2508 oz. AGW, 22 mm. **Ruler:**
Elizabeth II **Obv:** Head with tiara right **Obv. Designer:** Ian
Rank-Broadley **Rev:** Britannia portrait behind wavy lines **Rev.
Designer:** Philip Nathan **Edge:** Reeded

Date	Mintage	F	VF	XF	Unc	BU
2003	604	—	—	—	BV+35%	—
2003 Proof	3,250			Value: 225		

KM# 1069 25 POUNDS (1/4 Ounce - Britannia)
8.5100 g., 0.9167 Gold 0.2508 oz. AGW, 22 mm. **Ruler:**
Elizabeth II **Obv:** Head with tiara right **Obv. Designer:** Ian Rank-
Broadley **Rev:** Seated Britannia **Rev. Designer:** Philip Nathan
Edge: Reeded

Date	Mintage	F	VF	XF	Unc	BU
2005 Proof	2,750			Value: 300		

KM# 952 50 POUNDS (1/2 Ounce - Britannia)
17.0250 g., 0.9170 Gold .5000 oz. AGW **Ruler:** Elizabeth II **Obv:**
Crowned head right **Rev:** Britannia standing **Note:** Copper alloy.

Date	Mintage	F	VF	XF	Unc	BU
1987	—	—	—	—	BV+10%	—

Date	Mintage	F	VF	XF	Unc	BU
1987 Proof	2,486			Value: 375		
1988	—	—	—	—	BV+10%	—
1988 Proof	626			Value: 375		
1989	—	—	—	—	BV+10%	—
1989 Proof	338			Value: 375		

KM# 952a 50 POUNDS (1/2 Ounce - Britannia)
17.0250 g., 0.9170 Gold .5000 oz. AGW **Ruler:** Elizabeth II **Obv:** Crowned head right **Rev:** Britannia standing **Note:** Silver alloy.

Date	Mintage	F	VF	XF	Unc	BU
1990 Proof	527			Value: 375		
1991 Proof	509			Value: 400		
1992 Proof	500			Value: 425		
1993 Proof	462	—	—	—	—	—
1994 Proof	435			Value: 425		
1995 Proof	500			Value: 425		
1996 Proof	483			Value: 400		
1999 Proof	740			Value: 450		

KM# 984 50 POUNDS (1/2 Ounce - Britannia)
17.0300 g., 0.9167 Gold .5019 oz. AGW **Ruler:** Elizabeth II **Obv:** Crowned head right **Rev:** Britannia in chariot

Date	Mintage	F	VF	XF	Unc	BU
1997 Proof	Est. 1,500			Value: 400		

KM# 1010 50 POUNDS (1/2 Ounce - Britannia)
17.0300 g., 0.9167 Gold .5019 oz. AGW **Ruler:** Elizabeth II **Obv:** Head with tiara right **Obv. Designer:** Ian Rank-Broadley **Rev:** Britannia standing **Rev. Designer:** Philip Nathan **Edge:** Reeded

Date	Mintage	F	VF	XF	Unc	BU
1999 Proof	—			Value: 425		
2000 Proof	750			Value: 425		
2002 Proof	1,000			Value: 445		
2004	—	—	—	—	—	—
2004 Proof	—			Value: 500		

KM# 1022 50 POUNDS (1/2 Ounce - Britannia)
17.0200 g., 0.9167 Gold .5016 oz. AGW, 27 mm. **Ruler:** Elizabeth II **Subject:** Britannia Bullion **Obv:** Head with tiara right **Obv. Designer:** Ian Rank-Broadley **Rev:** Stylized "Britannia and the Lion" **Rev. Designer:** Philip Nathan **Edge:** Reeded

Date	Mintage	F	VF	XF	Unc	BU
2001	600	—	—	—	BV+35%	—
2001 Proof	1,000			Value: 435		

KM# 1042 50 POUNDS (1/2 Ounce - Britannia)
17.0200 g., 0.9167 Gold 0.5016 oz. AGW, 27 mm. **Ruler:**
Elizabeth II **Obv:** Head with tiara right **Obv. Designer:** Ian
Rank-Broadley **Rev:** Britannia portrait behind wavy lines **Rev.**
Designer: Philip Nathan **Edge:** Reeded

Date	Mintage	F	VF	XF	Unc	BU
2003	—	—	—	—	BV+25%	—
2003 Proof	2,500	Value: 450				

KM# 1070 50 POUNDS (1/2 Ounce - Britannia)
17.0300 g., 0.9167 Gold 0.5019 oz. AGW, 27 mm. **Ruler:** Elizabeth II
Obv: Head with tiara right **Obv. Designer:** Ian Rank-Broadley **Rev:**
Seated Britannia **Rev. Designer:** Philip Nathan **Edge:** Reeded

Date	Mintage	F	VF	XF	Unc	BU
2005 Proof	2,000	Value: 450				

KM# 953 100 POUNDS (1 Ounce - Britannia)
34.0500 g., 0.9170 Gold 1.0000 oz. AGW **Ruler:** Elizabeth II **Obv:**
Crowned head right **Rev:** Britannia standing **Note:** Copper alloy.

Date	Mintage	F	VF	XF	Unc	BU
1987	—	—	—	—	BV+12%	—
1987 Proof	13,000	Value: 765				
1988	—	—	—	—	BV+12%	—
1988 Proof	Est. 8,500	Value: 765				
1989	—	—	—	—	BV+12%	—
1989 Proof	Est. 2,600	Value: 765				

KM# 953a 100 POUNDS (1 Ounce - Britannia)
34.0500 g., 0.9170 Gold 1.0000 oz. AGW **Ruler:** Elizabeth II **Obv:**
Crowned head right **Rev:** Britannia standing **Note:** Silver alloy.

Date	Mintage	F	VF	XF	Unc	BU
1990 Proof	262	Value: 800				
1991 Proof	143	Value: 850				
1992 Proof	500	Value: 875				
1993 Proof	Est. 500	Value: 875				
1994 Proof	Est. 500	Value: 850				
1995 Proof	Est. 500	Value: 900				
1996 Proof	2,500	Value: 800				
1999 Proof	Est. 750	Value: 845				

KM# 985 100 POUNDS (1 Ounce - Britannia)
34.0500 g., 0.9167 Gold 1.0035 oz. AGW **Ruler:** Elizabeth II
Obv: Crowned head right **Rev:** Britannia in chariot

Date	Mintage	F	VF	XF	Unc	BU
1997	—	—	—	—	BV+15%	—
1997 Proof	164	Value: 865				

KM# 1011 100 POUNDS (1 Ounce - Britannia)
34.0500 g., 0.9167 Gold 1.0035 oz. AGW **Ruler:** Elizabeth II **Obv:** Head with tiara right **Obv. Designer:** Ian Rank-Broadley **Rev:** Britannia standing **Rev. Designer:** Philip Nathan **Edge:** Reeded

Date	Mintage	F	VF	XF	Unc	BU
1999 Proof	—			Value: 875		
2000 Proof	750			Value: 875		
2002 Proof	1,000			Value: 900		
2004	—	—	—	—	—	—
2004 Proof	—			Value: 875		

KM# 1023 100 POUNDS (1 Ounce - Britannia)
34.0500 g., 0.9167 Gold 1.0035 oz. AGW, 32.7 mm. **Ruler:** Elizabeth II **Subject:** Britannia Bullion **Obv:** Head with tiara right **Obv. Designer:** Ian Rank-Broadley **Rev:** Stylized "Britannia and the Lion" **Rev. Designer:** Philip Nathan **Edge:** Reeded

Date	Mintage	F	VF	XF	Unc	BU
2001	900	—	—	—	BV+15%	—
2001 Proof	1,000			Value: 875		

KM# 1043 100 POUNDS (1 Ounce - Britannia)
34.0500 g., 0.9167 Gold 1.0035 oz. AGW, 32.7 mm. **Ruler:** Elizabeth II **Obv:** Head with tiara right **Obv. Designer:** Ian Rank-Broadley **Rev:** Britannia portrait behind wavy lines **Rev. Designer:** Philip Nathan **Edge:** Reeded

Date	Mintage	F	VF	XF	Unc	BU
2003	—	—	—	—	BV+15%	—
2003 Proof	1,500			Value: 900		

KM# 1071 100 POUNDS (1 Ounce - Britannia)
34.0500 g., 0.9167 Gold 1.0035 oz. AGW, 32.7 mm. **Ruler:** Elizabeth II **Obv:** Head with tiara right **Obv. Designer:** Ian Rank-Broadley **Rev:** Seated Britannia **Edge:** Reeded

Date	Mintage	F	VF	XF	Unc	BU
2005 Proof	1,500			Value: 875		

ISLE OF MAN
ANGEL SERIES

KM# 166 1/20 ANGEL
1.6970 g., 0.9170 Gold .0500 oz. AGW **Ruler:** Elizabeth II **Obv:** Crowned bust right **Obv. Designer:** Raphael Maklouf **Rev:** Archangel Michael slaying dragon

Date	Mintage	F	VF	XF	Unc	BU
1986	—	—	—	—	37.50	—
1986 (pi) Proof	5,000			Value: 45.00		
1987	—	—	—	—	37.50	—
1987 Proof	—			Value: 45.00		

KM# 193 1/20 ANGEL
1.6970 g., 0.9170 Gold .0500 oz. AGW **Obv:** Crowned bust right
Obv. Designer: Raphael Maklouf **Rev:** Archangel Michael slaying
dragon **Rev. Designer:** Leslie Lindsay

Date	Mintage	F	VF	XF	Unc	BU
1988	—	—	—	—	37.50	—
1988 (pi)	—	—	—	—	50.00	—
1989 (h) Proof	Est. 5,000	Value: 50.00				
1989 (mt) Proof	3,000	Value: 50.00				
1990 (sg) Proof	Est. 3,000	Value: 50.00				
1991 (cc) Proof	1,000	Value: 50.00				
1992 (cb) Proof	1,000	Value: 50.00				
1993 Proof	Est. 1,000	Value: 50.00				

KM# 393 1/20 ANGEL
1.5551 g., 0.9999 Gold .0500 oz. AGW **Ruler:** Elizabeth II **Obv:**
Crowned bust right **Obv. Designer:** Raphael Maklouf **Rev:**
Archangel Michael slaying dragon right

Date	Mintage	F	VF	XF	Unc	BU
1994 (ns) Proof	—	Value: 45.00				
1995 (sc) Proof	—	Value: 50.00				
1996 (bs) Proof	Est. 1,000	Value: 50.00				
1997 (at) Proof	Est. 1,000	Value: 50.00				
1998 (x) Proof	Est. 1,000	Value: 50.00				
1999 (fw) Proof	Est. 1,000	Value: 50.00				
2000 (ch) Proof	Est. 1,000	Value: 50.00				
2000 Proof	—	Value: 45.00				
Note: Christmas candle privy mark						

KM# 1106 1/20 ANGEL
1.5552 g., 0.9999 Gold .0500 oz. AGW, 15 mm. **Ruler:**
Elizabeth II Bust with tiara right **Obv. Designer:** Ian Rank-
Broadley **Rev:** St. Michael slaying dragon, three crown privy
mark at right **Edge:** Reeded

Date	Mintage	F	VF	XF	Unc	BU
2001 (3c) Proof	1,000	Value: 50.00				
2002 Proof	—	Value: 50.00				
Note: With candy cane privy mark						

KM# 1252 1/20 ANGEL
1.5550 g., 0.9999 Gold 0.05 oz. AGW, 15 mm. **Ruler:** Elizabeth II
Obv: Bust with tiara right **Obv. Designer:** Ian Rank-Broadley
Rev: St. Michael and Christmas privy mark **Edge:** Reeded

Date	Mintage	F	VF	XF	Unc	BU
2004PM Proof	1,000	Value: 60.00				

KM# 138 1/10 ANGEL
3.3900 g., 0.9170 Gold .1000 oz. AGW **Ruler:** Elizabeth II **Obv:** Crowned bust right **Obv. Designer:** Raphael Maklouf **Rev:** Archangel Michael slaying dragon

Date	Mintage	F	VF	XF	Unc	BU
1984 Proof	5,000			Value: 75.00		

KM# 140 1/10 ANGEL
3.3900 g., 0.9170 Gold .1000 oz. AGW **Ruler:** Elizabeth II **Obv:** Crowned bust right **Obv. Designer:** Raphael Maklouf **Rev:** Archangel Michael slaying dragon left **Rev. Designer:** Leslie Lindsay

Date	Mintage	F	VF	XF	Unc	BU
1985 Proof	3,000			Value: 80.00		
1985	8,000	—	—	—	70.00	—
1986	—	—	—	—	70.00	—
1986 Proof	—			Value: 80.00		
1987	—	—	—	—	70.00	—
1987 Proof	—			Value: 80.00		

KM# 159 1/10 ANGEL
3.3900 g., 0.9170 Gold .1000 oz. AGW **Ruler:** Elizabeth II **Obv:** Crowned bust right **Obv. Designer:** Raphael Maklouf **Rev:** Archangel Michael slaying dragon left **Rev. Designer:** Leslie Lindsay

Date	Mintage	F	VF	XF	Unc	BU
1985 A	1,000	—	—	—	85.00	—
1985 C	1,000	—	—	—	85.00	—
1985 H	1,000	—	—	—	85.00	—
1985 L	1,000	—	—	—	85.00	—
1985	5,000	—	—	—	70.00	—
1986 A	1,000	—	—	—	85.00	—
1986 T	1,000	—	—	—	85.00	—
1986 X	1,000	—	—	—	85.00	—
1987 A	1,000	—	—	—	85.00	—
1987 F Proof	1,000			Value: 85.00		
1987 L	1,000	—	—	—	85.00	—
1987 (mt) Proof	3,000			Value: 85.00		
1988 A Proof	1,000			Value: 85.00		

KM# 194 1/10 ANGEL
3.3900 g., 0.9170 Gold .1000 oz. AGW **Ruler:** Elizabeth II **Obv:** Crowned bust right **Obv. Designer:** Raphael Maklouf **Rev:** Archangel Michael slaying dragon

Date	Mintage	F	VF	XF	Unc	BU
1988	—	—	—	—	70.00	—
1989 A Proof	250			Value: 100		
1990 A Proof	1,000			Value: 85.00		
1991 A Proof	400			Value: 95.00		
Note: 299 pieces have been melted						
1992 A	100	—	—	—	110	—

KM# 394 1/10 ANGEL
3.1103 g., 0.9999 Gold .1000 oz. AGW **Obv:** Crowned bust right
Obv. Designer: Raphael Maklouf **Rev:** Archangel Michael

Date	Mintage	F	VF	XF	Unc	BU
1994 Proof	—	Value: 75.00				

KM# 152.1 1/4 ANGEL
8.4830 g., 0.9170 Gold .2500 oz. AGW **Ruler:** Elizabeth II **Obv:**
Crowned bust right **Obv. Designer:** Raphael Maklouf **Rev:**
Archangel Michael slaying dragon left **Rev. Designer:** Leslie Lindsay

Date	Mintage	F	VF	XF	Unc	BU
1985	2,117	—	—	—	175	—
1985 Proof	51	Value: 200				
1986 L	1,000	—	—	—	175	—
1986 Proof	—	Value: 185				

KM# 152.2 1/4 ANGEL
8.4830 g., 0.9170 Gold .2500 oz. AGW **Ruler:** Elizabeth II **Obv:**
Crowned bust right **Obv. Designer:** Raphael Maklouf **Rev:**
Archangel Michael slaying dragon **Rev. Designer:** Leslie Lindsay

Date	Mintage	F	VF	XF	Unc	BU
1987	—	—	—	—	175	—
1987 Proof	—	Value: 185				
1987 (s) Proof	1,000	Value: 185				
1987 (SL) Proof	568	Value: 185				
1987 (bb) Proof	1,000	Value: 185				

KM# 195 1/4 ANGEL
8.4830 g., 0.9170 Gold .2500 oz. AGW **Ruler:** Elizabeth II **Obv:**
Crowned bust right **Obv. Designer:** Raphael Maklouf **Rev:**
Archangel Michael slaying dragon left **Rev. Designer:** Leslie Lindsay

Date	Mintage	F	VF	XF	Unc	BU
1988	—	—	—	—	175	—
1988 (f) Proof	1,000	Value: 200				
1988 (p) Proof	1,000	Value: 200				
1988 (ss) Proof	1,000	Value: 200				
1989 C (d) Proof	1,000	Value: 200				
1989 (p) Proof	500	Value: 200				
1989 (hk) Proof	1,000	Value: 200				
1989 (y)	—	—	—	—	175	—
1990 (ba) Proof	1,000	Value: 200				
Note: 513 pieces melted						
1990 (c) Proof	250	Value: 220				
1990 (fl)	1,000	—	—	—	175	—
Note: 9 pieces melted						
1990 (h) Proof	1,000	Value: 180				

Date	Mintage	F	VF	XF	Unc	BU
1990 (ma) Proof	200		Value: 250			
Note: 40 pieces melted						
1990 (tb)	1,000	—	—	—	175	—
Note: 10 pieces melted						
1991 (c) Proof	200		Value: 250			
Note: 57 pieces melted						
1991 (fr) Proof	500		Value: 200			
1993 Proof	—		Value: 175			

KM# 395 1/4 ANGEL
7.7758 g., 0.9999 Gold .2500 oz. AGW **Ruler:** Elizabeth II **Obv:** Crowned bust right **Obv. Designer:** Raphael Maklouf **Rev:** Archangel Michael slaying dragon

Date	Mintage	F	VF	XF	Unc	BU
1994 Proof	750		Value: 190			

KM# 155 1/2 ANGEL
16.9380 g., 0.9170 Gold .5000 oz. AGW **Ruler:** Elizabeth II **Obv:** Crowned bust right **Obv. Designer:** Raphael Maklouf **Rev:** Archangel Michael slaying dragon left **Rev. Designer:** Leslie Lindsay

Date	Mintage	F	VF	XF	Unc	BU
1985	1,776	—	—	—	350	—
1985 Proof	51		Value: 375			
1986	—	—	—	—	350	—
1986 Proof	3,000		Value: 365			
1987	—	—	—	—	350	—
1987 Proof	—		Value: 365			

KM# 196 1/2 ANGEL
16.9380 g., 0.9170 Gold .5000 oz. AGW **Ruler:** Elizabeth II **Obv:** Crowned bust right **Obv. Designer:** Raphael Maklouf **Rev:** Archangel Michael slaying dragon

Date	Mintage	F	VF	XF	Unc	BU
1988	—	—	—	—	350	—

KM# 396 1/2 ANGEL
15.5517 g., 0.9999 Gold .5000 oz. AGW **Ruler:** Elizabeth II **Obv:** Crowned bust right **Obv. Designer:** Raphael Maklouf **Rev:** Archangel Michael slaying dragon

Date	Mintage	F	VF	XF	Unc	BU
1994 Proof	—		Value: 350			

KM# 139 ANGEL
33.9300 g., 0.9170 Gold 1.0000 oz. AGW **Ruler:** Elizabeth II **Obv:** Young bust right **Obv. Designer:** Arnold Machin **Rev:** Archangel Michael slaying dragon left **Rev. Designer:** Leslie Lindsay

Date	Mintage	F	VF	XF	Unc	BU
1984 Proof	3,000		Value: 725			

KM# 141 ANGEL
33.9300 g., 0.9170 Gold 1.0000 oz. AGW **Ruler:** Elizabeth II
Obv: Crowned bust right **Obv. Designer:** Raphael Maklouf **Rev:**
Archangel Michael slaying dragon left **Rev. Designer:** Leslie Lindsay

Date	Mintage	F	VF	XF	Unc	BU
1985	28,000	—	—	—	700	—
1985 Prooflike	—	—	—	—	—	—
1985 Proof	3,000	Value: 725				
1986	—	—	—	—	700	—
1986 Proof	—	Value: 725				
1987	—	—	—	—	700	—
1987 Proof	—	Value: 725				

KM# 191 ANGEL
33.9300 g., 0.9170 Gold 1.0000 oz. AGW **Ruler:** Elizabeth II
Subject: Hong Kong Coin Show **Obv:** Crowned bust right **Rev:**
Archangel Michael slaying dragon left **Rev. Designer:** Leslie Lindsay

Date	Mintage	F	VF	XF	Unc	BU
1987 Proof	1,000	Value: 725				

KM# 191

KM# 197 ANGEL
33.9300 g., 0.9170 Gold 1.0000 oz. AGW **Ruler:** Elizabeth II
Obv: Crowned bust right **Obv. Designer:** Raphael Maklouf **Rev:**
Archangel Michael slaying dragon left **Rev. Designer:** Leslie Lindsay

Date	Mintage	F	VF	XF	Unc	BU
1988	—	—	—	—	700	—
1988 (ss) Proof	1,000	Value: 725				

KM# 397 ANGEL
31.1035 g., 0.9999 Gold 1.0000 oz. AGW **Ruler:** Elizabeth II
Obv: Crowned bust right **Obv. Designer:** Raphael Maklouf **Rev:**
Archangel Michael slaying dragon right

Date	Mintage	F	VF	XF	Unc	BU
1994 Proof	—	Value: 725				

KM# 156 5 ANGEL
169.6680 g., 0.9170 Gold 5.0000 oz. AGW **Ruler:** Elizabeth II
Obv: Crowned bust right **Obv. Designer:** Raphael Maklouf **Rev:**
Archangel Michael slaying dragon left **Rev. Designer:** Leslie
Lindsay

Date	Mintage	F	VF	XF	Unc	BU
1985	104	—	—	—	3,500	—
1985 Proof	90	Value: 3,500				
1986	89	—	—	—	3,500	—
1986 Proof	250	Value: 3,500				
1987	150	—	—	—	3,500	—
1987 Proof	27	Value: 3,500				

KM# 198 5 ANGEL
169.6680 g., 0.9170 Gold 5.0000 oz. AGW   **Ruler:** Elizabeth II
Obv: Crowned bust right **Obv. Designer:** Raphael Maklouf **Rev:**
Archangel Michael slaying dragon

Date	Mintage	F	VF	XF	Unc	BU
1988	250	—	—	—	3,500	—

KM# 157 10 ANGEL
339.3350 g., 0.9170 Gold 10.0000 oz. AGW   **Ruler:** Elizabeth II
Obv: Crowned bust right **Obv. Designer:** Raphael Maklouf **Rev:**
Archangel Michael slaying dragon left **Rev. Designer:** Leslie Lindsay

Date	Mintage	F	VF	XF	Unc	BU
1985	79	—	—	—	7,000	—
1985 Proof	68		Value: 7,000			
1986	47	—	—	—	7,000	—
1986 Proof	250		Value: 7,000			
1987	150	—	—	—	7,000	—
1987 Proof	30		Value: 7,000			

KM# 199 10 ANGEL
339.3350 g., 0.9170 Gold 10.0000 oz. AGW   **Ruler:** Elizabeth II
Obv: Crowned bust right **Obv. Designer:** Raphael Maklouf **Rev:**
Archangel Michael slaying dragon

Date	Mintage	F	VF	XF	Unc	BU
1988 Proof	250		Value: 7,000			

KM# 189 15 ANGEL
508.9575 g., 0.9170 Gold 15.0000 oz. AGW   **Ruler:** Elizabeth II
Obv: Crowned bust right **Obv. Designer:** Raphael Maklouf **Rev:**
Archangel Michael slaying dragon

Date	Mintage	F	VF	XF	Unc	BU
1987	150	—	—	—	10,500	—
1987 Proof	18		Value: 11,000			

KM# 200 15 ANGEL
508.9575 g., 0.9170 Gold 15.0000 oz. AGW   **Ruler:** Elizabeth II
Obv: Crowned bust right **Obv. Designer:** Raphael Maklouf **Rev:**
Archangel Michael slaying dragon left **Rev. Designer:** Leslie Lindsay

Date	Mintage	F	VF	XF	Unc	BU
1988 Proof	—		Value: 10,500			

KM# 201 20 ANGEL
678.6720 g., 0.9170 Gold 20.0000 oz. AGW, 75.2 mm.   **Ruler:**
Elizabeth II **Obv:** Crowned bust right **Obv. Designer:** Raphael
Maklouf **Rev:** Archangel Michael slaying dragon left **Rev.
Designer:** Leslie Lindsay

Date	Mintage	F	VF	XF	Unc	BU
1988	250	—	—	—	10,500	—
1988 Proof	100		Value: 11,000			

GOLD RUSH

KM# 301 25 ANGEL
848.2750 g., 0.9170 Gold 25.0000 oz. AGW **Ruler:** Elizabeth II
Obv: Crowned bust right **Obv. Designer:** Raphael Maklouf **Rev:**
Archangel Michael slaying dragon

Date	Mintage	F	VF	XF	Unc	BU
1989	—	—	—	—	17,500	—

SOVEREIGN SERIES

KM# 969 1/5 SOVEREIGN
1.0000 g., 0.9999 Gold .0321 oz. AGW **Ruler:** Elizabeth II **Obv:**
Head with tiara right **Obv. Designer:** Ian Rank-Broadley **Rev:**
Triskeles **Shape:** Rectangular

Date	Mintage	F	VF	XF	Unc	BU
1999	—	—	—	—	BV+40%	—

KM# 970 1/2 SOVEREIGN
2.5000 g., 0.9999 Gold .0804 oz. AGW **Ruler:** Elizabeth II **Obv:**
Head with tiara right **Obv. Designer:** Ian Rank-Broadley **Rev:**
Triskeles **Shape:** Rectangular

Date	Mintage	F	VF	XF	Unc	BU
1999	—	—	—	—	BV+30%	—

KM# 971 3/4 SOVEREIGN
3.5000 g., 0.9999 Gold .1125 oz. AGW **Ruler:** Elizabeth II **Obv:**
Head with tiara right **Obv. Designer:** Ian Rank-Broadley **Rev:**
Triskeles **Shape:** Rectangular

Date	Mintage	F	VF	XF	Unc	BU
1999	—	—	—	—	BV+25%	—

KM# 972 SOVEREIGN
5.0000 g., 0.9999 Gold .1607 oz. AGW **Ruler:** Elizabeth II Obv:
Head with tiara right **Obv. Designer:** Ian Rank-Broadley **Rev:**
Triskeles **Shape:** Rectangular

Date	Mintage	F	VF	XF	Unc	BU
1999	—	—	—	—	BV+20%	—

KM# 973 2 SOVEREIGNS
10.0000 g., 0.9999 Gold .3215 oz. AGW **Ruler:** Elizabeth II **Obv:**
Head with tiara right **Obv. Designer:** Ian Rank-Broadley **Rev:**
Triskeles **Shape:** Rectangular

Date	Mintage	F	VF	XF	Unc	BU
1999	—	—	—	—	—	—

KM# 974 5 SOVEREIGNS
31.1035 g., 0.9999 Gold .9999 oz. AGW **Ruler:** Elizabeth II **Obv:**
Head with tiara right **Obv. Designer:** Ian Rank-Broadley **Rev:**
Triskeles **Shape:** Rectangular

Date	Mintage	F	VF	XF	Unc	BU
1999	—	—	—	—	BV+5%	—

PLATINA SERIES

KM# 944 1/25 PLATINA
1.2447 g., 0.7500 White Gold .0300 oz. AGW **Ruler:** Elizabeth II **Obv:** Crowned bust right **Obv. Designer:** Raphael Maklouf **Rev:** Crowned arms

Date	Mintage	F	VF	XF	Unc	BU
1999 Proof	Est. 10,000			Value: 40.00		

KM# 945 1/10 PLATINA
3.1103 g., 0.7500 White Gold .0750 oz. AGW **Ruler:** Elizabeth II **Obv:** Crowned bust right **Obv. Designer:** Raphael Maklouf **Rev:** Crowned arms

Date	Mintage	F	VF	XF	Unc	BU
1999 Proof	Est. 7,500			Value: 75.00		

KM# 946 1/5 PLATINA
6.2200 g., 0.7500 White Gold .1500 oz. AGW **Ruler:** Elizabeth II **Obv:** Crowned bust right **Obv. Designer:** Raphael Maklouf **Rev:** Crowned arms flanked by falcons

Date	Mintage	F	VF	XF	Unc	BU
1999 Proof	Est. 5,000			Value: 135		

KM# 947 1/2 PLATINA
15.5517 g., 0.7500 White Gold .3750 oz. AGW **Ruler:** Elizabeth II **Obv:** Crowned bust right **Obv. Designer:** Raphael Maklouf **Rev:** Crowned arms

Date	Mintage	F	VF	XF	Unc	BU
1999 Proof	Est. 3,500			Value: 275		

GOLD AND PLATINUM BIMETALLIC SERIES

KM# 1065 1/4 ANGEL
Ring Weight: 3.8880 g. **Ring Composition:** 0.9995 Platinum .1244 oz. APW **Center Weight:** 3.8880 g. **Center Composition:** 0.9999 Gold .1249 oz. AGW , 22 mm. **Ruler:** Elizabeth II **Obv:** Crowned bust right **Obv. Designer:** Raphael Maklouf **Rev:** Archangel Michael slaying dragon **Edge:** Reeded

Date	Mintage	F	VF	XF	Unc	BU
1995 Proof	—			Value: 265		

KM# 1066 1/4 NOBLE
Bi-Metallic Platinum center in Gold ring, 22 mm. **Ruler:** Elizabeth II **Obv:** Crowned bust right **Obv. Designer:** Raphael Maklouf **Rev:** Viking ship **Edge:** Reeded

Date	Mintage	F	VF	XF	Unc	BU
1995 Proof	—			Value: 265		

SOUTH AFRICA
Mint mark: GRC - Gold Reef City

KM# 105 1/10 KRUGERRAND
3.3900 g., 0.9170 Gold .1000 oz. AGW

Date	Mintage	F	VF	XF	Unc	BU
1980	857,000	—	—	—	BV+15%	—
1980 Proof	60			Value: 2,500		
1981	1,321,000	—	—	—	BV+15%	—
1981 Proof	7,500			Value: 90.00		
1982	1,065,000	—	—	—	BV+15%	—
1982 Proof	11,000			Value: 85.00		
1983	508,000	—	—	—	BV+15%	—
1983 Proof	12,000			Value: 85.00		
1984	898,000	—	—	—	BV+15%	—
1984 Proof	13,000			Value: 85.00		
1985	282,000	—	—	—	BV+15%	—
1985 Proof	6,700			Value: 85.00		
1986	87,000	—	—	—	BV+15%	—
1986 Proof	8,001			Value: 85.00		
1987	53,000	—	—	—	BV+15%	—
1987 Proof	6,065			Value: 85.00		
1987 GRC Proof	1,126			Value: 400		
1988	87,000	—	—	—	BV+15%	—
1988 Proof	2,056			Value: 90.00		
1988 GRC Proof	949			Value: 400		
1989	—	—	—	—	BV+15%	—
1989 Proof	3,316			Value: 90.00		
1989 GRC Proof	377			Value: 1,000		
1990	—	—	—	—	BV+15%	—
1990 Proof	3,459			Value: 90.00		
1990 GRC Proof	1,096			Value: 275		
1991 Proof	3,524			Value: 90.00		
1991 GRC Proof	426			Value: 275		
1992 Proof	1,789			Value: 90.00		
1993	54,000	—	—	—	BV+15%	—
1993 Proof	3,811			Value: 90.00		
1994	86,000	—	—	—	BV+15%	—
1994 Proof	—			Value: 90.00		
1995	25,000	—	—	—	BV+15%	—
1995 Proof	750			Value: 120		
1996 Proof	4,000			Value: 90.00		
1997 Proof	3,410			Value: 90.00		
1997 Proof	30			Value: 300		
Note: 30th Anniversary of Krugerrand privy mark						
1998 Proof	—			Value: 90.00		
1999 Proof	—			Value: 90.00		

KM# 106 1/4 KRUGERRAND

8.4800 g., 0.9170 Gold .2500 oz. AGW **Obv:** Bust left **Rev:**
Springbok divides date **Rev. Designer:** Coert L. Steynberg

Date	Mintage	F	VF	XF	Unc	BU
1980	534,000	—	—	—	BV+10%	—
1980 Proof	60			Value: 3,000		
1981	726,000	—	—	—	BV+10%	—
1981 Proof	7,500			Value: 195		
1982	1,269,000	—	—	—	BV+10%	—
1982 Proof	11,000			Value: 195		
1983	64,000	—	—	—	BV+10%	—
1983 Proof	12,000			Value: 195		
1984	503,000	—	—	—	BV+10%	—
1984 Proof	13,000			Value: 195		
1985	594,000	—	—	—	BV+10%	—
1985 Proof	6,700			Value: 195		
1986 Proof	8,001			Value: 195		
1987 Proof	6,050			Value: 195		
1987 GRC Proof	1,121			Value: 500		
1988	5,946	—	—	—	BV+10%	—
1988 Proof	2,056			Value: 200		
1988 GRC Proof	835			Value: 500		
1989	5,943	—	—	—	BV+10%	—
1989 Proof	3,316			Value: 200		
1989 GRC Proof	318			Value: 1,400		
1990 Proof	2,750			Value: 200		
1990 GRC Proof	1,066			Value: 400		
1991 Proof	1,626			Value: 200		
1991 GRC Proof	426			Value: 400		
1992 Proof	1,629			Value: 200		
1993 Proof	3,061			Value: 200		
1994	39,000	—	—	—	BV+10%	—
1994 Proof	1,874			Value: 200		
1995	13,000	—	—	—	BV+10%	—
1995 Proof	1,095			Value: 215		
1996 Proof	1,853			Value: 200		
1997 Proof	1,440			Value: 200		
1997 Proof	30			Value: 450		
Note: 30th Anniversary of Krugerrand privy mark						
1998 Proof	—			Value: 200		
1999 Proof	—			Value: 200		

KM# 107 1/2 KRUGERRAND
16.9700 g., 0.9170 Gold .5000 oz. AGW **Obv:** Bust left **Rev:** Springbok divides date **Rev. Designer:** Coert L. Steynberg

Date	Mintage	F	VF	XF	Unc	BU
1980	374,000	—	—	—	BV+8%	—
1980 Proof	60			Value: 3,500		
1981	178,000	—	—	—	BV+8%	—
1981 Proof	9,000			Value: 375		
1982	429,000	—	—	—	BV+8%	—
1982 Proof	13,000			Value: 375		
1983	60,000	—	—	—	BV+8%	—
1983 Proof	14,000			Value: 375		
1984	187,000	—	—	—	BV+8%	—
1984 Proof	9,900			Value: 375		
1985	104,000	—	—	—	BV+8%	—
1985 Proof	5,945			Value: 375		
1986 Proof	8,002			Value: 375		
1987 Proof	5,389			Value: 375		
1987 GRC Proof	1,186			Value: 800		
1988	5,454	—	—	—	BV+8%	—
1988 Proof	2,282			Value: 400		
1988 GRC Proof	1,026			Value: 800		
1989	4,980	—	—	—	BV+8%	—
1989 Proof	3,727			Value: 400		
1989 GRC Proof	399			Value: 1,500		
1990 Proof	2,850			Value: 400		
1990 GRC Proof	1,066			Value: 500		
1991 Proof	3,459			Value: 400		
1991 GRC Proof	426			Value: 500		
1992 Proof	1,501			Value: 400		
1993	11,000	—	—	—	BV+8%	—
1993 Proof	2,439			Value: 400		
1994	16,000	—	—	—	BV+8%	—
1994 Proof	2,146			Value: 400		
1995	10,000	—	—	—	BV+8%	—
1995 Proof	1,012			Value: 400		
1996 Proof	1,788			Value: 400		
1997 Proof	2,000			Value: 400		
1997 Proof	30			Value: 550		
Note: 30th Anniversary of Krugerrand privy mark						
1998 Proof	—			Value: 375		
1999 Proof	—			Value: 400		

KM# 73 KRUGERRAND
33.9305 g., 0.9170 Gold 1.0000 oz. AGW   **Obv:** Bust left **Rev:**
Springbok divides date **Rev. Designer:** Coert L. Steynberg

Date	Mintage	F	VF	XF	Unc	BU
1967	40,000	—	—	—	BV+5%	—
1967 Proof	10,000			Value: 725		
1968	20,000	—	—	—	BV+5%	—
1968 Proof	5,000			Value: 1,000		
Note: Frosted bust and frosted reverse						
1968 Proof	8,956			Value: 745		
1969	20,000	—	—	—	BV+5%	—
1969 Proof	10,000			Value: 725		
1970	211,000	—	—	—	BV+5%	—
1970 Proof	10,000			Value: 720		
1971	550,000	—	—	—	BV+5%	—
1971 Proof	6,000			Value: 720		
1972	544,000	—	—	—	BV+5%	—
1972 Proof	6,625			Value: 720		
1973	859,000	—	—	—	BV+5%	—
1973 Proof	10,000			Value: 720		
1974	3,204,000	—	—	—	BV+5%	—
1974 Proof	6,352			Value: 720		
1975	4,804,000	—	—	—	BV+5%	—
1975 Proof	5,600			Value: 720		
1976	3,005,000	—	—	—	BV+5%	—
1976 Proof	6,600			Value: 720		
1977	3,331,000	—	—	—	BV+5%	—
Note: 188 serrations on edge						
1977 Proof	8,500			Value: 720		
Note: 188 serrations on edge						
1977	Inc. above	—	—	—	BV+5%	—
Note: 220 serrations on edge						
1977 Proof	Inc. above			Value: 720		
Note: 220 serrations on edge						
1978	6,012,000	—	—	—	BV+5%	—
1978 Proof	10,000			Value: 720		
1979	4,941,000	—	—	—	BV+5%	—
1979 Proof	12,000			Value: 720		
1980	3,143,000	—	—	—	BV+5%	—
1980 Proof	12,000			Value: 720		
1981	3,560,000	—	—	—	BV+5%	—
1981 Proof	13,000			Value: 720		
1982	2,566,000	—	—	—	BV+5%	—

Date	Mintage	F	VF	XF	Unc	BU
1982 Proof	17,000			Value: 720		
1983	3,368,000	—	—	—	BV+5%	—
1983 Proof	19,000			Value: 720		
1984	2,070,000	—	—	—	BV+5%	—
1984 Proof	14,000			Value: 720		
1985	875,000	—	—	—	BV+5%	—
1985 Proof	10,000			Value: 720		
1986 Proof	20,000			Value: 720		
1987	11,000	—	—	—	BV+5%	—
1987 Proof	11,000			Value: 720		
1987 GRC Proof	1,160			Value: 1,200		
1988	615,000	—	—	—	BV+5%	—
1988 Proof	4,268			Value: 725		
1988 GRC Proof	1,220			Value: 1,200		
1989	194,000	—	—	—	BV+5%	—
1989 Proof	5,070			Value: 725		
1989 GRC Proof	987			Value: 1,600		
1990	391,000	—	—	—	BV+5%	—
1990 Proof	3,032			Value: 725		
1990 GRC Proof	1,066			Value: 1,600		
1991	283,000	—	—	—	BV+5%	—
1991 Proof	2,181			Value: 725		
1991 GRC Proof	426			Value: 1,600		
1992	1,803	—	—	—	BV+5%	—
1992 Proof	2,067			Value: 725		
1993	162,000	—	—	—	BV+5%	—
1993 Proof	3,963			Value: 725		
1994	130,000	—	—	—	BV+5%	—
1994 Proof	1,761			Value: 725		
1995	59,000	—	—	—	BV+5%	—
1995 Proof	1,678			Value: 725		
1996 Proof	2,188			Value: 725		
1997 Proof	1,663			Value: 725		
1997 SS Proof	72			Value: 850		
1997 Proof	30			Value: 1,250		
Note: 30th Anniversary of Krugerrand privy mark						
1998 Proof	—			Value: 725		
1999 Proof	—			Value: 725		

CHAPTER 8

THE JEFFERSON PLAN

Mint profile: Carson City

The Carson City, Nevada, branch mint was established in 1863 and was another effort to bring coin production closer to bullion sources, specifically the Comstock Lode. The Civil War delayed the mint's opening until 1870. Until it ceased coinage production in 1893, the Carson City mint struck silver dime, 20-cent, quarter, half-dollar, and dollar coins, and gold $5, $10, and $20 coins. A "CC" mint mark denotes its production.

Mint profile: West Point

This facility was built in 1937 as the West Point Bullion Depository, an adjunct of the New York Assay Office. It produced one-cent coins without a mint mark from 1973 to 1986. It was officially designated a mint in 1988. In more recent years, it has produced commemorative coins and proof American Eagle bullion coins. Its "W" mint mark first appeared on the 1986 Statue of Liberty Centennial commemorative gold $5 coin.

Gold issues were included in some of the first proposals for a national coinage in the fledgling United States of the late 18th century. Gold coins from England, France, Portugal, and Spain circulated in the country at the end of the Revolutionary War. After the war, the Articles of Confederation granted individual states the right to issue coins, and the result was a wide range of copper and silver issues that saw some circulation, too.

Today's decimal monetary system in the United States is based largely on a proposal put forth by Thomas Jefferson. His original coinage plan called for the dollar as the basic monetary unit and included several minor coins and a gold $10. A Continental Congress committee generally favored Jefferson's plan in a report dated May 13, 1785, but substituted a gold $5 coin for the gold $10. Two months later, Congress approved the plan but failed to set a standard weight for the silver dollar or to establish a mint.

A more concerted effort at establishing a national coinage and mint commenced in September 1789, when Alexander Hamilton was named to head the new Treasury Department. He proposed a gold $10, gold dollar, silver dollar, silver dime, copper cent, and copper half cent. On April 2, 1792, Congress passed an act establishing the U.S. Mint and authorized the following denominations: a gold $10, gold $5, gold $2.50, silver dollar, silver half dollar, silver quarter dollar, silver dime (or "disme"), silver half dime, copper cent, and copper half cent. Hamilton suggested naming the gold $10 an "eagle," apparently for lack of anything better to call it. The gold $5 was to be a "half eagle" and the gold $2.50 a "quarter eagle."

Coinage began in earnest in 1793 with the striking of half cents and cents at the new mint located on Seventh Street, between Market and Arch streets, in Philadelphia. Silver half dimes, half dollars, and dollars followed in 1794. Gold coinage did not begin until 1795 with the minting of the first $5 and $10 coins. Gold $2.50 coins followed in 1796. The U.S. Mint produced 8,707 half eagles and 5,583 eagles dated 1795. It produced 1,395 quarter eagles dated 1796.

To give all the new U.S. coins credibility and a value reference, their specifications emulated those of foreign coins popularly circulating in the country at the time. The coins were based on a bimetallic system, which means gold and silver equally represented the basic unit of value. In other words, five silver dollars had the same intrinsic value as a gold $5 coin. The system was based on a gold-to-silver value ratio of 15-to-1.

Mint profile: Philadelphia

The Philadelphia Mint was established with the original coinage and mint act of 1792 and continues to be regarded today as the main U.S. mint. Historically, coins struck at Philadelphia do not have mint marks, but in more recent years, modern circulating coins, commemoratives, and some silver and gold American Eagle bullion coins struck at Philadelphia have included "P" mint marks.

Mint profile: Charlotte

The Charlotte, North Carolina, branch mint was established in 1835 to strike gold coins only. The bill establishing the mint was pushed by Southern representatives in Congress who argued that it was cheaper to strike coins closer to the source of gold bullion rather than ship it to Philadelphia. In various years from 1838 to 1861, the Charlotte mint struck gold dollar, $2.50, and $5 coins. A "C" mint mark denotes its production.

Mint profile: Dahlonega

The same bill that established the Charlotte branch mint also established a branch mint at Dahlonega, Georgia. Like Charlotte, Dahlonega was authorized to strike gold coins only. In various years from 1838 to 1861, it struck gold dollar, $2.50, $3, and $5 coins. A "D" mint mark denotes its production.

Mint profile: New Orleans

The same bill that established the Charlotte and Dahlonega branch mints also established a branch mint at New Orleans. Unlike Charlotte and Dahlonega, however, New Orleans was authorized to strike gold and silver coins. In various years from 1838 to 1861 and again from 1879 to 1909, it struck silver three-cent, half-dime, dime, quarter, half-dollar, and dollar coins, and gold dollar, $2.50, $3, $5, $10, and $20 coins. An "O" mint mark denotes its production.

For the next hundred years or so, gold and silver had a troubled marriage in the U.S. monetary system. At various times, the bimetallic system led to class warfare and private profiteering under the guise of public policy. From the beginning, some officials expressed concern about the system. They feared that world market fluctuations in the prices for the two metals would cause the more valuable metal to leave the country. Indeed, that's what happened in the early 1800s. The silver dollar intrinsically became less valuable than a dollar's worth of gold. Gold coins either disappeared quickly after minting or never entered circulation.

The situation was eased somewhat when gold was discovered in South Carolina in 1824 and Georgia in 1830. Then in 1834, a new law lowered the standard weight of all gold coins and established a gold-to-silver value ratio of 16.002-to-1. Five dollars in silver coins bought a new, lighter gold $5 coin. Speculators hoarded the older, heavier gold coins and hauled them to the melting pot at a profit of 4.7 percent. Follow-up legislation in 1837 established a uniform fineness of 0.900 for gold and silver coins and tweaked the ratio again, to 15.998-to-1.

By the 1850s, the situation reversed. The discovery of gold in California made silver the more valuable metal, and silver coins became scarce in circulation. New gold $1 and $20 coins were authorized in 1849. Four years later, Congress lowered the weights of the half dime, dime, quarter, and half dollar to try to keep silver coins in circulation.

But by the mid-1870s, the situation reversed again when the Comstock Lode near Virginia City, Nevada, dumped new, large supplies of silver on the market. Combined with European demonetization of silver, the bottom fell out of the metal's price.

The Coinage Act of 1873 brought sweeping changes to the U.S. monetary and coinage systems and to the Mint's governing structure. First, the act established the main mint at Philadelphia and the various branch mints as a bureau of the Treasury Department to be headed by a director appointed by the president. Second, it authorized the minting of the following gold coins: $2.50, $3, $5, $10, and $20. Third, it effectively put the nation on the gold standard, thus ending the bimetallic standard, and discontinued the silver dollar.

Those in favor of the legislation argued that the gold dollar was already the de facto standard for the U.S. monetary system and was consistent with the gold standard of Great Britain and most other European nations. Several years later, however, despite historical evidence to the contrary, silver interests

GOLD RUSH

insisted the gold standard and elimination of the silver dollar were secretly slipped into the legislation. Their cause was bolstered when a special congressional commission in 1877 concluded that the demonetization of silver had been effected solely to benefit the creditor classes.

The anti-gold-standard crowd advocated the resumption of large-scale silver-dollar production as a cheaper, more plentiful form of money in response to the era's economic woes. Their efforts resulted in the passage of what is commonly called today the Bland-Allison Act of 1878, which required the government to purchase $2 million to $4 million of silver monthly and resume the production of silver dollars for circulation.

In 1890, the Sherman Silver Purchase Act increased the required monthly purchases of silver to $4.5 million. By 1893, the intrinsic value of a silver dollar dropped to 52 cents. Holders of Treasury notes, redeemable in either silver or gold, choose the higher-valued gold for redemption and drained the Treasury's reserves of the yellow metal. President Grover Cleveland reported that from July 1, 1890, to July 15, 1893, the Treasury's gold reserves had decreased more than $132 million while its silver reserves increased more than $147 million. Later in 1893, Congress repealed the Sherman Silver Purchase Act.

In 1900, Congress confirmed the gold standard through legislation and directed the Treasury secretary to "maintain all forms of money in parity with this standard." The United States continued to strike gold coins into the 1900s, but the economic demands of World War I and then the economic challenges of the 1930s eventually led to the demise of the gold standard and the production of gold coins for circulation. In 1933, President Franklin D. Roosevelt banned the private ownership of gold bullion, and the production of U.S. gold coinage for circulation ceased. This and other actions effectively took the United States off the gold standard. In 1971, President Richard M. Nixon announced the United States would no longer exchange paper currency for gold in international transactions among central banks, which was the final step in the country abandoning the gold standard. In 1975, the United States lifted the restrictions on private ownership of gold bullion.

Since 1986, the United States has produced non-circulating, legal-tender commemorative gold coins in the traditional denominations of $5 and $10. It has also produced American Eagle bullion coins, which have legal-tender face values but are designed as a convenient way for private citizens to own gold bullion.

Mint profile: San Francisco

The San Francisco branch mint was authorized in 1852 to again bring coin production closer to bullion sources. Coinage commenced in 1854 but stopped in 1955. It resumed again in 1968, largely to produce proof coins for collector sets, and continues today. Over the years, San Francisco has produced a wide range of base-metal, silver, and gold coins, including gold dollar, $2.50, $3, $5, $10, and $20 coins. An "S" mint mark denotes its production.

Mint profile: Denver

An 1862 congressional act established a U.S. assay office in Denver, but full-fledged branch-mint status came later. Coin production began in 1906. Denver continues to produce all denominations of currently circulating coins. In various years in the early 1900s, it produced gold $2.50, $5, $10, and $20 coins. A "D" mint mark denotes its production and is not to be confused with the Dahlonega "D" mint mark of an earlier era.

CHAPTER 9

THE JOY OF COLLECTING U.S. GOLD COINS

GOLD RUSH

P re-1933 U.S. gold coins are popular with collectors and investors throughout the world. Many were saved by individuals or stored by banks. Some circulated, as originally intended, but many survive in uncirculated, or mint, condition.

The U.S. gold $20, or double eagle, enjoys steady demand from collectors and investors. As a bullion coin, the double eagle contains nearly one troy ounce of gold, which makes it easy to price in relation to its intrinsic value. Portability and liquidity also contribute to the coin's popularity. Double eagles are widely bought and sold and readily available through any dealer who stocks gold coins.

Gold bullion coins can be purchased in any quantity, from a single piece to hundreds or more at a time. The price for larger bullion trades is typically based on the London p.m. fix and is normally locked in before the fix comes in at about 10:30 a.m. Eastern time. Payment on bullion purchases is normally due immediately.

U.S. gold $5 and $10 coins are also popular with collectors and investors, and are widely available. The smaller U.S. gold denominations – dollar, $2.50, and $3 – are of greater interest to collectors than bullion investors. These coins sell for significantly higher premiums than the larger denominations.

Some pre-1933 U.S. gold $5, $10, and $20 coins may trade for a slightly higher premium over their bullion value in better grades or more scarce dates. These are commonly referred to as "seminumismatic" coins because they have some collector value, thus the higher premium, but their base value is still tied to their bullion value.

Following are some popular strategies for collecting gold coins.

COLLECTING BY SERIES

Gold coins present some challenges to the traditional pursuit of acquiring one of each date and mint mark within a series. For example, many coins within the Coronet Head gold $2.50 and $5 series are affordable for most collectors, even in uncirculated grades. But both of these series had long runs – the $2.50 from 1840 to 1907 and the $5 from 1839 to 1908. Add in varieties, multiple mint marks for a majority of dates, and premium prices for key dates, and the goal of a complete collection of either series is commendable but daunting for most collectors.

Series containing the first U.S. gold coins are shorter, but these late 18th-century pieces are rare and command prices that reflect that rarity. The Indian Head Type 2 gold dollar is another short series – just six date and mint-mark combinations – but two of those are key dates with prices topping five figures. The same is true of many other early 19th-century gold-coin series.

There are, however, some relatively affordable possibilities for gold-coin series collecting. The best may be the Indian Head $2.50, struck from 1908 to 1929. The series features only 15 date and mint-mark combinations, most of which are affordable to many collectors in grades as high as MS-60. Bela Lyon Pratt's design for this coin is a classic and artistically pleasing. The incised design features, however, present some grading nuances that should be studied through grading guides and examining coins at shows and shops.

The series also contains one key date – the 1911-D, with a mintage of only 55,680. The next lowest mintage in the series is 240,117 for the 1914. Still, the 1911-D is an achievable challenge for many collectors. Some saving and prudent management of a collecting budget can result in the acquisition of a 1911-D at the right time and the right price. The resulting complete collection of Indian Head gold $2.50 coins can be rewarding and satisfying to the viewer.

The Indian Head gold $5 – Pratt's counterpart to his $2.50 design – is more challenging to the series collector but still achievable with proper planning and management of a collecting budget. The series contains 24 date and mint-mark combinations from 1908 to 1916 and 1929. Most sell for under $500 in the high circulated grade of AU-50.

Two key dates provide the challenge. Only 34,200 of the 1909-O were struck. A total of 662,000 of the 1929 were struck, but the mintage occurred just a few short years before the discontinuation of U.S. gold coinage and the withdrawal of gold coins from circulation. It is believed many were melted; thus, surviving examples are scarce.

The Saint-Gaudens gold $10 and $20 series include some of the great rarities in numismatics. The series collector, however, will also find some obtainable if ambitious opportunities in both types.

A collection of Saint-Gaudens gold $10 coins could start with the most common variety of the 1907 issue – without periods between the words in "E Pluribus Unum" on the reverse – and continue to the 1932 issue. Most of the date and mint-mark combinations could be purchased for about $500 each in grade AU-50. A few of the scarce dates are a bit more but still relatively affordable. A step up in grade to MS-60 – the lowest uncirculated grade – is also within reach of many collectors.

GOLD RUSH

Three key dates will be encountered along the way – the 1915-S, 1920-S, and 1930-S. But again, prudent planning and management of a collecting budget could bring those dates within reach, particularly the 1915-S.

The 1933 Saint-Gaudens gold $10 commands six figures even in common circulated grades, but there would be no shame in a collection that stopped short of this rarity.

The Saint-Gaudens gold $20 series includes more date and mint-mark combinations than the Saint-Gaudens $10 series. It also includes a number of issues that are out of reach for most collectors. Many other issues in the series, however, are relatively affordable. A collector could pursue as many issues in the series that are within his or her reach now and may be able to fill in one or more of the scarce or even rare issues in the future.

COLLECTING BY TYPE

Because of the challenges in collecting gold coins by series, many turn to collecting gold coins by type. Collecting by type provides opportunities for almost any budget. Each of the headings under each denomination in the following pricing section represents a "type." For example, under gold $2.50 coins, there are the Liberty Cap type, three Turban Head types, Classic Head type, Coronet Head type, and Indian Head type. A type collection of gold $2.50 coins would include an example of each type listed. The type collector can chose an example that fits his or her budget from any of the date and mint-mark combinations under that type.

Following are some more ways to organize a type collection. Also available are quality holders that can provide a road map for various type collections and an attractive medium for viewing a collection.

One of everything. The ultimate U.S. gold type collection would be one example of each type produced, from the first circulating gold issues of the late 18th and early 19th century to the last of the early 20th century. Commemorative coins could be added to the set, too. Although this is an ambitious goal, it is achievable for many collectors over time.

A collector could work on one aspect of the collection at a time. For example, the acquisition of just three coins completes a type set of gold dollars. The completion of smaller sets such as this leads to the ultimate goal of one of everything.

By denomination. A collector could pursue an example of each type within a certain denomination. As noted above, a type set of gold dollars consists of just three coins. A type set of gold

$2.50 coins would consist of one of each type listed above. Gold $3 coins are pricey, but only one is required to complete a type set of that denomination.

A denomination type set of $2.50, $5, or $10 coins requires a collector to contend with some scarce early issues. Alternatives to this include concentrating first on the later issues or selecting denominations introduced later, such as the dollar and $20.

By century or year. Many type collectors focus on a particular time frame. For example, among gold collectors, a 20th-century type set is a popular focus. A 20th-century gold type set consists of one example of each type of circulating gold coin dated 1901 or later. The set consists of a (1) Coronet Head $2.50, (2) Indian Head $2.50, (3) Coronet Head $5, (4) Indian Head $5, (5) Coronet Head $10, (6) Saint-Gaudens $10, (7) Liberty $20, and (8) Saint-Gaudens $20.

The set is short yet complete and significant. It is also affordable to many collectors because they can choose examples of each type that best fit their budgets. Also, most dates from the 1900s are readily available and priced accordingly.

Completion of a 20th-century type set can prompt a collector to venture back further in time and start acquiring type coins from the 19th century.

A collector may also focus on a particular year or range of years that interests him or her. A historical event that interests the collector may have occurred in the year or years, or the era may have personal interest to the collector, such as the birth year of an ancestor.

By design. Many collectors like a particular design theme or the work of a particular designer and focus a collection on that interest. For example, some collectors focus on coins depicting Liberty or an Indian motif. Either theme could be combined with non-gold coins of the same theme for an attractive set with a strong Americana feel.

Coronet Head gold type set.

Some collectors focus on coins designed by Christian Gobrecht or James B. Longacre or one of the other legendary names from the U.S. Mint design staff. A type set of Augustus Saint-Gaudens circulating gold coins would consist of just two pieces – the $10 and $20. But those two pieces contain what many regard as the two most beautiful designs in U.S. coinage history.

By mint. The various U.S. branch mints are rich in history. Collectors interested in Western history may focus a type set on coins produced at the San Francisco or Carson City mints. An interest in Southern history may lead to a collection of coins produced by the Charlotte, Dahlonega, and New Orleans mints. Gold coins from these mints could again be combined with non-gold coins of the same theme for an attractive set or even with other types of Western or Southern collectibles.

By collector's choice. Collectors can combine various elements from the type-collecting strategies outlined above – a type set of 20th-century gold coins produced at San Francisco and Carson City, for example. Or, they can invent their own parameters that play to their historical and numismatic interests.

COLLECTING COMMEMORATIVES

As shown in the pricing section, commemoratives fall into two categories: (1) those issued from 1892 through 1954 and (2) those issued from 1982 to the present. In the first category, commemorative gold coins were issued in 1903-1905, 1915-1917, 1922, and 1926. Among the newer issues, commemorative gold coins have been issued in various years since 1984.

The older commemorative gold coins consist of seven dollar coins, two $2.50 coins, and two types of $50 coins. Any of these could be considered part of one of the type sets outlined above or as a type or series set by themselves. Most of the dollars and $2.50 coins are relatively affordable.

The two gold $50 types were issued in 1915 to commemorate the Panama-Pacific Exposition. One is round; the other is octagonal. Both types are scarce and command five-figure prices.

The modern gold commemoratives have been issued in $5 and $10 denominations, and can fall under any of the series or type collecting themes outlined previously. One or more individual coins could be acquired simply because the collector likes the design, the coin's subject, or wants to support the cause benefiting from the coin's initial sales. Upon issue, commemoratives can be purchased directly from the U.S. Mint with a portion of the sales proceeds benefiting a project related to the coin's theme.

Past and current modern gold commemoratives can also be purchased from coin dealers. Oftentimes prices for these coins on the secondary market drop from their original U.S. Mint issue price a year or more after their release.

AMERICAN EAGLE GOLD BULLION COINS

Although issued as a convenient way for private citizens to own gold bullion, some American Eagle coins also have collectible value. Uncirculated and proof examples are available either directly from the U.S. Mint for current issues or on the secondary market for past issues. Prices for most are tied to their bullion value and the current price of gold, but a few with lower mintages command premiums on the secondary market.

The U.S. Mint does not sell bulk quantities of business-strike American Eagle bullion coins directly to the public. Instead, they are sold to a small number of distributors worldwide at a small premium over the gold price. This premium covers the cost of production and distribution, along with a profit for the Mint. The distributors then sell the coins to dealers, who, in turn, retail them to collectors and investors. The dealer markup varies but typically ranges from 5 percent to 10 percent over the spot gold price.

Some states define gold bullion as coins selling at a premium of 15 percent or less over the coins' bullion value. Some states tax the sale of gold coins, and others do not.

CHAPTER 10

COLLECTING U.S. GOLD COINS

GOLD RUSH

U.S. GOLD $1
LIBERTY HEAD – TYPE 1

Designer: James B. Longacre.
Diameter: 13 millimeters.
Fineness: 0.9000.
Total weight: 1.672 grams.
Actual gold weight: 0.0484 ounces.
Mint marks: C – Charlotte. D – Dahlonega. O – New Orleans. S – San Francisco. None – Philadelphia.
Varieties: On the "closed wreath" variety of 1849, the wreath on the reverse extends closer to the numeral 1 in "1 Dollar."

KM# 73

Overview: A gold dollar coin was included in legislation proposed in 1836 but was opposed by U.S. Mint Director Robert Patterson and was dropped from the final bill. Patterson thought the coin's physical size was too small and had patterns struck apparently to illustrate his point. A gold dollar coin was proposed again in 1844. Patterson again had patterns produced, from the same dies used for the 1836 patterns, and again opposed the coin. He said small gold coins in general were not popular. A congressional committee failed to approve the 1844 proposal. A bill authorizing a gold dollar coin reappeared in early 1849 after gold was discovered in California in late 1848. Authorization of a gold $20 coin was added to the bill later. Patterson and others continued to object to a gold dollar coin because of its small size, but the legislation still passed on March 3, 1849.

Date	Mintage	F-12	VF-20	XF-40	AU-50	MS-60
1849 open wreath	688,567	110	140	200	235	425
1849 closed wreath	Inc. above	110	135	190	220	365
1849C closed wreath	11,634	800	950	1,250	1,900	8,000
1849C open wreath	Inc. above	—	—	—	—	—
1849D open wreath	21,588	950	1,300	1,800	2,350	7,000
1849O open wreath	215,000	125	175	240	325	1,000
1850	481,953	110	145	200	215	360
1850C	6,966	900	1,150	1,600	2,300	9,000
1850D	8,382	975	1,250	1,650	2,800	10,000
1850O	14,000	185	275	375	850	3,600
1851	3,317,671	110	145	190	215	315
1851C	41,267	840	1,150	1,500	1,950	4,900
1851D	9,882	950	1,200	1,600	2,500	5,650
1851O	290,000	135	175	225	265	750

Date	Mintage	F-12	VF-20	XF-40	AU-50	MS-60
1852	2,045,351	110	145	200	215	330
1852C	9,434	800	1,150	1,400	1,700	5,100
1852D	6,360	950	1,250	1,600	2,300	10,000
1852O	140,000	125	165	230	385	1,500
1853	4,076,051	110	135	190	200	245
1853C	11,515	900	1,100	1,400	1,750	6,200
1853D	6,583	975	1,150	1,600	2,400	9,700
1853O	290,000	135	160	235	270	665
1854	736,709	110	145	200	230	335
1854D	2,935	990	1,400	2,350	6,000	13,000
1854S	14,632	245	360	525	840	2,450

KM# 83

INDIAN HEAD – TYPE 2

Designer: James B. Longacre.
Diameter: 15 millimeters.
Fineness: 0.9000.
Total weight: 1.672 grams.
Actual gold weight: 0.0484 ounces.
Mint marks: C – Charlotte. D – Dahlonega. O – New Orleans. S
– San Francisco. None – Philadelphia.
Overview: The gold dollar's diameter was stretched 2
millimeters in 1854, but the total weight and gold content
remained the same. Design modifications added an Indian
headdress to the image of Liberty on the obverse and moved
the legend "United States of America" from the reverse to
the obverse. The moving of the legend allowed for a more
elaborate wreath to encircle the denomination on the reverse.

Date	Mintage	F-12	VF-20	XF-40	AU-50	MS-60
1854	902,736	210	315	440	650	3,600
1855	758,269	210	315	440	650	3,600
1855C	9,803	975	1,450	3,500	11,000	33,000
1855D	1,811	3,000	4,750	9,800	22,000	48,000
1855O	55,000	345	475	700	1,400	7,800
1856S	24,600	575	900	1,400	2,300	8,500

INDIAN HEAD – TYPE 3

Designer: James B. Longacre.
Diameter: 15 millimeters.
Fineness: 0.9000.
Total weight: 1.672 grams.
Actual gold weight: 0.0484 ounces.
Mint marks: C – Charlotte. D – Dahlonega. S – San Francisco.
None – Philadelphia.

Varieties: The 1856 varieties are distinguished by whether the 5 in the date is slanted or upright. The 1873 varieties are distinguished by the amount of space between the upper left and lower left serifs in the 3.

Overview: Design modifications in 1856 reworked the image of Liberty on the obverse but retained an Indian headdress. Legislation passed September 26, 1890, discontinued the gold dollar.

KM# 86

Date	Mintage	F-12	VF-20	XF-40	AU-50	MS-60	Prf-65
1856 upright 5	1,762,936	135	170	210	275	575	—
1856 slanted 5	Inc. above	140	160	195	250	400	50,000
1856D	1,460	2,950	3,800	5,800	8,000	32,000	—
1857	774,789	130	166	200	215	290	31,000
1857C	13,280	900	1,150	1,750	3,750	14,000	—
1857D	3,533	1,000	1,300	2,300	4,400	11,000	—
1857S	10,000	250	500	615	1,300	5,800	—
1858	117,995	135	160	200	220	325	27,500
1858D	3,477	925	1,250	1,600	2,750	10,000	—
1858S	10,000	300	400	575	1,300	5,500	—
1859	168,244	145	170	200	215	260	17,000
1859C	5,235	885	1,050	1,700	4,000	15,000	—
1859D	4,952	1,000	1,400	1,800	3,100	11,000	—
1859S	15,000	185	225	480	1,050	5,000	—
1860	36,668	135	170	190	240	400	14,500
1860D	1,566	2,000	2,800	3,800	7,000	23,000	—
1860S	13,000	280	380	480	750	2,300	—
1861	527,499	140	155	190	215	325	14,000
1861D mintage unrecorded	—	4,600	7,000	10,000	18,000	47,500	—
1862	1,361,390	130	150	200	240	325	15,000
1863	6,250	370	500	925	2,100	3,750	18,000
1864	5,950	270	350	440	750	950	18,000
1865	3,725	270	350	570	750	1,600	18,000
1866	7,130	275	360	470	670	950	18,000
1867	5,250	300	400	515	675	1,100	17,500
1868	10,525	265	290	415	490	950	19,000
1869	5,925	315	335	530	800	1,300	17,000
1870	6,335	245	285	400	480	850	16,000
1870S	3,000	290	475	750	1,150	2,300	—
1871	3,930	250	285	380	470	750	18,000
1872	3,530	245	275	400	480	975	18,000

Date	Mintage	F-12	VF-20	XF-40	AU-50	MS-60	Prf-65
1873 closed 3	125,125	300	425	800	950	1,600	—
1873 open 3	Inc. above	130	160	200	250	325	—
1874	198,820	130	160	200	245	340	18,000
1875	420	1,600	2,350	3,850	4,700	340	32,500
1876	3,245	220	275	345	475	650	16,750
1877	3,920	145	190	345	450	800	18,000
1878	3,020	180	250	350	465	675	15,500
1879	3,030	170	225	325	350	525	14,000
1880	1,636	150	180	200	240	440	14,000
1881	7,707	150	175	200	250	550	11,500
1882	5,125	160	180	200	265	600	9,500
1883	11,007	150	175	200	275	600	9,400
1884	6,236	140	155	200	260	550	9,400
1885	12,261	140	165	215	265	585	9,400
1886	6,016	150	175	215	285	550	9,400
1887	8,543	145	170	200	260	550	9,400
1888	16,580	145	170	200	250	550	9,400
1889	30,729	150	180	200	240	400	9,000

U.S. GOLD $2.50

LIBERTY CAP

Designer: Robert Scot.
Diameter: 20 millimeters.
Fineness: 0.9160.
Total weight: 4.37 grams.
Actual gold weight: 0.1289 ounces.
Mint marks: None – Philadelphia.
Varieties: The 1796 "no stars" variety does not have stars on the obverse. The 1804 varieties are distinguished by the number of stars on the obverse.
Overview: Authorization for a gold $2.50 coin, or quarter eagle, was part of the original U.S. Mint act, passed April 2, 1792. Early proposals by Alexander Hamilton, Thomas Jefferson, and others had included only $5 or $10 coins, or both, but Congress added the $2.50 coin.

KM# 27

Date	Mintage	F-12	VF-20	XF-40	MS-60
1796 no stars	963	30,000	42,000	70,000	165,000
1796 stars	432	28,000	40,000	63,000	140,000
1797	427	17,000	23,000	27,500	120,000
1798	1,094	4,750	10,000	12,500	55,000
1802/1	3,035	4,400	8,000	9,500	32,000

GOLD RUSH

Date	Mintage	F-12	VF-20	XF-40	MS-60
1804 13-star reverse	3,327	23,500	36,500	72,000	200,000
1804 14-star reverse	Inc. above	4,800	7,400	9,000	27,500
1805	1,781	6,000	7,500	9,000	21,000
1806/4	1,616	5,750	8,000	9,500	23,000
1806/5	Inc. above	6,000	8,000	18,000	77,000
1807	6,812	5,500	7,000	9.00	21,000

TURBAN HEAD

Designer: John Reich.

Diameter: 20 millimeters.

Fineness: 0.9160.

Total weight: 4.37 grams.

Actual gold weight: 0.1289 ounces.

Mint marks: None – Philadelphia.

Overview: A redesign turned Liberty around – from right facing to left facing – on the obverse and adorned her in a turban. On the reverse, a more natural-looking eagle and the denomination, "2 1/2 D.", was added. The design, however, was short-lived as the U.S. Mint turned its attention to striking low-denomination silver coins rather than gold coins, which were largely exported at a profit.

KM# 40

Date	Mintage	F-12	VF-20	XF-40	MS-60
1808	2,710	22,500	31,000	45,000	125,000

TURBAN HEAD

Designer: John Reich.

Diameter: 18.5 millimeters.

Fineness: 0.9160.

Total weight: 4.37 grams.

Actual gold weight: 0.1289 ounces.

Mint marks: None – Philadelphia.

Overview: Gold $2.50 coinage resumed for one year in 1821 and then again in 1824 after gold was discovered in South Carolina that year. The diameter was reduced slightly, but the gold content remained the same. The obverse design was modified, although the basic design concept of a turban-head Liberty was retained. The same reverse design from 1808 was used with minor modification.

KM# 46

Date	Mintage	F-12	VF-20	XF-40	MS-60
1821	6,448	5,500	6,250	7,500	23,000
1824/21	2,600	5,500	6,250	7,250	22,000
1825	4,434	5,500	6,500	7,800	21,000
1826/25	760	6,000	7,000	8,500	36,000
1827	2,800	5,500	7,500	9,000	22,500

KM# 49

TURBAN HEAD

Designer: John Reich.
Diameter: 18.2 millimeters.
Fineness: 0.9160.
Total weight: 4.37 grams.
Actual gold weight: 0.1289 ounces.
Mint marks: None – Philadelphia.
Overview: The diameter was reduced slightly again in 1829, and the obverse again saw some modification of the basic turban-head concept.

Date	Mintage	F-12	VF-20	XF-40	MS-60
1829	3,403	4,900	5,850	6,700	12,500
1830	4,540	4,950	5,850	6,700	12,500
1831	4,520	4,950	5,850	6,700	12,500
1832	4,400	4,950	5,850	6,700	12,500
1833	4,160	4,950	5,850	6,800	12,750
1834	4,000	8,800	12,000	16,000	36,000

KM# 56

CLASSIC HEAD

Designer: William Kneass.
Diameter: 18.2 millimeters.
Fineness: 0.8990.
Total weight: 4.18 grams.
Actual gold weight: 0.1209 ounces.
Mint marks: C – Charlotte. D – Dahlonega. O – New Orleans. None – Philadelphia.
Overview: Coinage reform legislation passed in 1834 increased the gold-to-silver value ratio in the U.S. bimetallic monetary system from 15-to-1 to 16.002-to-1. Thus, the fineness and gold content of the $2.50 decreased. A new rendering of Liberty appeared on the obverse; minor design modifications appeared on the reverse.

Date	Mintage	VF-20	XF-40	AU-50	MS-60	MS-65
1834	112,234	475	675	965	3,300	27,000
1835	131,402	475	675	950	3,200	32,000
1836	547,986	475	675	940	3,100	29,000
1837	45,080	500	800	1,500	4,000	35,000
1838	47,030	500	625	1,100	3,200	30,000
1838C	7,880	1,700	3,000	8,000	27,000	55,000
1839	27,021	500	900	1,900	5,500	—
1839C	18,140	1,500	2,650	4,500	26,500	—
1839D	13,674	1,750	3,450	8,000	24,000	—
1839O	17,781	700	1,100	2,500	7,250	—

GOLD RUSH

CORONET HEAD

Designer: Christian Gobrecht.

Diameter: 18 millimeters.

Fineness: 0.9000.

Total weight: 4.18 grams.

Actual gold weight: 0.121 ounces.

Mint marks: C – Charlotte. D – Dahlonega. O – New Orleans. S – San Francisco. None – Philadelphia.

Varieties: Varieties for 1843 are distinguished by the size of the numerals in the date. One 1848 variety has "Cal." Inscribed on the reverse, indicating it was made from California gold. The 1873 "closed-3" and "open-3" varieties are distinguished by the amount of space between the upper-left and lower-left serifs in the 3 in the date.

Overview: Legislation passed in 1837 set the fineness of all U.S. gold and silver coins at 0.9000 and revised the gold-to-silver value ratio to 15.998-to-1. Thus, the size and actual gold weight of the $2.50 coin changed slightly in 1840. A new image of Liberty appeared on the obverse. With some modification, the basic reverse design used since 1808 was retained.

KM# 72

Date	Mintage	F-12	VF-20	XF-40	AU-50	MS-60	Prf-65
1840	18,859	160	190	900	2,950	6,000	—
1840C	12,822	975	1,400	1,600	6,000	13,000	—
1840D	3,532	2,000	3,200	8,700	15,500	35,000	—
1840O	33,580	250	400	825	2,100	11,000	—
1841	—	—	48,000	85,000	96,000	—	—
1841C	10,281	750	1,500	2,000	3,500	18,500	—
1841D	4,164	950	2,100	4,750	11,000	25,000	—
1842	2,823	500	900	2,600	6,500	20,000	140,000
1842C	6,729	700	1,700	3,500	8,000	27,000	—
1842D	4,643	900	2,100	4,000	11,750	38,000	—
1842O	19,800	240	370	1,200	2,500	14,000	—
1843	100,546	160	180	450	915	3,000	140,000
1843C small date	26,064	1,500	2,400	5,500	9,000	29,000	—
1843C large date	Inc. above	800	1,600	2,200	3,500	8,800	—
1843D small date	36,209	920	1,800	2,350	3,250	10,500	—
1843O small date	288,002	165	190	250	350	1,700	—

Date	Mintage	F-12	VF-20	XF-40	AU-50	MS-60	Prf-65
1843O large date	76,000	210	260	465	1,600	8,000	—
1844	6,784	225	365	850	2,000	7,500	140,000
1844C	11,622	700	1,600	2,600	7,000	20,000	—
1844D	17,332	785	1,650	2,200	3,200	7,800	—
1845	91,051	190	250	350	600	1,275	140,000
1845D	19,460	950	1,900	2,600	3,900	15,000	—
1845O	4,000	550	1,050	2,300	9,000	20,000	—
1846	21,598	200	275	500	950	6,000	140,000
1846C	4,808	725	1,575	3,500	9,250	18,750	—
1846D	19,303	800	1,400	2,000	3,000	12,000	—
1846O	66,000	170	280	400	1,150	6,500	—
1847	29,814	140	220	360	825	3,800	—
1847C	23,226	900	1,800	2,300	3,500	7,250	—
1847D	15,784	800	1,650	2,250	3,250	10,500	—
1847O	124,000	160	240	400	1,000	4,000	—
1848	7,497	315	500	850	2,400	7,000	125,000
1848 "Cal."	1,389	8,000	15,000	26,000	36,000	50,000	—
1848C	16,788	800	1,600	2,100	3,800	14,000	—
1848D	13,771	1,000	2,000	2,500	4,500	12,000	—
1849	23,294	180	275	475	1,000	2,600	—
1849C	10,220	800	1,475	2,150	5,150	23,500	—
1849D	10,945	950	2,000	2,500	4,500	18,000	—
1850	252,923	160	180	275	350	1,100	—
1850C	9,148	800	1,500	2,100	3,400	17,500	—
1850D	12,148	950	1,800	2,500	4,000	15,000	—
1850O	84,000	170	225	450	1,200	4,900	—
1851	1,372,748	145	180	200	225	325	—
1851C	14,923	900	1,750	2,300	4,800	13,000	—
1851D	11,264	950	1,700	2,600	4,200	13,000	—
1851O	148,000	160	200	220	1,000	4,650	—
1852	1,159,681	150	175	200	250	325	—
1852C	9,772	675	1,500	2,100	4,250	18,000	—
1852D	4,078	840	1,600	2,800	7,250	17,000	—
1852O	140,000	160	190	300	950	5,000	—
1853	1,404,668	150	180	200	225	350	—
1853D	3,178	950	2,100	3,400	4,900	18,000	—
1854	596,258	150	180	215	240	350	—
1854C	7,295	800	1,500	2,400	5,000	14,750	—
1854D	1,760	1,750	2,900	6,950	12,000	27,500	—

Date	Mintage	F-12	VF-20	XF-40	AU-50	MS-60	Prf-65
1854O	153,000	150	185	240	425	1,600	—
1854S	246	32,500	70,000	115,000	215,000	300,000	—
1855	235,480	145	180	225	250	360	—
1855C	3,677	800	1,675	3,300	6,500	25,000	—
1855D	1,123	1,750	3,250	7,500	24,000	46,000	—
1856	384,240	145	175	210	250	390	75,000
1856C	7,913	650	1,150	2,200	4,400	15,500	—
1856D	874	3,500	6,700	12,500	30,000	72,500	—
1856O	21,100	180	240	750	1,500	8,000	—
1856S	71,120	160	250	375	950	4,500	—
1857	214,130	150	190	205	230	380	75,000
1857D	2,364	875	1,750	2,900	3,850	13,000	—
1857O	34,000	155	210	350	1,100	4,600	—
1857S	69,200	160	210	340	900	5,500	—
1858	47,377	150	200	250	360	1,350	59,000
1858C	9,056	825	1,500	2,100	3,350	9,250	—
1859	39,444	150	185	265	400	1,250	61,000
1859D	2,244	1,000	1,900	3,300	4,900	20,000	—
1859S	15,200	200	350	1,000	2,800	7,000	—
1860	22,675	150	200	265	470	1,300	58,000
1860C	7,469	815	1,550	2,200	3,950	21,000	—
1860S	35,600	170	250	675	1,200	4,000	—
1861	1,283,878	150	180	210	230	325	31,500
1861S	24,000	200	400	1,000	3,700	7,400	—
1862	98,543	160	200	300	520	1,375	32,500
1862/1	Inc. above	450	950	2,000	4,000	8,000	—
1862S	8,000	500	1,000	2,100	4,500	17,000	—
1863	30	—	—	—	—	—	95,000
1863S	10,800	250	500	1,500	3,200	13,500	—
1864	2,874	2,500	5,500	8,800	21,500	37,500	27,000
1865	1,545	2,400	6,000	8,000	19,000	38,000	30,000
1865S	23,376	160	225	650	1,650	5,000	—
1866	3,110	650	1,300	3,500	6,000	11,500	25,000
1866S	38,960	180	300	650	1,600	6,250	—
1867	3,250	190	385	900	1,250	4,800	27,000
1867S	28,000	170	250	625	1,750	4,000	—
1868	3,625	170	235	400	675	1,600	27,000
1868S	34,000	150	200	300	1,100	4,000	—
1869	4,345	170	250	450	715	3,000	24,500
1869S	29,500	160	240	440	775	5,000	—
1870	4,555	165	225	425	740	3,800	22,750

Date	Mintage	F-12	VF-20	XF-40	AU-50	MS-60	Prf-65
1870S	16,000	155	215	400	800	4,900	—
1871	5,350	160	230	325	600	2,200	24,000
1871S	22,000	150	185	280	530	2,200	—
1872	3,030	200	400	750	1,100	4,650	22,000
1872S	18,000	155	225	415	900	4,500	—
1873 closed 3	178,025	155	170	210	260	535	22,500
1873 open 3	Inc. above	155	165	195	250	300	—
1873S	27,000	160	225	425	900	2,800	—
1874	3,940	170	240	380	720	2,100	32,000
1875	420	1,750	3,500	5,000	11,000	21,500	32,500
1875S	11,600	150	200	300	850	4,500	—
1876	4,221	170	275	675	925	3,200	22,000
1876S	5,000	170	225	525	980	3,300	—
1877	1,652	275	400	800	1,100	3,250	22,000
1877S	35,400	150	160	200	230	635	—
1878	286,260	150	160	200	225	275	26,000
1878S	178,000	150	160	200	235	340	—
1879	88,990	150	160	195	235	300	26,000
1879S	43,500	155	200	300	550	2,150	—
1880	2,996	170	210	335	600	1,300	20,250
1881	691	900	2,200	3,400	5,000	10,000	19,000
1882	4,067	160	210	290	400	700	15,000
1883	2,002	175	220	440	1,000	2,600	15,500
1884	2,023	175	225	420	600	1,600	16,000
1885	887	400	715	1,800	2,500	4,400	15,000
1886	4,088	170	190	270	425	1,100	16,500
1887	6,282	175	200	245	325	700	16,500
1888	16,098	160	180	240	285	340	15,000
1889	17,648	155	180	230	250	325	17,000
1890	8,813	170	190	240	280	500	13,750
1891	11,040	165	175	215	230	400	14,000
1892	2,545	170	180	250	325	765	15,000
1893	30,106	165	175	200	240	300	14,000
1894	4,122	170	180	225	325	800	13,500
1895	6,199	150	175	225	275	395	12,500
1896	19,202	150	175	225	235	285	12,500

Date	Mintage	F-12	VF-20	XF-40	AU-50	MS-60	Prf-65
1897	29,904	150	175	210	235	285	12,500
1898	24,165	150	175	210	235	285	12,500
1899	27,350	150	175	210	235	300	12,500
1900	67,205	150	175	240	320	415	12,500
1901	91,322	150	175	200	235	275	12,500
1902	133,733	150	170	200	235	275	12,500
1903	201,257	150	170	200	235	275	13,000
1904	160,960	150	170	200	240	275	12,500
1905	217,944	150	170	200	240	275	12,500
1906	176,490	150	170	200	240	275	12,500
1907	336,448	150	170	200	240	275	12,500

INDIAN HEAD

Designer: Bela Lyon Pratt.
Diameter: 18 millimeters.
Fineness: 0.9000.
Total weight: 4.18 grams.
Actual gold weight: 0.121 ounces.
Mint marks: D – Denver. None – Philadelphia.
Overview: A completely new design replaced the long-running Coronet Head in 1908. Its intaglio features were unusual and controversial. Legislation passed April 11, 1930, discontinued the gold $2.50.

KM# 128

Date	Mintage	XF-40	AU-50	MS-60	MS-63	MS-65
1908	565,057	220	230	275	1,800	8,500
1909	441,899	220	230	275	2,600	11,000
1910	492,682	220	230	275	2,600	12,500
1911	704,191	220	230	280	1,600	12,500
1911D	55,680	3,650	5,000	10,500	24,500	90,000
1912	616,197	220	230	275	2,800	16,000
1913	722,165	220	230	280	1,725	14,000
1914	240,117	235	260	480	8,500	34,000
1914D	448,000	220	230	300	2,650	40,000
1915	606,100	220	230	275	1,650	13,500
1925D	578,000	220	230	275	1,450	7,000
1926	446,000	220	230	275	1,450	7,000
1927	388,000	220	230	275	1,450	7,000
1928	416,000	220	230	275	1,450	7,000
1929	532,000	230	250	340	1,600	10,000

KM# 84

GOLD $3

Designer: James B. Longacre.
Diameter: 20.5 millimeters.
Fineness: 0.9000.
Total weight: 5.015 grams.
Actual gold weight: 0.1452 ounces.
Mint marks: D – Dahlonega. O – New Orleans. S – San Francisco. None – Philadelphia.
Varieties: The 1873 "closed-3" and "open-3" varieties are distinguished by the amount of space between the upper-left and lower-left serifs of the 3 in the date.
Overview: The country's gold interests promoted and achieved authorization for a $3 coin in 1853. Longacre described the denomination as "anomalous" among the gold $1, $2.50, $5, $10, and $20 issues of the time. He struggled with creating a design that would sufficiently distinguish it from the $2.50 coin, which was just slightly smaller in physical size. The result depicts Liberty in a feathered tiara on the obverse and a wreath surrounding the denomination, as opposed to the $2.50's eagle, on the reverse. Legislation passed September 26, 1890, discontinued the gold $3 coin.

Date	Mintage	VF-20	XF-40	AU-50	MS-60	MS-65	Prf-65
1854	138,618	850	1,100	2,000	3,400	18,000	125,000
1854D	1,120	8,300	15,000	29,000	65,000	—	—
1854O	24,000	1,000	2,000	4,000	20,000	—	—
1855	50,555	900	1,100	2,000	3,300	32,000	120,000
1855S	6,600	1,025	2,150	5,700	25,000	—	—
1856	26,010	880	1,100	2,150	3,500	27,000	—
1856S	34,500	900	1,500	2,350	10,000	—	—
1857	20,891	900	1,100	2,100	3,500	—	62,500
1857S	14,000	950	2,200	5,500	18,000	—	—
1858	2,133	950	1,800	3,000	9,000	—	62,500
1859	15,638	900	1,800	1,800	3,000	—	60,000
1860	7,155	900	1,600	2,000	3,600	21,000	46,000
1860S	7,000	950	2,000	7,000	17,000	—	—
1861	6,072	925	1,500	2,200	3,600	27,000	46,000
1862	5,785	925	1,850	2,200	3,600	28,000	46,500
1863	5,039	900	1,450	2,200	3,600	20,000	43,000
1864	2,680	950	1,500	2,300	3,600	29,000	42,000
1865	1,165	1,350	2,500	6,000	10,000	39,000	40,000
1866	4,030	970	1,100	2,000	3,600	27,500	42,000
1867	2,650	950	1,100	2,400	4,000	28,000	41,500
1868	4,875	740	1,100	2,100	3,000	22,000	42,000
1869	2,525	1,150	2,200	2,600	4,000	—	46,000
1870	3,535	1,000	1,500	2,400	5,000	—	47,000
1870S unique	—	—	—	—	—	—	—
Note: H. W. Bass Collection. AU50, cleaned. Est. value, $1,250,000.							

GOLD RUSH

Date	Mintage	VF-20	XF-40	AU-50	MS-60	MS-65	Prf-65
1871	1,330	1,000	1,500	2,000	4,000	27,500	47,000
1872	2,030	900	1,800	2,250	3,600	—	33,000
1873 open 3, proof only	25	3,300	5,000	8,700	—	—	—
1873 closed 3, mintage unknown	—	4,000	6,000	10,000	—	—	42,000
1874	41,820	800	1,300	1,900	3,000	16,000	42,000
1875 proof only	20	20,000	28,000	47,500	—	—	175,000
1876	45	6,000	10,000	16,500	—	—	60,000
1877	1,488	1,200	2,900	5,200	12,000	60,000	43,500
1878	82,324	800	1,300	1,900	3,000	16,000	43,000
1879	3,030	850	1,300	2,000	2,650	19,000	32,000
1880	1,036	850	1,700	3,000	4,000	20,000	29,500
1881	554	1,400	2,750	5,500	8,000	24,000	25,000
1882	1,576	925	1,400	2,000	3,500	22,000	25,000
1883	989	1,000	1,600	3,500	3,600	24,000	25,000
1884	1,106	1,250	1,700	2,200	3,600	24,000	24,000
1885	910	1,300	1,800	2,850	3,900	24,000	25,000
1886	1,142	1,250	1,800	3,000	4,000	20,000	24,000
1887	6,160	900	1,300	2,000	3,000	18,000	21,000
1888	5,291	950	1,500	2,000	3,300	20,000	23,000
1889	2,429	925	1,300	1,700	3,100	18,000	22,000

GOLD $5
LIBERTY CAP

Designer: Robert Scot.
Diameter: 25 millimeters.
Fineness: 0.9160.
Total weight: 8.75 grams.
Actual gold weight: 0.258 ounces.
Mint marks: None – Philadelphia.
Varieties: From 1795 through 1798, varieties exist with either a "small eagle" or a "large (heraldic) eagle" on the reverse. After 1798, only the heraldic eagle was used. Two 1797 varieties are distinguished by the size of the 8 in the date. 1806 varieties are distinguished by whether the top of the 6 has a serif.
Overview: Authorization for a gold $5 coin, or half eagle, was part of the original U.S. Mint act, passed April 2, 1792. The Continental Congress also included a gold $5 coin in its failed attempt to establish a mint and coinage in 1786. The design emulated the $2.50 coin but in a larger size.

KM# 19

Date	Mintage	F-12	VF-20	XF-40	MS-60
1795 small eagle	8,707	11,500	17,000	19,000	47,000

Date	Mintage	F-12	VF-20	XF-40	MS-60
1795 large eagle	Inc. above	8,800	14,000	20,000	75,000
1796/95 small eagle	6,196	12,000	17,500	24,000	75,000
1797/95 large eagle	3,609	8,600	14,000	22,000	150,000
1797 15 stars, small eagle	Inc. above	14,000	21,000	35,000	150,000
1797 16 stars, small eagle	Inc. above	13,000	17,500	34,000	145,000
1798 small eagle	—	90,000	155,000	275,000	—
1798 large eagle, small 8	24,867	3,300	4,500	6,000	21,000
1798 large eagle, large 8, 13-star reverse	Inc. above	3,000	3,700	4,500	17,500
1798 large eagle, large 8, 14-star reverse	Inc. above	3,000	4,200	7,000	35,000
1799	7,451	3,000	3,800	5,300	16,500
1800	37,628	3,000	3,800	5,000	8,800
1802/1	53,176	3,000	4,000	4,300	8,900
1803/2	33,506	3,000	3,800	4,300	8,700
1804 small 8	30,475	3,000	3,800	4,300	8,700
1804 large 8	Inc. above	3,000	3,800	4,300	9,600
1805	33,183	3,000	3,800	4,300	8,600
1806 pointed 6	64,093	3,200	3,700	4,300	9,000
1806 round 6	Inc. above	3,000	3,700	4,300	8,600
1807	32,488	3,000	3,800	4,300	8,700

TURBAN HEAD, CAPPED DRAPED BUST

Designer: John Reich.

Diameter: 25 millimeters.

Fineness: 0.9160.

Total weight: 8.75 grams.

Actual gold weight: 0.258 ounces.

Mint marks: None – Philadelphia.

Varieties: The 1810 varieties are distinguished by the size of the numerals in the date and the size of the 5 in the "5D." on the reverse. The 1811 varieties are distinguished by the size of the 5 in the "5D." on the reverse.

Overview: A redesign turned Liberty around – from right facing to left facing – on the obverse and adorned her in a turban. On the reverse, a more natural-looking eagle and the denomination, "5 D.", was added. A similar change on the $2.50 coin followed in 1808. The mint continued to strike $5 coins despite the suspension of $2.50 production from 1809

KM# 38

GOLD RUSH

through 1820 and $10 production from 1805 through 1837 to concentrate on striking small-denomination silver coins.

Date	Mintage	F-12	VF-20	XF-40	MS-60
1807	51,605	2,400	3,000	4,300	8,400
1808	55,578	2,400	3,000	4,300	8,250
1808/7	Inc. above	3,000	3,800	4,500	13,000
1809/8	33,875	2,500	3,000	3,750	8,500
1810 small date, small 5	100,287	9,600	22,500	32,000	95,000
1810 small date, large 5	Inc. above	2,300	3,000	3,800	8,500
1810 large date, small 5	Inc. above	13,500	24,000	32,000	115
1810 large date, large 5	Inc. above	2,600	3,000	3,750	8,500
1811 small 5	99,581	2,600	3,000	3,750	8,500
1811 large 5	Inc. above	2,500	2,900	38,000	9,000
1812	58,087	2,400	2,850	4,000	8,000

TURBAN HEAD, CAPPED HEAD

Designer: John Reich.

Diameter: 25 millimeters.

Fineness: 0.9160.

Total weight: 8.75 grams.

Actual gold weight: 0.258 ounces.

Mint marks: None – Philadelphia.

Varieties: 1820 varieties are distinguished by whether the 2 in the date has a curved base or square base and by the size of the letters in the reverse inscriptions. 1832 varieties are distinguished by whether the 2 in the date has a curved base or square base and by the number of stars on the reverse. 1834 varieties are distinguished by whether the 4 has a serif at its far right.

Overview: Some minor redesign of Liberty on the obverse resulted in the image being shortened to the neckline.

KM# 43

Date	Mintage	F-12	VF-20	XF-40	MS-60
1813	95,428	2,400	2,750	3,800	7,800
1814/13	15,454	2,500	2,800	3,500	10,000
1815	635	27,000	33,000	70,000	—
Note: 1815, private sale, Jan. 1994, MS-61, $150,000					
1818	48,588	2,475	3,100	4,000	8,250
1819	51,723	9,600	16,500	275,000	62,000
1820 curved-base 2, small letters	263,806	2,600	3,000	4,500	11,000
1820 curved-base 2, large letters	Inc. above	2,600	3,000	4,150	20,000

Date	Mintage	F-12	VF-20	XF-40	MS-60
1820 square-base 2	Inc. above	2,600	3,000	3,800	14,000
1821	34,641	7,000	15,000	23,000	70,000
1822 3 known	—	—	—	—	1,000,000
Note: 1822, private sale, 1993, VF-30, $1,000,000.					
1823	14,485	2,500	3,400	5,000	16,000
1824	17,340	5,000	10,000	16,000	38,000
1825/21	29,060	5,150	9,500	12,000	38,000
1825/24	Inc. above	—	—	250,000	350,000
Note: 1825/4, Bowers & Merena, March 1989, XF, $148,500.					
1826	18,069	4,000	7,500	9,300	32,000
1827	24,913	6,000	10,000	12,250	34,000
1828/7	28,029	15,000	27,500	41,000	125,000
Note: 1828/7, Bowers & Merena, June 1989, XF, $20,900.					
1828	Inc. above	6,000	13,000	21,000	7,000
1829 large planchet	57,442	15,000	27,500	50,000	135,000
Note: 1829 large planchet, Superior, July 1985, MS-65, $104,500.					
1829 small planchet	Inc. above	37,500	50,000	82,500	140,000
Note: 1829 small planchet, private sale, 1992 (XF-45), $89,000.					
1830 small "5D."	126,351	14,500	17,500	21,000	40,000
1830 large "5D."	Inc. above	14,500	17,500	21,000	40,000
1831	140,594	14,500	17,500	21,000	42,500
1832 curved-base 2, 12 stars	157,487	50,000	80,000	135,000	—
1832 square-base 2, 13 stars	Inc. above	14,500	17,500	21,000	40,000
1833	193,630	14,500	17,500	21,000	40,000
1834 plain 4	50,141	14,500	17,500	21,000	40,000
1834 crosslet 4	Inc. above	14,500	17,500	21,000	40,000

CLASSIC HEAD

Designer: William Kneass.
Diameter: 22.5 millimeters.
Fineness: 0.8990.
Total weight: 8.36 grams.
Actual gold weight: 0.2418 ounces.
Mint marks: C – Charlotte. D – Dahlonega. None – Philadelphia.
Varieties: 1834 varieties are distinguished by whether the 4 has a serif at its far right.
Overview: Coinage reform legislation passed in 1834 increased the gold-to-silver value ratio in the U.S. bimetallic monetary system from 15-to-1 to 16.002-to-1. Thus, the fineness and gold

KM# 57

GOLD RUSH

content of the $5 decreased. Obverse and reverse designs were modified slightly.

Date	Mintage	VF-20	XF-40	AU-50	MS-60	MS-65
1834 plain 4	658,028	390	550	950	3,000	48,000
1834 crosslet 4	Inc. above	1,650	2,900	6,000	20,000	—
1835	371,534	390	560	1,000	3,150	70,000
1836	553,147	390	550	1,000	2,950	70,000
1837	207,121	390	585	1,200	3,500	75,000
1838	286,588	390	5,500	1,000	3,700	58,000
1838C	17,179	2,200	4,000	13,000	38,500	—
1838D	20,583	2,000	3,850	9,000	25,000	—

CORONET HEAD, NO MOTTO ABOVE EAGLE

Designer: Christian Gobrecht.

Diameter: 21.6 millimeters.

Fineness: 0.9000.

Total weight: 8.359 grams.

Actual gold weight: 0.242 ounces.

Mint marks: C – Charlotte. D – Dahlonega. O – New Orleans. S – San Francisco. None – Philadelphia.

Varieties: Varieties for the 1842 Philadelphia strikes are distinguished by the size of the letters in the reverse inscriptions. Varieties for the 1842-C and -D strikes are distinguished by the size of the numerals in the date. Varieties for the 1843-O strikes are distinguished by the size of the letters in the reverse inscriptions.

Overview: Legislation passed in 1837 set the fineness of all U.S. gold and silver coins at 0.9000 and revised the gold-to-silver value ratio to 15.998-to-1. Thus, the diameter and actual gold weight of the $5 coin changed slightly in 1839. A new image of Liberty appeared on the obverse. With some modification, the basic reverse design used since 1807 was retained.

KM# 69

Date	Mintage	F-12	VF-20	XF-40	MS-60	Prf-65
1839	118,143	250	275	480	4,000	—
1839/8 curved date	Inc. above	275	325	700	2,250	—
1839C	17,205	1,250	2,300	2,900	24,000	—
1839D	18,939	1,125	2,200	3,200	22,000	—
1840	137,382	200	230	360	3,700	—
1840C	18,992	1,200	2,200	3,000	26,000	—
1840D	22,896	1,200	2,200	3,000	16,000	—
1840O	40,120	200	365	875	11,000	—

Date	Mintage	F-12	VF-20	XF-40	MS-60	Prf-65
1841	15,833	200	400	875	5,500	—
1841C	21,467	1,200	1,850	2,400	20,000	—
1841D	30,495	1,400	1,800	2,350	15,000	—
1841O 2 known	50	—	—	—	—	—
1842 small letters	27,578	2,000	345	1,100	—	—
1842 large letters	Inc. above	350	750	2,000	11,000	—
1842C small date	28,184	4,500	10,000	23,000	110,000	—
1842C large date	Inc. above	900	1,800	2,200	18,000	—
1842D small date	59,608	1,000	2,000	2,300	15,000	—
1842D large date	Inc. above	1,400	2,350	6,500	48,000	—
1842O	16,400	550	1,000	3,400	22,000	—
1843	611,205	200	230	330	1,850	—
1843C	44,201	1,250	1,850	2,500	14,000	—
1843D	98,452	1,250	1,950	2,600	13,000	—
1843O small letters	19,075	300	660	1,700	26,000	—
1843O large letters	82,000	200	265	1,175	12,000	—
1844	340,330	200	230	330	2,000	—
1844C	23,631	1,300	1,900	3,000	24,000	—
1844D	88,982	1,500	1,950	2,400	12,000	—
1844O	364,600	220	250	375	4,700	—
1845	417,099	200	235	260	2,000	—
1845D	90,629	1,300	1,900	2,400	12,500	—
1845O	41,000	235	415	800	9,900	—
1846	395,942	200	230	330	2,400	—
1846C	12,995	1,350	1,900	3,000	24,000	—
1846D	80,294	1,250	1,800	2,400	13,000	—
1846O	58,000	215	375	1,000	11,500	—
1847	915,981	200	230	250	1,650	—

Date	Mintage	F-12	VF-20	XF-40	MS-60	Prf-65
1847C	84,151	1,350	1,800	2,400	13,000	—
1847D	64,405	1,400	2,000	2,000	10,000	—
1847O	12,000	550	2,200	6,750	28,000	—
1848	260,775	200	230	275	1,500	—
1848C	64,472	1,400	1,900	2,250	19,250	—
1848D	47,465	1,450	2,000	2,350	14,500	—
1849	133,070	200	230	280	2,800	—
1849C	64,823	1,500	1,900	2,400	14,000	—
1849D	39,036	1,550	2,000	2,600	16,500	—
1850	64,491	200	300	625	4,250	—
1850C	63,591	1,350	1,850	2,300	14,000	—
1850D	43,984	1,450	1,950	2,500	33,000	—
1851	377,505	200	230	250	2,800	—
1851C	49,176	1,300	1,900	2,350	17,500	—
1851D	62,710	1,400	1,950	2,400	15,000	—
1851O	41,000	280	590	1,500	13,000	—
1852	573,901	200	230	260	1,400	—
1852C	72,574	1,350	1,900	2,450	7,750	—
1852D	91,584	1,450	2,000	2,450	13,000	—
1853	305,770	200	230	250	1,400	—
1853C	65,571	1,500	1,950	2,350	8,500	—
1853D	89,678	1,550	2,000	2,500	11,000	—
1854	160,675	200	230	260	2,000	—
1854C	39,283	1,400	1,900	2,300	14,000	—
1854D	56,413	1,400	1,875	2,200	11,500	—
1854O	46,000	225	300	525	8,250	—
1854S	268	—	—	—	—	—
Note: 1854S, Bowers & Merena, Oct. 1982, AU-55, $170,000.						
1855	117,098	200	230	250	1,800	—
1855C	39,788	1,400	1,900	2,300	16,000	—
1855D	22,432	1,500	1,950	2,400	19,000	—
1855O	11,100	315	675	2,100	20,000	—
1855S	61,000	200	390	1,000	15,500	—
1856	197,990	200	230	240	2,300	—
1856C	28,457	1,450	1,875	2,400	20,000	—
1856D	19,786	1,475	1,950	2,600	15,000	—
1856O	10,000	370	650	1,600	14,000	—
1856S	105,100	200	300	700	6,750	—
1857	98,188	200	230	260	1,600	123,500
1857C	31,360	1,400	1,900	2,500	9,500	—
1857D	17,046	1,500	2,000	2,650	14,500	—

Date	Mintage	F-12	VF-20	XF-40	MS-60	Prf-65
1857O	13,000	340	640	1,400	15,000	—
1857S	87,000	200	300	700	11,000	—
1858	15,136	200	240	550	3,850	190,000
1858C	38,856	1,400	1,900	2,350	11,000	—
1858D	15,362	1,500	2,000	2,450	12,500	—
1858S	18,600	400	825	2,350	31,000	—
1859	16,814	200	325	625	7,000	—
1859C	31,847	1,400	1,900	2,450	16,000	—
1859D	10,366	1,600	2,150	2,600	16,000	—
1859S	13,220	615	1,800	4,150	30,000	—
1860	19,825	200	280	575	3,500	100,000
1860C	14,813	1,500	2,100	3,000	15,000	—
1860D	14,635	1,500	1,900	2,600	15,000	—
1860S	21,200	500	1,100	2,100	27,000	—
1861	688,150	200	230	245	1,450	100,000
1861C	6,879	1,500	2,400	3,900	25,000	—
1861D	1,597	3,000	4,700	7,000	50,000	—
1861S	18,000	500	1,100	4,500	36,500	—
1862	4,465	400	800	1,850	20,000	96,000
1862S	9,500	1,500	3,000	6,000	62,000	—
1863	2,472	450	1,200	3,750	27,500	90,000
1863S	17,000	600	1,450	4,100	35,500	—
1864	4,220	350	650	1,850	15,000	72,000
1864S	3,888	2,300	4,750	16,000	55,000	—
1865	1,295	500	1,450	4,100	20,000	82,500
1865S	27,612	475	1,400	2,400	20,000	—
1866S	9,000	750	1,750	4,000	40,000	—

CORONET HEAD, "IN GOD WE TRUST" ABOVE EAGLE

Designer: Christian Gobrecht.
Diameter: 21.6 millimeters.
Fineness: 0.9000.
Total weight: 8.359 grams.
Actual gold weight: 0.242 ounces.
Mint marks: CC – Carson City. D – Denver. O – New Orleans. S – San Francisco. None – Philadelphia.
Varieties: The 1873 "closed-3 and "open-3" varieties are distinguished by the amount of space between the upper-left and lower-left serifs of the 3 in the date.
Overview: A congressional act passed March 3, 1865, allowed the addition of the motto "In God We Trust" to all U.S. gold and silver coins.

KM# 101

Date	Mintage	XF-40	AU-50	MS-60	MS-63	MS-65
1866	6,730	1,650	3,500	16,500	—	—

GOLD RUSH

Date	Mintage	XF-40	AU-50	MS-60	MS-63	MS-65
1866S	34,920	2,600	8,800	25,000	—	—
1867	6,920	1,500	3,300	11,500	—	—
1867S	29,000	2,900	8,000	34,500	—	—
1868	5,725	1,000	3,500	11,500	—	—
1868S	52,000	1,550	4,000	20,000	—	—
1869	1,785	2,400	3,500	17,500	34,000	—
1869S	31,000	1,750	4,000	26,000	—	—
1870	4,035	2,000	2,850	18,000	—	—
1870CC	7,675	15,000	30,000	110,000	137,500	200,000
1870S	17,000	2,600	8,250	29,000	—	—
1871	3,230	1,700	3,300	12,500	—	—
1871CC	20,770	3,000	12,000	60,000	—	—
1871S	25,000	950	2,950	13,000	—	—
1872	1,690	1,925	3,000	15,000	18,000	—
1872CC	16,980	5,000	20,000	60,000	—	—
1872S	36,400	800	3,400	13,500	—	—
1873 closed 3	49,305	225	440	1,200	6,500	24,000
1873 open 3	63,200	220	350	850	3,650	
1873CC	7,416	12,500	27,500	60,000	—	—
1873S	31,000	1,400	3,250	21,000	—	—
1874	3,508	1,675	2,500	13,000	26,000	—
1874CC	21,198	1,700	9,500	36,000	—	—
1874S	16,000	2,100	4,800	22,500	—	—
1875	220	45,000	60,000	190,000	—	—
1875CC	11,828	4,500	11,500	52,000	—	—
1875S	9,000	2,250	5,000	16,500	32,500	—
1876	1,477	2,500	4,125	11,000	14,500	55,000
1876CC	6,887	5,000	14,000	46,500	82,500	165,000
1876S	4,000	3,600	9,500	30,000	—	—
1877	1,152	2,750	4,000	13,750	29,000	—
1877CC	8,680	3,300	11,000	52,500	—	—
1877S	26,700	650	1,400	9,200	—	—
1878	131,740	220	240	425	2,000	—
1878CC	9,054	7,200	20,000	60,000	—	—
1878S	144,700	220	3,000	675	4,250	—
1879	301,950	220	225	400	2,000	12,000
1879CC	17,281	1,500	3,150	22,000	—	—
1879S	426,200	225	240	950	3,300	—
1880	3,166,436	225	225	235	840	7,500
1880CC	51,017	815	1,375	9,900	—	—

Date	Mintage	XF-40	AU-50	MS-60	MS-63	MS-65
1880S	1,348,900	220	225	235	800	5,750
1881	5,708,802	220	225	235	775	4,800
1881/80	Inc. above	600	750	1,500	4,500	—
1881CC	13,886	1,500	7,000	22,500	60,000	—
1881S	969,000	220	225	235	775	7,150
1882	2,514,568	220	225	235	800	6,150
1882CC	82,817	625	900	7,500	40,000	—
1882S	969,000	220	225	235	800	4,500
1883	233,461	220	225	260	1,200	—
1883CC	12,958	1,100	3,200	18,000	—	—
1883S	83,200	240	315	1,000	2,950	—
1884	191,078	220	225	650	2,250	—
1884CC	16,402	975	3,000	17,000	—	—
1884S	177,000	220	225	345	2,000	—
1885	601,506	220	225	260	825	4,800
1885S	1,211,500	220	225	235	790	4,000
1886	388,432	220	225	235	1,125	5,600
1886S	3,268,000	220	225	235	815	4,500
1887	87	14,500	20,000	—	—	—
1887S	1,912,000	220	225	235	800	4,800
1888	18,296	230	300	550	1,500	—
1888S	293,900	220	320	1,200	4,000	—
1889	7,565	440	515	1,150	2,400	—
1890	4,328	475	550	2,200	6,500	—
1890CC	53,800	460	615	1,600	8,000	55,000
1891	61,413	220	230	450	1,900	5,400
1891CC	208,000	415	525	750	3,150	31,500
1892	753,572	220	225	235	880	7,000
1892CC	82,968	400	575	1,500	6,000	33,500
1892O	10,000	1,000	1,375	3,300	—	—
1892S	298,400	220	225	525	3,300	—
1893	1,528,197	220	225	235	800	3,900
1893CC	60,000	465	770	1,400	6,350	—
1893O	110,000	315	480	950	6,500	—
1893S	224,000	220	225	245	825	9,000
1894	957,955	220	225	235	800	2,600
1894O	16,600	360	570	1,300	5,500	—
1894S	55,900	375	575	2,900	10,000	—
1895	1,345,936	220	225	235	800	4,500
1895S	112,000	275	400	3,150	6,500	26,000
1896	59,063	220	225	235	9,750	4,500

Date	Mintage	XF-40	AU-50	MS-60	MS-63	MS-65
1896S	155,400	240	300	1,150	6,000	24,500
1897	867,883	220	225	235	825	4,500
1897S	354,000	220	235	865	5,150	—
1898	633,495	220	225	235	885	6,000
1898S	1,397,400	220	225	230	950	—
1899	1,710,729	220	225	235	730	3,600
1899S	1,545,000	220	225	235	1,000	9,600
1900	1,405,730	220	225	235	790	3,600
1900S	329,000	220	230	245	900	14,000
1901	616,040	220	225	235	750	3,650
1901S	3,648,000	220	225	235	730	3,600
1902	172,562	220	225	235	730	4,400
1902S	939,000	220	225	235	730	3,600
1903	227,024	220	225	235	730	4,000
1903S	1,855,000	220	225	235	730	3,600
1904	392,136	220	225	235	730	3,600
1904S	97,000	240	285	900	3,850	9,600
1905	302,308	220	225	235	740	4,000
1905S	880,700	225	250	235	1,500	9,600
1906	348,820	220	225	235	745	3,600
1906D	320,000	220	225	235	930	3,200
1906S	598,000	220	230	240	900	4,400
1907	626,192	220	225	235	730	3,400
1907D	888,000	220	225	235	730	3,400
1908	421,874	220	225	235	730	3,400

INDIAN HEAD

Designer: Bela Lyon Pratt.
Diameter: 21.6 millimeters.
Fineness: 0.9000.
Total weight: 8.359 grams.
Actual gold weight: 0.242 ounces.
Mint marks: D – Denver. O – New Orleans. S – San Francisco. None – Philadelphia.
Overview: A completely new design replaced the long-running Coronet Head in 1908. Its intaglio features were unusual and controversial. The Gold Reserve Act of January 30, 1934, discontinued all U.S. gold coinage.

KM# 129

Date	Mintage	XF-40	AU-50	MS-60	MS-63	MS-65
1908	578,012	355	385	460	4,350	25,000
1908D	148,000	355	385	460	4,350	27,500
1908S	82,000	415	430	1,275	4,350	24,000

Date	Mintage	XF-40	AU-50	MS-60	MS-63	MS-65
1909	627,138	355	385	460	4,350	25,000
1909D	3,423,560	355	385	460	4,350	25,000
1909O	34,200	3,400	6,000	21,000	66,000	260,000
1909S	297,200	355	385	1,400	11,000	45,000
1910	604,250	355	385	460	4,350	25,000
1910D	193,600	355	385	460	4,350	42,500
1910S	770,200	355	385	1,000	6,000	44,000
1911	915,139	355	385	460	4,350	25,000
1911D	72,500	535	515	4,500	37,000	200,000
1911S	1,416,000	355	385	560	4,350	41,500
1912	790,144	355	385	460	4,350	25,000
1912S	392,000	365	400	1,700	13,500	93,500
1913	916,099	355	385	460	4,350	25,000
1913S	408,000	350	385	1,400	11,500	120,000
1914	247,125	355	385	460	4,350	25,000
1914D	247,000	355	385	460	4,350	26,000
1914S	263,000	365	400	1,375	13,500	100,000
1915	588,075	355	385	460	4,350	25,000
1915S	164,000	400	385	2,000	17,000	110,000
1916S	240,000	355	385	560	4,350	25,000
1929	662,000	9,600	10,500	13,250	17,500	45,000

GOLD $10
LIBERTY CAP, SMALL EAGLE

Designer: Robert Scot.
Diameter: 33 millimeters.
Fineness: 0.9160.
Total weight: 17.5 grams.
Actual gold weight: 0.5159 ounces.
Mint marks: None – Philadelphia.
Varieties: The 1795 varieties are distinguished by the number of leaves in the branch held in the eagle's talons on the reverse.
Overview: Authorization for a gold $10 coin, or eagle, was part of the original U.S. Mint act, passed April 2, 1792. The Continental Congress also included a gold $10 coin in its failed attempt to establish a mint and coinage in 1786. The obverse design emulated the $2.50 and $5 coins but in a larger size. On the reverse, only the "small eagle" design was used during the first two years of production.

KM# 21

Date	Mintage	F-12	VF-20	XF-40	MS-60
1795 13 leaves	5,583	18,000	24,000	33,000	70,000
1795 9 leaves	Inc. above	26,000	40,000	60,000	230,000
1796	4,146	23,000	27,500	38,000	80,000
1797 small eagle	3,615	30,000	38,000	45,000	185,000

LIBERTY CAP, HERALDIC EAGLE

Designer: Robert Scot.
Diameter: 33 millimeters.
Fineness: 0.9160.
Total weight: 17.5 grams.
Actual gold weight: 0.5159 ounces.
Mint marks: None – Philadelphia.
Varieties: The 1798/97 varieties are distinguished by the positioning of the stars on the obverse.
Overview: The reverse design was switched to the "heraldic eagle" in 1797, and it continued through 1804. The U.S. Mint suspended production of gold $10 coins in 1805 and turned its attention to striking low-denomination silver coins rather than gold coins, which were largely exported at a profit.

KM# 30

Date	Mintage	F-12	VF-20	XF-40	MS-60
1797 large eagle	10,940	9,000	11,000	14,000	40,000
1798/97 9 stars left, 4 right	900	11,000	19,000	29,000	100,000
1798/97 7 stars left, 6 right	842	23,000	30,000	65,000	—
1799	37,449	8,000	10,000	12,500	31,000
1800	5,999	8,200	11,000	12,000	33,000
1801	44,344	8,200	11,000	12,000	29,000
1803	15,017	8,200	11,000	12,000	32,000
1804	3,757	9,500	11,500	14,000	38,000

CORONET HEAD, OLD-STYLE HEAD

Designer: Christian Gobrecht.
Diameter: 27 millimeters.
Fineness: 0.9000.
Total weight: 16.718 grams.
Actual gold weight: 0.4839 ounces.
Mint marks: None – Philadelphia.
Overview: The discovery of gold in Southern states and later in California prompted the resumption of $10 coin production. Legislation passed in 1837 set the fineness of all U.S. gold and silver coins at 0.9000 and revised the gold-to-silver value ratio to 15.998-to-1. Thus, the diameter and actual gold weight of the new $10 coin decreased from the previous issue.

KM# 66.1

Date	Mintage	F-12	VF-20	XF-40	MS-60	Prf-65
1838	7,200	800	1,200	2,900	35,500	—
1839 large letters	38,248	800	1,150	1,950	32,000	—

KM# 66.2

CORONET HEAD, NEW-STYLE HEAD, NO MOTTO ABOVE EAGLE

Designer: Christian Gobrecht.
Diameter: 27 millimeters.
Fineness: 0.9000.
Total weight: 16.718 grams.
Actual gold weight: 0.4839 ounces.
Mint marks: O – New Orleans. S – San Francisco. None – Philadelphia.
Varieties: The 1842 varieties are distinguished by the size of the numerals in the date.
Overview: Some minor redesign of Liberty on the obverse resulted in the image being tilted backward.

Date	Mintage	F-12	VF-20	XF-40	MS-60	Prf-65
1839 small letters	Inc. above	825	1,600	3,500	30,000	—
1840	47,338	410	435	650	10,500	—
1841	63,131	410	435	500	9,500	—
1841O	2,500	1,400	2,400	5,000	30,000	—
1842 small date	81,507	410	435	650	16,500	—
1842 large date	Inc. above	410	435	475	9,500	—
1842O	27,400	410	450	500	22,500	—
1843	75,462	410	435	500	19,000	—
1843O	175,162	410	435	475	12,000	—
1844	6,361	800	1,350	2,900	16,750	—
1844O	118,700	410	435	475	15,000	—
1845	26,153	410	600	775	14,000	—
1845O	47,500	410	435	700	16,500	—
1846	20,095	435	625	900	20,000	—
1846O	81,780	410	435	770	14,750	—
1847	862,258	410	435	380	3,000	—
1847O	571,500	410	435	450	4,850	—
1848	145,484	410	435	450	4,300	—
1848O	38,850	410	525	1,050	14,000	—
1849	653,618	410	435	450	3,400	—
1849O	23,900	425	710	2,100	25,000	—
1850	291,451	410	435	450	3,600	—
1850O	57,500	410	440	880	—	—
1851	176,328	410	435	500	5,150	—
1851O	263,000	410	435	450	5,750	—
1852	263,106	410	435	370	5,000	—

Date	Mintage	F-12	VF-20	XF-40	MS-60	Prf-65
1852O	18,000	425	650	1,100	19,000	—
1853	201,253	410	435	450	3,500	—
1853O	51,000	410	435	500	13,000	—
1854	54,250	410	435	450	6,000	—
1854O small date	52,500	410	435	675	11,000	—
1854O large date	Inc. above	420	475	875	—	—
1854S	123,826	410	435	450	5,500	—
1855	121,701	410	435	450	4,150	—
1855O	18,000	415	435	1,250	20,000	—
1855S	9,000	800	1,500	2,500	29,500	—
1856	60,490	410	435	450	4,500	—
1856O	14,500	425	725	1,250	10,000	—
1856S	68,000	410	435	515	8,500	—
1857	16,606	410	515	850	12,000	—
1857O	5,500	600	1,000	1,850	20,000	—
1857S	26,000	410	450	1,000	10,000	—
1858	2,521	3,000	5,200	8,200	35,000	—
1858O	20,000	410	460	750	10,000	—
1858S	11,800	900	1,600	3,100	34,000	—
1859	16,093	410	435	800	10,500	—
1859O	2,300	2,000	4,000	8,200	47,500	—
1859S	7,000	1,200	1,800	4,500	40,000	—
1860	15,105	410	475	800	8,000	—
1860O	11,100	425	600	1,300	8,250	—
1860S	5,000	1,400	3,250	6,100	40,500	—
1861	113,233	410	435	450	4,000	—
1861S	15,500	690	1,600	2,950	32,500	—
1862	10,995	410	550	1,200	13,500	—
1862S	12,500	700	2,000	3,000	37,000	—
1863	1,248	2,400	3,650	10,000	42,500	—
1863S	10,000	700	1,600	3,350	24,000	—
1864	3,580	775	1,600	4,500	18,000	—
1864S	2,500	2,600	5,100	13,000	50,000	—
1865	4,005	900	1,950	3,500	32,000	—
1865S	16,700	1,700	5,500	12,000	45,000	—
1865S /inverted 186	—	1,300	3,000	6,100	50,000	—
1866S	8,500	1,000	2,800	3,800	44,000	—

KM# 102

CORONET HEAD, NEW-STYLE HEAD, "IN GOD WE TRUST" ABOVE EAGLE

Designer: Christian Gobrecht.
Diameter: 27 millimeters.
Fineness: 0.9000.
Total weight: 16.718 grams.
Actual gold weight: 0.4839 ounces.
Mint marks: CC – Carson City. D – Denver. O – New Orleans. S – San Francisco. None – Philadelphia.
Varieties: The 1873 "closed-3" and "open-3" varieties are distinguished by the amount of space between the upper-left and lower-left serifs of the 3 in the date.
Overview: A congressional act passed March 3, 1865, allowed the addition of the motto "In God We Trust" to all U.S. gold and silver coins.

Date	Mintage	XF-40	AU-50	MS-60	MS-63	MS-65
1866	3,780	1,800	5,000	17,000	—	—
1866S	11,500	4,000	8,000	26,000	—	—
1867	3,140	2,600	5,000	26,000	—	—
1867S	9,000	6,000	12,000	40,000	—	—
1868	10,655	800	2,000	18,000	—	—
1868S	13,500	2,600	4,000	24,000	—	—
1869	1,855	3,000	6,000	36,000	—	—
1869S	6,430	2,700	6,250	25,000	—	—
1870	4,025	1,500	2,500	18,000	—	—
1870CC	5,908	22,000	42,000	90,000	—	—
1870S	8,000	3,000	7,000	34,000	—	—
1871	1,820	3,000	5,000	25,000	—	—
1871CC	8,085	6,000	21,000	60,000	—	—
1871S	16,500	1,700	6,000	30,000	—	—
1872	1,650	3,600	11,000	18,000	33,000	—
1872CC	4,600	11,000	24,000	60,000	—	—
1872S	17,300	950	1,800	22,000	—	—
1873 closed 3	825	1,000	17,500	55,000	—	—
1873CC	4,543	12,500	28,000	58,000	—	—
1873S	12,000	2,350	5,100	25,000	—	—
1874	53,160	425	450	2,100	8,750	—
1874CC	16,767	3,100	10,500	40,000	—	—
1874S	10,000	3,250	7,250	4,000	—	—
1875	120	59,000	80,000	95,000	—	—
Note: 1875, Akers, Aug. 1990, Proof, $115,000.						
1875CC	7,715	11,000	25,000	65,000	—	—
1876	732	6,250	17,000	55,000	—	—

GOLD RUSH

Date	Mintage	XF-40	AU-50	MS-60	MS-63	MS-65
1876CC	4,696	7,950	23,000	50,000	—	—
1876S	5,000	2,000	6,500	40,000	—	—
1877	817	5,750	9,250	—	—	—
1877CC	3,332	6,400	15,000	48,000	—	—
1877S	17,000	850	2,200	23,000	—	—
1878	73,800	425	450	1,000	5,000	—
1878CC	3,244	10,000	16,000	47,000	—	—
1878S	26,100	615	2,150	16,000	—	—
1879	384,770	425	450	665	2,850	—
1879/78	Inc. above	450	800	1,250	2,000	—
1879CC	1,762	15,000	26,000	60,000	—	—
1879O	1,500	3,750	10,000	28,750	—	—
1879S	224,000	425	450	1,100	7,750	—
1880	1,644,876	425	450	465	2,250	—
1880CC	11,190	900	1,800	14,500	—	—
1880O	9,200	800	1,400	13,000	—	—
1880S	506,250	425	450	465	3,300	—
1881	3,877,260	425	450	465	1,200	—
1881CC	24,015	800	950	7,000	20,000	—
1881O	8,350	820	1,600	6,750	—	—
1881S	970,000	425	450	465	—	—
1882	2,324,480	425	450	465	1,200	—
1882CC	6,764	1,300	3,000	13,000	35,000	—
1882O	10,820	575	1,200	7,700	16,750	—
1882S	132,000	425	450	465	4,200	—
1883	208,740	425	450	465	2,400	—
1883CC	12,000	915	2,600	14,000	35,000	—
1883O	800	7,200	10,500	33,500	—	—
1883S	38,000	425	450	1,350	13,000	—
1884	76,905	425	450	750	4,000	—
1884CC	9,925	1,100	2,250	13,000	35,000	—
1884S	124,250	425	450	575	6,500	—
1885	253,527	425	450	465	4,200	—
1885S	228,000	425	450	465	4,300	22,000
1886	236,160	425	450	465	1,800	—
1886S	826,000	425	450	465	1,500	—
1887	53,680	425	450	800	4,750	—
1887S	817,000	425	450	465	1,950	—
1888	132,996	425	450	850	5,700	—
1888O	21,335	425	450	675	4,500	—
1888S	648,700	425	450	465	2,700	—

Date	Mintage	XF-40	AU-50	MS-60	MS-63	MS-65
1889	4,485	700	1,100	2,700	7,200	—
1889S	425,400	425	450	465	1,500	22,000
1890	58,043	425	450	825	5,200	22,000
1890CC	17,500	450	650	2,000	13,500	—
1891	91,868	425	450	465	1,900	—
1891CC	103,732	575	770	1,350	6,000	—
1892	797,552	425	450	465	1,300	13,000
1892CC	40,000	600	825	3,800	9,000	22,000
1892O	28,688	425	450	465	6,000	—
1892S	115,500	425	450	465	4,500	—
1893	1,840,895	425	450	465	850	
1893CC	14,000	900	1,800	8,500	18,000	—
1893O	17,000	425	450	625	5,300	—
1893S	141,350	425	450	500	4,400	—
1894	2,470,778	425	450	465	1,400	22,000
1894O	107,500	425	475	1,200	5,250	—
1894S	25,000	450	900	3,500	8,800	—
1895	567,826	425	450	465	1,400	22,000
1895O	98,000	425	475	525	4,800	—
1895S	49,000	425	700	2,250	9,500	—
1896	76,348	425	450	465	2,100	—
1896S	123,750	425	485	2,500	11,000	—
1897	1,000,159	425	450	465	1,400	22,000
1897O	42,500	425	450	750	4,200	—
1897S	234,750	425	450	870	5,000	—
1898	812,197	425	450	465	1,450	22,000
1898S	473,600	425	450	465	4,250	—
1899	1,262,305	425	450	465	1,400	22,000
1899O	37,047	425	450	550	4,750	—
1899S	841,000	425	450	465	3,250	—
1900	293,960	425	450	465	1,400	22,000
1900S	81,000	425	450	850	5,200	—
1901	1,718,825	425	450	465	1,400	22,000
1901O	72,041	425	450	465	3,700	—
1901S	2,812,750	425	450	465	1,400	22,000
1902	82,513	425	450	465	2,450	—
1902S	469,500	425	450	465	1,400	22,000
1903	125,926	425	450	465	2,500	—
1903O	112,771	425	450	465	3,250	—
1903S	538,000	425	450	465	1,400	22,000
1904	162,038	425	450	465	2,400	—

Date	Mintage	XF-40	AU-50	MS-60	MS-63	MS-65
1904O	108,950	425	450	465	3,700	—
1905	201,078	425	450	465	1,450	22,000
1905S	369,250	425	450	1,100	4,500	—
1906	165,497	425	450	465	2,275	22,000
1906D	981,000	425	450	465	1,450	22,000
1906O	86,895	425	450	470	3,400	—
1906S	457,000	425	450	515	4,400	22,000
1907	1,203,973	425	450	465	1,400	—
1907D	1,030,000	425	450	465	1,400	—
1907S	210,500	425	450	600	4,650	—

INDIAN HEAD, NO MOTTO NEXT TO EAGLE

Designer: Augustus Saint-Gaudens.
Diameter: 27 millimeters.
Fineness: 0.9000.
Total weight: 16.718 grams.
Actual gold weight: 0.4839 ounces.
Mint marks: D – Denver. None – Philadelphia.
Varieties: 1907 varieties are distinguished by whether the edge is rolled or wired, and whether the legend "E Pluribus Unum" has periods between each word.
Overview: Augustus Saint-Gaudens designed President Theodore Roosevelt's inaugural medal. Roosevelt liked the result so much that he commissioned the sculptor to improve the design of U.S. coinage. The results included a striking new design for the gold $10 coin in 1907.

Date	Mintage	XF-40	AU-50	MS-60	MS-63	MS-65
1907 wire edge, periods before and after legend	500	12,000	13,500	18,000	31,500	47,000
1907 same, without stars on edge, unique	—	—	—	—	—	—
1907 rolled edge, periods	42	35,000	42,500	65,000	90,000	95,000
1907 without periods	239,406	550	595	625	2,750	7,200
1908 without motto	33,500	550	595	850	4,000	14,000
1908D without motto	210,000	550	595	715	6,400	40,000

KM# 125

KM# 130

INDIAN HEAD, "IN GOD WE TRUST" LEFT OF EAGLE

Designer: Augustus Saint-Gaudens.
Diameter: 27 millimeters.
Fineness: 0.9000.
Total weight: 16.718 grams.
Actual gold weight: 0.4839 ounces.
Mint marks: D – Denver. S – San Francisco. None – Philadelphia.
Overview: Congressional acts of March 3, 1865, and February 12, 1873, allowed the motto "In God We Trust" to be placed on U.S. coins but did not mandate it. According to author Don Taxay, President Theodore Roosevelt considered it sacrilege to use a religious motto on coinage. When the new 1907 gold $10 and $20 coins appeared without the motto, Congress passed legislation on May 18, 1908, mandating its use on all coins on which it had previously appeared. The Gold Reserve Act of January 30, 1934, discontinued all U.S. gold coinage.

Date	Mintage	XF-40	AU-50	MS-60	MS-63	MS-65
1908	341,486	550	595	625	2,100	8,000
1908D	836,500	550	595	770	7,000	30,000
1908S	59,850	550	595	2,700	9,500	24,000
1909	184,863	550	595	625	2,300	10,000
1909D	121,540	550	595	680	3,850	44,000
1909S	292,350	550	595	690	4,350	13,500
1910	318,704	550	595	625	2,100	8,000
1910D	2,356,640	550	595	625	2,100	8,000
1910S	811,000	550	595	625	7,000	55,000
1911	505,595	550	595	625	2,100	7,000
1911D	30,100	800	950	4,000	19,000	120,000
1911S	51,000	600	650	1,300	8,200	13,000
1912	405,083	550	595	625	2,100	8,500
1912S	300,000	550	595	715	5,300	48,500
1913	442,071	550	595	625	2,100	8,000
1913S	66,000	650	775	3,850	27,500	100,000
1914	151,050	550	595	625	2,100	9,000
1914D	343,500	550	595	625	2,100	13,000
1914S	208,000	550	595	750	7,000	39,000
1915	351,075	550	595	625	2,100	8,000
1915S	59,000	725	1,000	3,300	12,000	65,000
1916S	138,500	550	595	900	4,400	19,000
1920S	126,500	7,500	9,000	19,000	6,500	275,000
1926	1,014,000	550	595	600	2,100	8,000
1930S	96,000	7,000	9,000	12,000	28,000	60,000
1932	4,463,000	550	595	6,235	2,100	8,000
1933	312,500	140,000	150,000	185,000	230,000	650,000

GOLD RUSH

GOLD $20
LIBERTY, "TWENTY D." BELOW EAGLE, NO MOTTO ABOVE EAGLE

Designer: James B. Longacre.
Diameter: 34 millimeters.
Fineness: 0.9000.
Total weight: 33.436 grams.
Actual gold weight: 0.9677 ounces.
Mint marks: O – New Orleans. S – San Francisco. None – Philadelphia.
Overview: An amendment authorizing a gold $20 coin, or "double eagle," was added to proposed congressional legislation authorizing a gold dollar coin. It passed March 3, 1849. Both coins were advanced by gold interests after the discovery of the precious metal in California in 1848.

KM# 74.1

Date	Mintage	XF-40	AU-50	MS-60	MS-63	MS-65
1849 unique, in Smithsonian collection	1	—	—	—	—	—
1850	1,170,261	1,150	3,000	7,000	46,000	—
1850O	141,000	2,400	7,600	36,000	—	—
1851	2,087,155	865	970	3,600	23,000	—
1851O	315,000	1,400	2,600	26,000	—	—
1852	2,053,026	865	1,000	3,650	14,000	—
1852O	190,000	1,100	3,800	19,000	—	—
1853	1,261,326	875	1,000	5,000	24,000	—
1853O	71,000	2,200	3,600	36,000	—	—
1854	757,899	865	1,050	6,000	24,000	—
1854O	3,250	70,000	165,000	350,000	—	—
1854S	141,468	900	1,500	5,000	13,000	44,000
1855	364,666	900	1,450	10,000	—	—
1855O	8,000	9,500	23,000	88,000	—	—
1855S	879,675	900	1,500	7,200	17,000	—
1856	329,878	865	1,200	8,900	30,000	—
1856O	2,250	90,000	200,000	425,000	—	—
1856S	1,189,750	865	1,300	5,500	14,000	35,000
1857	439,375	865	975	3,400	30,000	—
1857O	30,000	2,650	4,800	30,000	130,000	—
1857S	970,500	865	1,200	4,800	8,000	—
1858	211,714	1,000	1,500	5,800	40,000	—
1858O	35,250	2,600	7,600	29,000	—	—
1858S	846,710	875	1,700	10,500	—	—
1859	43,597	2,450	4,400	32,000	—	—

KM# 93

Date	Mintage	XF-40	AU-50	MS-60	MS-63	MS-65
1859O	9,100	9,000	22,000	85,000	—	—
1859S	636,445	865	1,800	5,000	—	—
1860	577,670	865	1,000	4,400	23,000	—
1860O	6,600	9,000	23,000	89,000	—	—
1860S	544,950	865	1,000	6,400	23,000	—
1861	2,976,453	865	1,000	3,000	11,000	40,000
1861O	17,741	6,500	23,000	88,000	—	—
1861S	768,000	950	2,450	11,000	35,000	—

LIBERTY, PAQUET DESIGN

Designer: Anthony C. Paquet.
Diameter: 34 millimeters.
Fineness: 0.9000.
Total weight: 33.436 grams.
Actual gold weight: 0.9677 ounces.
Mint marks: S – San Francisco. None – Philadelphia.
Overview: This design by the U.S. Mint's assistant engraver was withdrawn soon after its release. The letters in the inscriptions on the Paquet-designed coins are taller than the ones on the regular reverse.

Date	Mintage	XF-40	AU-50	MS-60	MS-63	MS-65
1861 2 Known	—	—	—	—	—	—
Note: 1861 Paquet reverse, Bowers & Merena, Nov. 1988, MS-67, $660,000.						
1861S	—	24,000	52,000	185,000	—	—
Note: Included in mintage of 1861S, KM#74.1						

KM# A74.1

LIBERTY, LONGACRE DESIGN RESUMED

Designer: James B. Longacre.
Diameter: 34 millimeters.
Fineness: 0.9000.
Total weight: 33.436 grams.
Actual gold weight: 0.9677 ounces.
Mint marks: S – San Francisco. None – Philadelphia.
Overview: The Longacre-designed gold $20, introduced into circulation in 1850, was resumed in 1862 after the ill-fated Paquet design was discontinued.

Date	Mintage	XF-40	AU-50	MS-60	MS-63	MS-65
1862	92,133	1,600	4,000	15,500	34,000	—
1862S	854,173	1,500	2,100	13,000	—	—
1863	142,790	1,450	2,600	17,000	38,000	—
1863S	966,570	1,400	1,950	16,000	34,000	—

GOLD RUSH

Date	Mintage	XF-40	AU-50	MS-60	MS-63	MS-65
1864	204,285	1,000	1,750	14,000	—	—
1864S	793,660	865	1,700	6,600	—	—
1865	351,200	865	1,000	6,000	29,500	—
1865S	1,042,500	865	1,000	4,000	7,850	18,000
1866S	Inc. below	2,850	11,000	60,000	—	—

LIBERTY, "TWENTY D." BELOW EAGLE, "IN GOD WE TRUST" ABOVE EAGLE

Designer: James B. Longacre.
Diameter: 34 millimeters.
Fineness: 0.9000.
Total weight: 33.436 grams.
Actual gold weight: 0.9677 ounces.
Mint marks: CC – Carson City. S – San Francisco. None – Philadelphia.
Varieties: The 1873 "closed-3" and "open-3" varieties are distinguished by the amount of space between the upper-left and lower-left serif in the 3 in the date.
Overview: A congressional act passed March 3, 1865, allowed the addition of the motto "In God We Trust" to all U.S. gold and silver coins.

KM# 74.2

Date	Mintage	XF-40	AU-50	MS-60	MS-63	MS-65
1866	698,775	900	2,100	6,000	32,000	—
1866S	842,250	850	2,000	16,000	—	—
1867	251,065	850	925	2,400	23,000	—
1867S	920,750	850	1,600	15,000	—	—
1868	98,600	950	2,000	10,000	44,000	—
1868S	837,500	850	1,900	9,500	—	—
1869	175,155	850	1,250	6,000	24,000	—
1869S	686,750	850	1,100	5,300	33,000	—
1870	155,185	1,000	1,750	10,000	—	—
1870CC	3,789	150,000	260,000	700,000	—	—
1870S	982,000	850	860	5,300	27,000	—
1871	80,150	850	1,500	4,500	30,000	—
1871CC	17,387	11,000	27,000	45,000	—	—
1871S	928,000	850	860	4,400	22,000	—
1872	251,880	850	860	3,000	25,000	—
1872CC	26,900	2,500	7,000	33,000	—	—
1872S	780,000	850	860	3,000	24,000	—
1873 closed 3	Est. 208,925	850	1,100	2,600	—	—
1873 open 3	Est. 1,500,900	850	860	990	12,000	—

Date	Mintage	XF-40	AU-50	MS-60	MS-63	MS-65
1873CC	22,410	4,750	8,000	36,000	100,000	—
1873S	1,040,600	850	860	1,800	23,000	—
1874	366,800	850	860	1,400	22,000	—
1874CC	115,085	1,900	2,650	9,200	—	—
1874S	1,214,000	850	860	1,700	28,000	—
1875	295,740	850	860	1,000	13,000	—
1875CC	111,151	1,500	1,850	3,000	19,000	—
1875S	1,230,000	850	860	1,100	18,000	—
1876	583,905	850	860	1,000	13,000	—
1876CC	138,441	1,500	1,900	5,750	37,000	—
1876S	1,597,000	850	860	990	12,000	—

LIBERTY, "TWENTY DOLLARS" BELOW EAGLE

Designer: James B. Longacre.
Diameter: 34 millimeters.
Fineness: 0.9000.
Total weight: 33.436 grams.
Actual gold weight: 0.9677 ounces.
Mint marks: CC – Carson City. D – Denver. O – New Orleans. S – San Francisco. None – Philadelphia.
Overview: The reverse design was modified so the denomination read "Twenty Dollars" instead of "Twenty D."

KM# 74.3

Date	Mintage	XF-40	AU-50	MS-60	MS-63	MS-65
1877	397,670	830	840	850	5,250	—
1877CC	42,565	1,900	2,600	17,500	—	—
1877S	1,735,000	830	840	875	12,500	—
1878	543,645	830	840	850	5,600	—
1878CC	13,180	3,000	6,000	26,000	—	—
1878S	1,739,000	830	840	850	22,000	—
1879	207,630	830	840	1,000	14,000	—
1879CC	10,708	4,000	7,000	34,000	—	—
1879O	2,325	9,000	24,000	75,000	120,000	—
1879S	1,223,800	830	840	1,200	—	—
1880	51,456	830	840	3,000	16,500	—
1880S	836,000	830	840	950	16,000	—
1881	2,260	6,750	13,750	52,000	—	—
1881S	727,000	830	840	900	17,500	—
1882	630	22,000	35,000	80,000	135,000	—
1882CC	39,140	1,500	2,200	7,000	—	—
1882S	1,125,000	830	840	850	16,000	—
1883 proof only	92	—	14,000	—	—	—

GOLD RUSH

Date	Mintage	XF-40	AU-50	MS-60	MS-63	MS-65
1883CC	59,962	1,600	2,000	4,800	21,500	—
1883S	1,189,000	830	840	850	9,000	—
1884 proof only	71	—	15,000	—	—	—
1884CC	81,139	1,550	1,900	3,100	—	—
1884S	916,000	830	840	850	7,000	—
1885	828	8,500	12,000	35,000	—	—
1885CC	9,450	4,000	6,000	13,000	—	—
1885S	683,500	830	840	850	7,000	—
1886	1,106	12,000	33,000	45,000	57,500	—
1887	121	—	8,000	—	—	—
1887S	283,000	830	840	850	14,000	—
1888	226,266	830	840	850	4,500	32,000
1888S	859,600	8,300	840	850	5,500	—
1889	44,111	860	875	850	11,000	—
1889CC	30,945	1,600	2,200	4,700	17,500	—
1889S	774,700	830	840	850	7,250	—
1890	75,995	860	840	850	6,500	—
1890CC	91,209	1,600	2,000	4,750	22,000	—
1890S	802,750	830	840	850	8,800	—
1891	1,442	5,000	9,500	40,000	—	—
1891CC	5,000	7,250	9,500	20,000	45,000	—
1891S	1,288,125	830	840	850	3,500	—
1892	4,523	2,000	2,600	6,000	20,000	—
1892CC	27,265	1,600	2,200	5,000	31,000	—
1892S	930,150	830	840	850	4,000	—
1893	344,339	830	840	850	2,600	—
1893CC	18,402	1,900	2,500	5,000	18,000	—
1893S	996,175	830	840	850	4,000	—
1894	1,368,990	830	840	850	1,700	—
1894S	1,048,550	830	840	850	2,600	—
1895	1,114,656	830	840	850	1,300	13,000
1895S	1,143,500	830	840	850	2,500	15,000
1896	792,663	830	840	850	2,000	13,000
1896S	1,403,925	830	840	850	2,400	—
1897	1,383,261	830	840	850	1,350	—
1897S	1,470,250	830	840	850	1,400	14,000
1898	170,470	830	840	850	5,250	—
1898S	2,575,175	830	840	850	1,300	11,000
1899	1,669,384	830	840	850	1,050	8,500
1899S	2,010,300	830	840	850	1,900	12,500

Date	Mintage	XF-40	AU-50	MS-60	MS-63	MS-65
1900	1,874,584	830	840	850	1,000	6,000
1900S	2,459,500	830	840	850	2,300	—
1901	111,526	830	840	850	1,000	6,500
1901S	1,596,000	830	840	850	3,850	—
1902	31,254	830	840	850	10,000	—
1902S	1,753,625	830	840	850	4,000	—
1903	287,428	830	840	850	1,000	6,000
1903S	954,000	830	840	850	1,800	12,000
1904	6,256,797	830	840	850	1,000	5,000
1904S	5,134,175	830	840	850	1,000	6,600
1905	59,011	830	840	850	15,000	—
1905S	1,813,000	830	840	850	3,850	16,500
1906	69,690	830	840	850	6,600	15,000
1906D	620,250	830	840	850	2,350	15,000
1906S	2,065,750	830	840	850	2,300	19,000
1907	1,451,864	830	840	850	1,000	7,500
1907D	842,250	830	840	850	2,350	7,000
1907S	2,165,800	830	840	850	2,400	17,000

SAINT-GAUDENS, ROMAN NUMERALS IN DATE, NO MOTTO BELOW EAGLE

Designer: Augustus Saint-Gaudens.
Diameter: 34 millimeters.
Fineness: 0.9000.
Total weight: 33.436 grams.
Actual gold weight: 0.9677 ounces.
Mint marks: None – Philadelphia.

Overview: Augustus Saint-Gaudens designed President Theodore Roosevelt's inaugural medal. Roosevelt liked the result so much that he commissioned the sculptor to improve the design of U.S. coinage. The results included a striking new design for the gold $20 coin in 1907, considered by many to be the most beautiful coin in U.S. history. Roosevelt wanted the new $20 coin to emulate the high-relief style of ancient Greek coins.

KM# 126

Date	Mintage	VF-20	XF-40	AU-50	MS-60	MS-63	MS-65
MCMVII (1907) high relief, unique, AU- 55, $150,000	—	—	—	—	—	—	—

GOLD RUSH

Date	Mintage	VF-20	XF-40	AU-50	MS-60	MS-63	MS-65
MCMVII (1907) high relief, wire rim	11,250	7,000	10,000	11,000	16,500	29,000	54,500
MCMVII (1907) high relief, flat rim	Inc. above	7,250	10,500	11,500	17,000	29,500	55,000

SAINT-GAUDENS, ARABIC NUMERALS IN DATE, NO MOTTO BELOW EAGLE

Designer: Augustus Saint-Gaudens.

Diameter: 34 millimeters.

Fineness: 0.9000.

Total weight: 33.436 grams.

Actual gold weight: 0.9677 ounces.

Mint marks: D – Denver. None – Philadelphia.

Varieties: The 1907 varieties are distinguished by the size of the letters in the motto "E Pluribus Unum" lettered on the coin's edge.

Overview: Although an artistic triumph, the high relief of the first 1907 Saint-Gaudens gold $20 coins caused production problems and would not allow the coins to stack properly. Thus, the relief was lowered, and Arabic numerals were used in the date instead of Roman numerals.

KM# 127

Date	Mintage	XF-40	AU-50	MS-60	MS-63	MS-65
1907 large letters on edge, unique	—	—	—	—	—	—
1907 small letters on edge	361,667	845	850	905	1,100	3,400
1908	4,271,551	845	850	875	1,000	1,950
1908D	663,750	845	850	910	1,075	10,500

SAINT-GAUDENS, "IN GOD WE TRUST" BELOW EAGLE

Designer: Augustus Saint-Gaudens.

Diameter: 34 millimeters.

Fineness: 0.9000.

Total weight: 33.436 grams.

Actual gold weight: 0.9677 ounces.

Mint marks: D – Denver. S – San Francisco. None – Philadelphia.

Overview: Congressional acts of March 3, 1865, and February 12, 1873, allowed the motto "In God We Trust" to be placed on U.S. coins but did not mandate it. According to author Don Taxay, President Theodore Roosevelt considered it sacrilege to use a religious motto on coinage. When the new 1907 gold $10 and $20

KM# 131

coins appeared without the motto, Congress passed legislation on May 18, 1908, mandating its use on all coins on which it had previously appeared. The Gold Reserve Act of January 30, 1934, discontinued all U.S. gold coinage. Most of the 1933 mintage of gold $20 coins were still in government vaults at the time and were melted, but a few examples illicitly found their way into private hands. The U.S. government allowed one of them to be sold in 2002, but any others that turn up are still subject to confiscation.

Date	Mintage	XF-40	AU-50	MS-60	MS-63	MS-65
1908	156,359	845	850	870	1,800	23,500
1908D	349,500	845	850	870	1,300	5,600
1908S	22,000	1,800	2,100	7,000	17,500	43,000
1909/8	161,282	900	950	1,300	6,000	35,000
1909	Inc. above	850	875	925	3,450	41,000
1909D	52,500	845	850	1,750	8,250	37,500
1909S	2,774,925	845	850	870	1,000	6,250
1910	482,167	845	850	870	1,000	8,600
1910D	429,000	845	850	870	1,100	3,100
1910S	2,128,250	845	850	870	1,000	10,000
1911	197,350	845	850	870	2,100	15,500
1911D	846,500	845	850	870	1,000	1,980
1911S	775,750	845	850	870	1,000	6,200
1912	149,824	845	850	870	1,800	19,500
1913	168,838	845	850	870	3,000	34,000
1913D	393,500	845	850	870	1,100	6,500
1913S	34,000	950	1,000	1,350	4,200	42,500
1914	95,320	845	850	870	3,100	23,000
1914D	453,000	845	850	870	1,000	3,250
1914S	1,498,000	845	850	870	1,000	2,000
1915	152,050	845	850	870	2,100	28,000
1915S	567,500	845	850	870	1,000	2,000
1916S	796,000	845	850	870	1,000	3,200
1920	228,250	845	850	870	1,000	62,500
1920S	558,000	14,000	21,000	41,000	95,000	210,000
1921	528,500	23,000	30,000	90,000	200,000	950,000
1922	1,375,500	845	850	870	1,000	3,600
1922S	2,658,000	845	850	2,200	4,500	43,000
1923	566,000	875	900	870	1,000	6,350
1923D	1,702,250	845	850	870	1,000	1,980
1924	4,323,500	845	850	870	1,000	1,980
1924D	3,049,500	1,500	1,700	2,800	8,250	75,000

GOLD RUSH

Date	Mintage	XF-40	AU-50	MS-60	MS-63	MS-65
1924S	2,927,500	1,500	1,750	3,000	8,000	47,500
1925	2,831,750	845	850	870	1,000	1,980
1925D	2,938,500	2,100	2,300	3,800	10,000	96,000
1925S	3,776,500	1,900	2,700	8,500	26,000	96,000
1926	816,750	845	850	870	1,000	1,980
1926D	481,000	6,000	7,000	15,500	34,000	115,000
1926S	2,041,500	1,500	1,650	2,200	4,800	36,000
1927	2,946,750	845	850	870	1,000	1,980
1927D	180,000	210,000	265,000	340,000	1,600,000	2,100,000
1927S	3,107,000	7,000	7,000	15,000	57,500	115,000
1928	8,816,000	845	850	870	1,000	1,980
1929	1,779,750	8,000	10,000	13,500	26,000	70,000
1930S	74,000	20,000	22,000	28,000	130,000	150,000
1931	2,938,250	12,000	15,000	20,000	45,000	75,000
1931D	106,500	12,000	20,000	30,000	47,500	80,000
1932	1,101,750	13,500	15,000	21,000	34,000	70,000
1933	445,500	—	—	—	—	7,590,000
Note: Sotheby/Stack's Sale, July 2002. Eleven known, only one currently available.						

U.S. COMMEMORATIVE GOLD COINS, 1903-1926

From 1892 to 1954, the U.S. Mint struck commemorative coins to honor historic events or people. The coins were legal tender and struck to current specifications for the denomination but were not intended for circulation. Instead, they were sold at a premium as collectibles with a portion of the proceeds benefiting a project related to the event or person being commemorated. Most of the issues were silver half dollars, but the following gold coins were also issued.

U.S. COMMEMORATIVE GOLD $1

Diameter: 15 millimeters.
Fineness: 0.9000.
Total weight: 1.672 grams.
Actual gold weight: 0.0484 ounces.
Mint marks: S – San Francisco. None – Philadelphia.

Louisiana Purchase Exposition

Designer: Charles E. Barber.
Obverse: Portrait of President William McKinley.

Date	Mintage	AU-50	MS-60	MS-63	MS-64	MS-65
1903	17,500	730	780	975	2,450	3,600

KM# 120

KM# 119

KM# 121

KM# 136

KM# 144

KM# 152.1

KM# 152.2

LOUISIANA PURCHASE EXPOSITION

Designer: Charles E. Barber.
Obverse: Portrait of Thomas Jefferson.

Date	Mintage	AU-50	MS-60	MS-63	MS-64	MS-65
1903	17,500	725	780	1,100	2,600	3,800

LEWIS & CLARK EXPOSITION

Designer: Charles E. Barber.

Date	Mintage	AU-50	MS-60	MS-63	MS-64	MS-65
1904	10,025	1,075	1,125	2,300	6,400	12,250
1905	10,041	1,300	1,550	2,800	8,000	18,500

PANAMA-PACIFIC EXPOSITION

Designer: Charles E. Barber.

Date	Mintage	AU-50	MS-60	MS-63	MS-64	MS-65
1915S	15,000	675	770	950	1,600	3,000

MCKINLEY MEMORIAL

Obverse designer: Charles E. Barber.
Reverse designer: George T. Morgan.

Date	Mintage	AU-50	MS-60	MS-63	MS-64	MS-65
1916	9,977	650	705	850	1,550	3,000
1917	10,000	800	850	1,200	2,700	4,250

GRANT MEMORIAL

Designer: Laura G. Fraser.
Obverse: No star above the word "Grant."

Date	Mintage	AU-50	MS-60	MS-63	MS-64	MS-65
1922	5,016	1,800	1,900	2,400	4,200	5,000

GRANT MEMORIAL

Designer: Laura G. Fraser.
Obverse: Star above the word "Grant."

Date	Mintage	AU-50	MS-60	MS-63	MS-64	MS-65
1922	5,000	1,900	2,000	2,300	3,500	4,250

U.S. COMMEMORATIVE GOLD $2.50

Diameter: 18 millimeters.
Fineness: 0.9000.
Total weight: 4.18 grams.
Actual gold weight: 0.121 ounces.
Mint marks: S – San Francisco. None – Philadelphia.

GOLD RUSH

PANAMA PACIFIC EXPOSITION

Obverse designer: Charles E. Barber.
Reverse designer: George T. Morgan.

Date	Mintage	AU-50	MS-60	MS-63	MS-64	MS-65
1915S	6,749	1,750	2,100	4,200	6,300	8,000

KM# 137

PHILADELPHIA SESQUICENTENNIAL

Designer: John R. Sinnock.

Date	Mintage	AU-50	MS-60	MS-63	MS-64	MS-65
1926	46,019	585	600	900	1,600	4,850

KM# 161

U.S. COMMEMORATIVE GOLD $50

Panama-Pacific Exposition
Designer: Robert Aitken.
Diameter: 44 millimeters.
Fineness: 0.9000.
Total weight: 83.59 grams.
Actual gold weight: 2.419 ounces.
Mint marks: S – San Francisco.

ROUND

Date	Mintage	AU-50	MS-60	MS-63	MS-64	MS-65
1915S	483	41,500	52,500	78,000	95,000	155,000

OCTAGON

Date	Mintage	AU-50	MS-60	MS-63	MS-64	MS-65
1915S	645	39,500	50,000	69,000	90,000	140,000

KM# 138

U.S. COMMEMORATIVE GOLD COINS, 1986-PRESENT

U.S. commemorative coinage resumed in 1982 with a silver half dollar to commemorate the 250th anniversary of George Washington's birth. Like the earlier commemoratives, the modern commemoratives are legal tender but not intended for circulation. They are sold by the U.S. Mint to collectors at a premium with a portion of the proceeds benefiting a project related to the event or person being commemorated.

U.S. COMMEMORATIVE GOLD $5

Diameter: 21.6 millimeters.
Fineness: 0.9000.
Total weight: 8.359 grams.
Actual gold weight: 0.242 ounces.
Mint marks: W – West Point. None – Philadelphia.

KM# 139

KM# 215

KM# 221

KM# 223

KM# 226

KM# 230

KM# 239

KM# 235

STATE OF LIBERTY CENTENNIAL
Designer: Elizabeth Jones.

Date	Mintage	Proof	MS-65	Prf-65
1986W	95,248	—	150	—
1986W	—	404,013	—	150

CONSTITUTION BICENTENNIAL
Designer: Marcel Jovine.

Date	Mintage	Proof	MS-65	Prf-65
1987W	214,225	—	150	—
1987W	—	651,659	—	150

OLYMPICS
Designer: Elizabeth Jones.

Date	Mintage	Proof	MS-65	Prf-65
1988W	62,913	—	150	—
1988W	—	281,456	—	150

BICENTENNIAL OF THE CONGRESS
Designer: John Mercanti.

Date	Mintage	Proof	MS-65	Prf-65
1989W	46,899	—	150	—
1989W	—	164,690	—	150

MOUNT RUSHMORE GOLDEN ANNIVERSARY
Obverse designer: John Mercanti.
Reverse designers: Robert Lamb and William C. Cousins.

Date	Mintage	Proof	MS-65	Prf-65
1991W	31,959	—	220	—
1991W	—	111,991	—	195

COLUMBUS QUINCENTENARY
Obverse designer: T. James Ferrell.
Reverse designer: Thomas D. Rogers Sr.

Date	Mintage	Proof	MS-65	Prf-65
1992W	—	79,730	—	200
1992W	24,329	—	240	—

OLYMPICS
Obverse designers: James C. Sharpe and T. James Ferell.
Reverse designer: James M. Peed.

Date	Mintage	Proof	MS-65	Prf-65
1992W	27,732	—	200	—
1992W	—	77,313	—	180

GOLD RUSH

JAMES MADISON AND BILL OF RIGHTS
Obverse designer: Scott R. Blazek.
Reverse designer: Joseph D. Peña. .

Date	Mintage	Proof	MS-65	Prf-65
1993W	—	78,651	—	215
1993W	22,266	—	240	—

KM# 242

WORLD WAR II 50TH ANNIVERSARY
Obverse designer: Charles J. Madsen.
Reverse designer: Edward S. Fisher.

Date	Mintage	Proof	MS-65	Prf-65
1993W	—	65,461	—	240
1993W	23,089	—	250	—

KM# 245

WORLD CUP SOCCER
Obverse designer: William J. Krawczewicz.
Reverse designer: Dean McMullen.

Date	Mintage	Proof	MS-65	Prf-65
1994W	22,464	—	215	—
1994W	—	89,619	—	185

KM# 248

CIVIL WAR
Obverse designer: Don Troiani.
Reverse designer: Alfred Maletsky.

Date	Mintage	Proof	MS-65	Prf-65
1995W	12,735	—	660	—
1995W	—	55,246	—	435

KM# 256

OLYMPICS

Date	Mintage	Proof	MS-65	Prf-65
1995W	—	57,442	—	450
1995W	14,675	—	550	—

KM# 261

OLYMPICS

Date	Mintage	Proof	MS-65	Prf-65
1995W	—	43,124	—	340
1995W	10,579	—	460	—

KM# 265

ATLANTA OLYMPICS

Date	Mintage	Proof	MS-65	Prf-65
1996W	—	38,555	—	435
1996W	9,210	—	535	—

KM# 270

KM# 274

KM# 277

KM# 282

KM# 280

KM# 300

KM# 326

OLYMPICS

Date	Mintage	Proof	MS-65	Prf-65
1996W	—	32,886	—	435
1996W	9,174	—	535	—

SMITHSONIAN INSTITUTION 150TH ANNIVERSARY

Obverse designer: Alfred Maletsky.
Reverse designer: T. James Ferrell.

Date	Mintage	Proof	MS-65	Prf-65
1996W	9,068	—	1,050	—
1996W	—	29,474	—	450

FRANKLIN DELANO ROOSEVELT

Obverse designer: T. James Ferrell.
Reverse designers: James M. Peed and Thomas D. Rogers Sr.

Date	Mintage	Proof	MS-65	Prf-65
1997W	11,894	—	400	—
1997W	—	29,474	—	400

JACKIE ROBINSON 50TH ANNIVERSARY

Obverse designer: William C. Cousins.
Reverse designer: James M. Peed.

Date	Mintage	Proof	MS-65	Prf-65
1997W	5,202	—	3,300	—
1997W	—	24,546	—	680

GEORGE WASHINGTON DEATH BICENTENNIAL

Designer: Laura G. Fraser.

Date	Mintage	Proof	MS-65	Prf-65
1999W	22,511	—	360	—
1999W	—	41,693	—	360

FIRST CONVENING OF CONGRESS IN WASHINGTON

Designer: Elizabeth Jones.

Date	Mintage	Proof	MS-65	Prf-65
2001W	6,761	—	735	—
2001W	—	27,652	—	375

GOLD RUSH

SALT LAKE CITY WINTER OLYMPICS

Designer: Donna Weaver.

Date	Mintage	Proof	MS-65	Prf-65
2002	10,585	—	450	—
2002W	—	32,877	—	350

JAMESTOWN 400TH ANNIVERSARY

Date	Mintage	Proof	MS-65	Prf-65
2007W	—	—	450	—
2007W	—	—	—	350

KM 337

U.S. COMMEMORATIVE GOLD $10
LOS ANGELES XXIII OLYMPIAD

Obverse designers: James M. Peed and John Mercanti.
Reverse designer: John Mercanti.
Diameter: 27 millimeters.
Fineness: 0.9000.
Total weight: 16.718 grams.
Actual gold weight: 0.4839 ounces.
Mint marks: D – Denver. P – Philadelphia. S – San Francisco. W – West Point.

Date	Mintage	Proof	MS-65	Prf-65
1984W	75,886	—	275	—
1984P	—	33,309	—	275
1984D	—	34,533	—	290
1984S	—	48,551	—	275
1984W	—	381,085	—	275

KM# 211

LIBRARY OF CONGRESS

Obverse designer: John Mercanti.
Reverse designer: Thomas D. Rogers Sr.
Diameter: 27 millimeters.
Total weight: 16.259 grams.
Composition: 48-percent platinum, 48-percent gold, 4-percent alloy.

Date	Mintage	Proof	MS-65	Prf-65
2000W	6,683	—	3,000	—
2000W	—	27,167	—	750

KM# 312

KM# 350

FIRST FLIGHT CENTENNIAL
Designer: Donna Weaver.
Diameter: 27 millimeters.
Fineness: 0.9000 gold.
Total weight: 16.718 grams.
Actual gold weight: 0.4839 ounces.

Date	Mintage	Proof	MS-65	Prf-65
2003P	—	—	470	—
2003P	—	—	—	1,200

AMERICAN EAGLE GOLD BULLION COINS

In 1986, the U.S. Mint introduced American Eagle gold and silver bullion coins as a convenient means for private citizens to own bullion. In 1997, American Eagle platinum bullion coins were introduced. American Eagle coins are legal tender and carry nominal face values, but they are bought and sold primarily for their bullion value. Augustus Saint-Gaudens' classic design from the 1907-1933 $20 coins was revived for the American Eagle gold bullion coins. They come in four sizes containing either a tenth, quarter, half, or full ounce of gold.

AMERICAN EAGLE GOLD $5
Obverse designer: Augustus Saint-Gaudens.
Reverse designer: Miley Busiek.
Diameter: 16.5 millimeters.
Fineness: 0.9167.
Total weight: 3.393 grams.
Actual gold weight: 0.1 ounces.
Mint marks: P – Philadelphia. W – West Point. None – Philadelphia.

KM# 216

Date	Mintage	Unc	Prf.
MCMLXXXVI (1986)	912,609	85.00	—
MCMLXXXVII (1987)	580,266	80.00	—
MCMLXXXVIII (1988)	159,500	200	—
MCMLXXXVIII (1988)P	(143,881)	—	80.00
MCMLXXXIX (1989)	264,790	85.00	—
MCMLXXXIX (1989)P	(82,924)	—	80.00
MCMXC (1990)	210,210	90.00	—
MCMXC (1990)P	(99,349)	—	80.00
MCMXCI (1991)	165,200	110	—
MCMXCI (1991)P	(70,344)	—	80.00
1992	209,300	95.00	—
1992P	(64,902)	—	80.00

GOLD RUSH

Date	Mintage	Unc	Prf.
1993	210,709	90.00	—
1993P	(58,649)	—	80.00
1994	206,380	90.00	—
1994W	(62,100)	—	80.00
1995	223,025	80.00	—
1995W	(62,650)	—	80.00
1996	401,964	80.00	—
1996W	(58,440)	—	80.00
1997	528,515	80.00	—
1997W	(35,000)	—	91.00
1998	1,344,520	70.00	—
1998W	(39,653)	—	80.00
1999	2,750,338	70.00	—
1999W	(48,426)	—	80.00
2000	569,153	85.00	—
2000W	(50,000)	—	90.00
2001	269,147	85.00	—
2001W	(37,547)	—	80.00
2002	230,027	85.00	—
2002W	(40,864)	—	80.00
2003	245,029	85.00	—
2003W	(40,634)	—	85.00
2004	250,016	85.00	—
2004W	(35,481)	—	90.00
2005	300,043	80.00	—
2005W	48,455	—	95.00
2006	—	75.00	—
2006W	—	—	80.00

AMERICAN EAGLE GOLD $10

Obverse designer: Augustus Saint-Gaudens.
Reverse designer: Miley Busiek.
Diameter: 22 millimeters.
Fineness: 0.9167.
Total weight: 8.483 grams.
Actual gold weight: 0.25 ounces.
Mint marks: P – Philadelphia. W – West Point. None – Philadelphia.

Date	Mintage	Unc	Prf.
MCMLXXXVI (1986)	726,031	175	—
MCMLXXXVII (1987)	269,255	175	—

KM# 217

Date	Mintage	Unc	Prf.
MCMLXXXVIII (1988)	49,000	175	—
MCMLXXXVIII (1988)P	(98,028)	—	200
MCMLXXXIX (1989)	81,789	175	—
MCMLXXXIX (1989P)	(53,593)	—	200
MCMXC (1990)	41,000	175	—
MCMXC (1990)P	(62,674)	—	200
MCMXCI (1991)	36,100	425	—
MCMXCI (1991)P	(50,839)	—	200
1992	59,546	175	—
1992P	(46,290)	—	200
1993	71,864	175	—
1993P	(46,271)	—	200
1994	72,650	175	—
1994W	(47,600)	—	200
1995	83,752	175	—
1995W	(47,545)	—	200
1996	60,318	175	—
1996W	(39,190)	—	200
1997	108,805	175	—
1997W	(29,800)	—	200
1998	309,829	175	—
1998W	(29,733)	—	200
1999	564,232	175	—
1999W	(34,416)	—	200
2000	128,964	175	—
2000W	(36,000)	—	200
2001	71,280	175	—
2001W	(25,630)	—	200
2002	62,027	175	—
2002W	(29,242)	—	200
2003	74,029	175	—
2003W	(31,000)	—	200
2004	72,014	175	—
2004W	(29,127)	—	200
2005	72,015	175	—
2005W	34,637	—	200
2006	—	175	—
2006W	—	—	200

AMERICAN EAGLE GOLD $25

Obverse designer: Augustus Saint-Gaudens.
Reverse designer: Miley Busiek.
Diameter: 27 millimeters.
Fineness: 0.9167.
Total weight: 16.966 grams.
Actual gold weight: 0.5 ounces.
Mint marks: P – Philadelphia. W – West Point. None – Philadelphia.

Date	Mintage	Unc	Prf.
MCMLXXXVI (1986)	599,566	500	—
MCMLXXXVII (1987)	131,255	350	—
MCMLXXXVII (1987)P	(143,398)	—	400
MCMLXXXVIII (1988)	45,000	550	—
MCMLXXXVIII (1988)P	(76,528)	—	400
MCMLXXXIX (1989)	44,829	650	—
MCMLXXXIX (1989)P	(44,264)	—	400
MCMXC (1990)	31,000	800	—
MCMXC (1990)P	(51,636)	—	400
MCMXCI (1991)	24,100	1,300	—
MCMXCI (1991)P	(53,125)	—	400
1992	54,404	500	—
1992P	(40,982)	—	400
1993	73,324	350	—
1993P	(43,319)	—	400
1994	62,400	350	—
1994W	(44,100)	—	400
1995	53,474	385	—
1995W	(45,511)	—	400
1996	39,287	525	—
1996W	(35,937)	—	400
1997	79,605	350	—
1997W	(26,350)	—	400
1998	169,029	350	—
1998W	(25,896)	—	400

KM# 218

Date	Mintage	Unc	Prf.
1999	263,013	350	—
1999W	(30,452)	—	400
2000	79,287	350	—
2000W	(32,000)	—	400
2001	48,047	500	—
2001W	(23,261)	—	400
2002	70,027	350	—
2002W	(26,646)	—	400
2003	79,029	350	—
2003W	(29,000)	—	400
2004	98,040	350	—
2004W	(27,731)	—	400
2005	80,023	350	—
2005W	33,598	—	400
2006	—	345	—
2006W	—	—	400

AMERICAN EAGLE GOLD $50

Obverse designer: Augustus Saint-Gaudens.
Reverse designer: Miley Busiek.
Diameter: 32.7 millimeters.
Fineness: 0.9167.
Total weight: 33.931 grams.
Actual gold weight: 1.0 ounce.
Mint marks: W – West Point. None – Philadelphia.

KM# 219

Date	Mintage	Unc	Prf.
MCMLXXXVI (1986)	1,362,650	715	—
MCMLXXXVI (1986)W	(446,290)	—	725
MCMLXXXVII (1987)	1,045,500	715	—
MCMLXXXVII (1987)W	(147,498)	—	725
MCMLXXXVIII (1988)	465,000	715	—
MCMLXXXVIII (1988)W	(87,133)	—	725
MCMLXXXIX (1989)	415,790	715	—
MCMLXXXIX (1989)W	(53,960)	—	725
MCMXC (1990)	373,210	715	—

GOLD RUSH

Date	Mintage	Unc	Prf.
MCMXC (1990)W	(62,401)	—	725
MCMXCI (1991)	243,100	715	—
MCMXCI (1991)W	(50,411)	—	725
1992	275,000	715	—
1992W	(44,835)	—	725
1993	480,192	715	—
1993W	(34,389)	—	725
1994	221,633	715	—
1994W	(36,300)	—	725
1995	200,636	715	—
1995W	(46,553)	—	725
1996	189,148	715	—
1996W	(37,302)	—	725
1997	664,508	715	—
1997W	(28,000)	—	725
1998	1,468,530	710	—
1998W	(26,060)	—	725
1999	1,505,026	710	—
1999W	(31,446)	—	725
2000	433,319	715	—
2000W	(33,000)	—	725
2001	143,605	715	—
2001W	(24,580)	—	725
2002	222,029	715	—
2002W	(24,242)	—	725
2003	416,032	715	—
2003W	(29,000)	—	725
2004	417,019	715	—
2004W	(28,731)	—	725
2005	356,555	715	—
2005W	34,695	—	725
2006	—	710	—
2006W	—	—	725
2006W Reverse Proof	(10,000)	—	—

CHAPTER 11

THE PRIVATE WORLD OF U.S. GOLD COINS

GOLD RUSH

fficial U.S. coinage production was unable to keep up with demand when gold was discovered in the West and South in the 1800s, especially in California. Commerce thrived in those areas as a result of the discoveries, increasing the need for mediums of exchange. Gold dust and nuggets were inconvenient forms requiring assaying and weighing with each transaction. Neither was accepted for payments of customs duties, and those transactions quickly absorbed the official U.S. coinage that did make it to the West.

A number of private companies stepped in and began producing gold coinlike pieces with official-looking designs and denominations. Federal law prevented states from coining money, but until 1864, it did not specifically prevent private individuals from coining money as long as it did not closely resemble official U.S. coinage. The Private Coinages Act of 1864 outlawed all private coinage, but the law was not enforced in California until 1883, when the Secret Service finally halted the practice. Non-denominated tokens continued to be struck after 1883.

Private firms also processed gold into ingots and bars, which were assayed, refined, and stamped with the appropriate weight, fineness, and value. These also circulated as mediums of exchange.

Today, these private issues are a specialty area of gold-coin collecting, appealing to those interested in Western history. Many of the fractional pieces are affordable for those who want to obtain one or more specimens as curiosity items or as part of an organized collection. Many of the larger denominations are scarce or rare and command prices commensurately.

CALIFORNIA FRACTIONAL AND DOLLAR GOLD COINAGE

By 1852, California jewelers were producing gold 25-cent, 50-cent, and dollar pieces in round and octagonal shapes. Makers included Herman J. Brand, M. Deriberpe, Eugene Deviercy, Pierre Frontier, Robert B. Gray, Antoine Louis Nouizillet, and Isadore Routhier. Herman and Jacob Levison, Reuben N. Hershfield, and Noah Mitchell made coins in Leavenworth, Kansas, for distribution in California. Most of their production was seized in August 1871. Herman Kroll made California gold coins in New York City in the 1890s.

Only two or three of these companies produced coins at any one time. Many varieties bear the maker's initials. Most of the earlier coins were struck from gold alloys and had intrinsic values of about 50 percent to 60 percent of face value. Imperfect production methods resulted in many thin coins.

About 25,000 small-denomination California gold coins are estimated to exist in more than 500 varieties. Some are undated; a few struck in the 1880s are backdated. The prices given in the following listings are for the most common variety in each group.

Counterfeits of California fractional gold coins exist. Collectors should be wary of 1854 and 1858 round half dollars and 1871 round dollars with designs that do not match any of the published varieties. They should also be wary of reeded-edge Kroll coins being sold as originals.

1/4 DOLLAR (OCTAGONAL)

KM# 1.1

KM# 1.1 Obverse: Large Liberty head **Reverse:** Value and date within beaded circle

Date	XF	AU	Unc	BU
1853	100	150	200	300
1854	100	150	250	350
1855	100	150	250	350
1856	100	150	260	375

KM# 1.2

KM# 1.2 Reverse: Value and date within wreath

Date	XF	AU	Unc	BU
1859	65.00	110	200	450
1864	75.00	125	250	400
1866	75.00	125	250	400
1867	65.00	110	250	400
1868	70.00	125	200	350
1869	70.00	125	200	350
1870	65.00	110	200	350
1871	65.00	110	200	350

KM# 1.3

KM# 1.3 Obverse: Large Liberty head above date **Reverse:** Value and CAL within wreath

Date	XF	AU	Unc	BU
1872	65.00	110	250	400
1873	50.00	85.00	175	300

KM# 1.4

KM# 1.4 Obverse: Small Liberty head **Reverse:** Value and date within beaded circle

Date	XF	AU	Unc	BU
1853	125	250	325	425

KM# 1.5

KM# 1.5 Obverse: Small Liberty head above date **Reverse:** Value within wreath

Date	XF	AU	Unc	BU
1854	125	250	300	350

KM# 1.6 Obverse: Small Liberty head **Reverse:** Value and date within wreath

Date	XF	AU	Unc	BU
1855	—	—	—	—
1856	—	—	—	—
1857 Plain edge	—	—	—	—
Note: Kroll type date				
1857 Reeded edge	—	—	—	—
Note: Kroll type date				
1860	—	—	—	—
1870	—	—	—	—

KM# 1.6

KM# 1.7 Reverse: Value in shield and date within wreath

Date	XF	AU	Unc	BU
1863	150	350	500	—
1864	65.00	110	240	—
1865	85.00	145	250	550
1866	85.00	145	250	400
1867	75.00	125	200	400
1868	75.00	125	200	—
1869	75.00	125	190	300
1870	75.00	125	200	350

KM# 1.7

KM# 1.8 Obverse: Small Liberty head above date **Reverse:** Value and CAL within wreath

Date	XF	AU	Unc	BU
1870	65.00	110	200	300
1871	65.00	110	175	250
1871	65.00	110	175	250
1873	175	250	400	—
1874	65.00	110	175	275
1875/3	350	700	1,000	—
1876	65.00	110	200	300

KM# 1.8

KM# 1.9 Obverse: Goofy Liberty head **Reverse:** Value and date within wreath

Date	XF	AU	Unc	BU
1870	85.00	145	200	300

KM# 1.9

KM# 1.10 Obverse: Oriental Liberty head above date **Reverse:** 1/4 CALDOLL withn wreath

Date	XF	AU	Unc	BU
1881	—	—	1,000	3,000

KM# 1.10

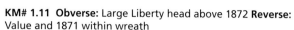

KM# 1.11 Obverse: Large Liberty head above 1872 **Reverse:** Value and 1871 within wreath

Date	XF	AU	Unc	BU
1872-71	—	—	1,000	3,000

KM# 2.1

KM# 2.1 Obverse: Large Indian head above date **Reverse:** Value within wreath

Date	XF	AU	Unc	BU
1852	100	175	240	450
Note: Back dated issue				
1868	100	175	240	450
Note: Back dated issue				
1874	85.00	160	220	400
Note: Back dated issue				
1876	85.00	160	220	400
1880	75.00	150	200	350
1881	85.00	160	220	400

KM# 2.2

KM# 2.2 Reverse: Value and CAL within wreath

Date	XF	AU	Unc	BU
1872	65.00	110	210	300
1873/2	200	350	550	800
1873	90.00	160	250	350
1874	65.00	110	210	300
1875	90.00	160	250	350
1876	90.00	160	250	350

KM# 2.3

KM# 2.3 Obverse: Small Indian head above date

Date	XF	AU	Unc	BU
1875	90.00	160	250	350
1876	90.00	160	250	500
1881	—	—	500	1,100

KM# 2.4

KM# 2.4 Obverse: Aztec Indian head above date

Date	XF	AU	Unc	BU
1880	65.00	110	210	300

KM# 2.6

KM# 2.6 Obverse: Dumb Indian head above date **Reverse:** Value and CAL within wreath

Date	XF	AU	Unc	BU
1881	—	—	650	—

KM# 2.7

KM# 2.7 Obverse: Young Indian head above date **Reverse:** Value within wreath

Date	XF	AU	Unc	BU
1881	—	—	450	—

GOLD RUSH

KM# 2.8 Reverse: Value and CAL within wreath

Date	XF	AU	Unc	BU
1882	—	—	500	750

KM# 2.8

KM# 3 Obverse: Washington head above date

Date	XF	AU	Unc	BU
1872	—	—	400	950

KM# 3

1/4 DOLLAR (ROUND)

KM# 4 Obverse: Defiant eagle above date **Reverse:** 25¢ within wreath

Date	XF	AU	Unc	BU
1854	11,000	22,000	33,000	44,000

KM# 4

KM# 5.1 Obverse: Large Liberty head **Reverse:** Value and date within wreath

Date	XF	AU	Unc	BU
1853	400	700	1,000	1,500
1854	150	250	400	600
1859	70.00	120	225	275
1865	90.00	160	250	350
1866	—	—	200	300
1867	—	—	200	300
1868	—	—	200	300
1870	—	—	200	300
1871	—	—	200	300

KM# 5.1

KM# 5.2 Obverse: Large Liberty head above date **Reverse:** Value and CAL within wreath

Date	XF	AU	Unc	BU
1871	—	—	200	275
1872	—	—	200	275
1873	—	—	180	260

KM# 5.2

KM# 5.3 Obverse: Small Liberty head **Reverse:** 25¢ in wreath

Date	XF	AU	Unc	BU
	1,000	1,650	2,450	3,500

KM# 5.4 Reverse: 1/4 DOLL. or DOLLAR and date in wreath

Date	XF	AU	Unc	BU
	90.00	150	200	350
Note: Rare counterfeit exists				
1853	500	800	1,200	2,500
1853 10 stars	120	200	275	365
Note: Kroll type				

KM# 5.4

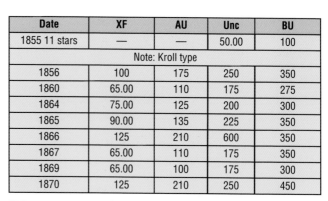

Date	XF	AU	Unc	BU
1855 11 stars	—	—	50.00	100
Note: Kroll type				
1856	100	175	250	350
1860	65.00	110	175	275
1864	75.00	125	200	300
1865	90.00	135	225	350
1866	125	210	600	350
1867	65.00	110	175	350
1869	65.00	100	175	300
1870	125	210	250	450

KM# 5.5 Reverse: Value in shield and date within wreath

Date	XF	AU	Unc	BU
1863	80.00	160	200	—

KM# 5.6 Obverse: Small Liberty head above date **Reverse:** Value and CAL within wreath

KM# 5.6

Date	XF	AU	Unc	BU
1870	80.00	160	200	250
	100	175	500	—
1871	80.00	160	200	250
1871	—	—	210	350
1873	—	—	300	500
1874	—	—	300	500
1875	—	—	250	475
1876	—	—	225	450

KM# 5.7 Obverse: Goofy Liberty head **Reverse:** Value and date within wreath

KM# 5.7

Date	XF	AU	Unc	BU
1870	110	160	220	250

KM# 5.8 Obverse: Liberty head with H and date below **Reverse:** Value and CAL in wreath

Date	XF	AU	Unc	BU
1871	80.00	125	160	250

KM# 6.1 Obverse: Large Indian head above date **Reverse:** Value within wreath

KM# 6.1

Date	XF	AU	Unc	BU
1852	—	—	200	300
Note: Back dated issue				
1868	—	—	250	375
Note: Back dated issue				
1874	—	—	190	275

GOLD RUSH

Date	XF	AU	Unc	BU
Note: Back dated issue				
1876	—	—	200	325
1878/6	—	—	200	300
1880	—	—	200	325
1881	—	—	200	325

KM# 6.2 Reverse: Value and CAL within wreath

Date	XF	AU	Unc	BU
1872/1	—	—	200	300
1873	—	—	180	275
1874	—	—	180	275
1875	—	—	200	300
1876	—	—	200	300

KM# 6.2

KM# 6.3 Obverse: Small Indian head above date

Date	XF	AU	Unc	BU
1875	75.00	125	250	400
1876	65.00	110	200	350
1881 Rare	—	—	—	—

KM# 6.3

KM# 6.4 Obverse: Young Indian head above date

Date	XF	AU	Unc	BU
1882	400	725	1,225	1,750

KM# 6.4

KM# 7 Obverse: Washington head above date

Date	XF	AU	Unc	BU
1872	—	—	600	900

KM# 7

1/2 DOLLAR (OCTAGONAL)

KM# 8.1 Obverse: Liberty head above date **Reverse:** 1/2 DOLLAR in beaded circle, CALIFORNIA GOLD around circle

Date	XF	AU	Unc	BU
1853	165	280	350	450
1854	110	225	285	350
Note: Rare counterfeit exists				
1854	165	280	350	450
1856	165	285	365	450

KM# 8.1

KM# 8.2 Reverse: Small eagle with rays ("peacock")

Date	XF	AU	Unc	BU
1853	400	600	1,000	1,500

KM# 8.2

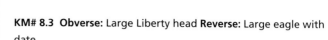

KM# 8.3 Obverse: Large Liberty head **Reverse:** Large eagle with date

Date	XF	AU	Unc	BU
1853	750	1,350	2,250	—

KM# 8.4 Reverse: Value and date within wreath

Date	XF	AU	Unc	BU
1859	—	130	200	275
1866	—	200	300	400
1867	—	130	225	300
1868	—	130	225	300
1869	—	130	250	350
1870	—	130	250	350
1871	—	130	225	300

KM# 8.4

KM# 8.5 Obverse: Large Liberty head above date **Reverse:** Value and CAL within wreath

Date	XF	AU	Unc	BU
1872	—	130	250	350
1873	—	130	225	300

KM# 8.5

KM# 8.6 Obverse: Liberty head **Reverse:** Date in wreath, HALF DOL. CALIFORNIA GOLD around wreath

Date	XF	AU	Unc	BU
1854	100	250	350	500
1855	90.00	200	300	400
1856	90.00	200	265	325
1856	165	350	1,100	—
Note: Back date issue struck in 1864				
1868	60.00	110	185	275
Note: Kroll type date				

KM# 8.6

KM# 8.7 Obverse: Small Liberty head **Reverse:** HALF DOLLAR and date in wreath

Date	XF	AU	Unc	BU
1864	—	175	275	350
1870	—	175	275	—

KM# 8.7

KM# 8.8 Reverse: CAL. GOLD HALF DOL and date in wreath

Date	XF	AU	Unc	BU
1869	—	175	200	350
1870	—	175	200	350

KM# 8.8

GOLD RUSH

KM# 8.9 Obverse: Small Liberty head above date **Reverse:** Value and CAL in wreath

Date	XF	AU	Unc	BU
1870	55.00	110	200	300
1871	55.00	110	200	250
1871	55.00	100	165	250
1873	85.00	200	300	600
1874	85.00	200	300	600
1875	250	475	1,000	—
1876	55.00	110	200	250

KM# 8.9

KM# 8.10 Obverse: Goofy Liberty head **Reverse:** Value and date within wreath

Date	XF	AU	Unc	BU
1870	55.00	110	200	300

KM# 8.10

KM# 8.11 Obverse: Oriental Liberty head above date **Reverse:** 1/2 CALDOLL within wreath

Date	XF	AU	Unc	BU
1881	250	450	750	1,150

KM# 8.11

KM# 9.1 Obverse: Large Indian head above date **Reverse:** Value within wreath

Date	XF	AU	Unc	BU
1852	—	—	500	900
Note: Back dated issue				
1868	—	—	650	1,000
Note: Back dated issue				
1874	—	175	500	900
Note: Back dated issue				
1876	—	—	300	400
1880	—	—	300	400
1881	—	—	300	400

KM# 9.1

KM# 9.2 Reverse: Value and CAL within wreath

Date	XF	AU	Unc	BU
1852	—	—	450	700
Note: Back dated issue				
1868	—	—	260	550
Note: Back dated issue				
1872	—	—	200	300
1873/2	—	—	200	400
1873	—	—	200	300
1874/3	—	—	250	350

KM# 9.2

Date	XF	AU	Unc	BU
1874	—	—	200	300
1875	—	—	250	425
1876	—	—	250	400
1878/6	—	—	250	400
1880	—	—	500	1,000
1881	—	—	250	400

KM# 9.3

KM# 9.3 Obverse: Small Indian head above date

Date	XF	AU	Unc	BU
1875	—	175	225	350
1876	—	175	225	350

KM# 9.4

KM# 9.4 Obverse: Young Indian head above date

Date	XF	AU	Unc	BU
1881	—	—	550	850
1882 Rare	—	—	—	—

1/2 DOLLAR (ROUND)

KM# 10 Obverse: Arms of California and date **Reverse:** Eagle and legends

KM# 10

Date	XF	AU	Unc	BU
1853	1,250	3,500	4,500	5,500

KM# 11.1 Obverse: Liberty head **Reverse:** Large eagle and legends

KM# 11.1

Date	XF	AU	Unc	BU
1854	1,000	2,700	6,000	—

KM# 11.2 Obverse: Liberty head and date **Reverse:** HALF DOL. CALIFORNIA GOLD around wreath

KM# 11.2

Date	XF	AU	Unc	BU
1854	175	210	300	450

KM# 11.3 Obverse: Liberty head **Reverse:** Date in wreath, value and CALIFORNIA GOLD around wreath

KM#11.3

Date	XF	AU	Unc	BU
1852	145	180	275	400
1852	145	180	275	400
1853	145	180	275	400
1853	165	200	300	425
1853	165	200	300	425
1853 Date on reverse	125	160	225	300

GOLD RUSH

Date	XF	AU	Unc	BU
Note: Kroll type				
1854 Large head	300	600	1,000	1,600
1854 Small head	—	—	100	200
Note: Common counterfeits exist				
1855 Date on reverse	175	210	325	550
Note: Kroll type				
1856	100	135	225	325
1860/56	125	185	250	400

KM# 11.4 Reverse: Small eagle and legends

Date	XF	AU	Unc	BU
1853 Rare	—	—	—	—
1853	5,000	8,000	10,000	15,000

KM# 11.5 Reverse: Value in wreath; CALIFORNIA GOLD and date around wreath

Date	XF	AU	Unc	BU
1853	150	250	750	1,500

KM# 11.5

KM# 11.6 Reverse: Value and date within wreath

Date	XF	AU	Unc	BU
Rare	—	—	—	—
1854	850	2,000	—	—
Note: Common counterfeit without FD beneath truncation				
1855	155	300	450	600
1859	140	250	350	500
1859	—	150	175	250
1865	—	150	225	350
1866	—	165	250	400
1867	—	150	225	350
1868	—	165	250	400
1869	—	165	250	400
1870	—	132	225	350
1871	—	125	200	300
1873	—	170	250	450

KM# 11.6

KM# 11.7 Obverse: Liberty head above date **Reverse:** Value and CAL within wreath

Date	XF	AU	Unc	BU
1870	—	125	250	400
1871	—	125	250	400
1871	—	200	400	—

Date	XF	AU	Unc	BU
1872	—	—	250	400
1873	—	200	400	1,000
1874	—	125	250	750
1875	—	125	300	800
1876	—	100	250	—

KM# 11.8 Obverse: Liberty head **Reverse:** Value and date within wreath, CALIFORNIA GOLD outside

KM# 11.8

Date	XF	AU	Unc	BU
1863	265	425	675	950
Note: This issue is a rare Kroll type. All 1858 dates of this type are counterfeits				

KM# 11.9 Obverse: Liberty head **Reverse:** HALF DOLLAR and date in wreath

KM# 11.9

Date	XF	AU	Unc	BU
1864	100	165	250	350
1866	200	330	500	700
1867	100	165	250	350
1868	100	165	250	350
1869	125	200	300	—
1870	—	200	350	—

KM# 11.11 Obverse: Goofy Liberty head **Reverse:** Value and date within wreath

KM# 11.11

Date	XF	AU	Unc	BU
1870	125	225	400	700

KM# 11.12 Obverse: Liberty head with H and date below **Reverse:** Value and CAL within wreath

KM# 11.12

Date	XF	AU	Unc	BU
1871	90.00	175	200	275

KM# 12.1 Obverse: Large Indian head above date **Reverse:** Value within wreath

KM# 12.1

Date	XF	AU	Unc	BU
1852	—	—	350	675
1868	—	—	300	600
1874	—	—	300	600
1876	—	—	200	250
1878/6	—	—	300	450
1880	—	—	250	400
1881	—	—	250	400

GOLD RUSH

KM# 12.2 Reverse: Value and CAL within wreath

Date	XF	AU	Unc	BU
1872	—	—	200	300
1873/2	—	—	350	650
1873	—	—	200	300
1874/3	—	—	300	450
1874	—	—	200	300
1875/3	—	—	200	300
1875	—	—	300	500
1876/5	—	—	200	300
1876	—	—	340	600

KM# 12.2

KM# 12.3 Obverse: Small Indian head above date

Date	XF	AU	Unc	BU
1875	100	165	250	450
1876	75.00	100	200	300

KM# 12.3

KM# 12.4 Obverse: Young Indian head above date

Date	XF	AU	Unc	BU
1882	—	350	850	—

KM# 12.4

DOLLAR (OCTAGONAL)

KM# 13.1 Obverse: Liberty head **Reverse:** Large eagle and legends

Date	XF	AU	Unc	BU
	1,000	1,500	2,000	4,000
1853	3,000	3,500	5,500	—
1854	1,000	1,500	2,000	4,000

KM# 13.1

KM# 13.2 Reverse: Value and date in beaded circle; CALIFORNIA GOLD, initials around circle

Date	XF	AU	Unc	BU
1853	275	500	750	1,100
1853	450	800	1,100	—
1853	300	450	900	—
1853	275	450	750	1,200
1854	450	800	1,100	—
1854	300	500	900	1,600
1855	350	600	900	—
1856	2,100	3,300	5,000	—
1863 Reeded edge	150	225	325	500
1863 Plain edge	—	—	40.00	80.00
Note: Reeded edge 1863 dates are Kroll types, while plain edge examples are Kroll restrikes				

KM# 13.2

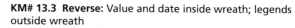

KM# 13.3

KM# 13.3 Reverse: Value and date inside wreath; legends outside wreath

Date	XF	AU	Unc	BU
1854 Rare	—	—	—	—
Note: Bowers and Marena sale 5-99, XF $9,775				
1854	275	500	750	1,100
1855	275	500	750	1,100
1858	150	250	350	600
Note: 1858 dates are Kroll types				
1859	1,900	—	—	—
1860	—	450	750	100
1868	—	450	750	1,100
1869	—	350	6,600	900
1870	—	350	600	900
1871	—	300	400	850

KM# 13.4 Obverse: Goofy Liberty head **Reverse:** Value and date inside wreath

Date	XF	AU	Unc	BU
1870	—	250	1,000	1,500

KM# 13.5

KM# 13.5 Obverse: Liberty head above date **Reverse:** Value and date within wreath; CALIFORNIA GOLD around wreath

Date	XF	AU	Unc	BU
1871	—	350	600	900
1874	—	3,000	—	—
1875	—	3,000	—	—
1876	—	2,000	—	—

KM# 14.1

KM# 14.1 Obverse: Large Indian head above date **Reverse:** 1 DOLLAR inside wreath; CALIFORNIA GOLD around wreath

Date	XF	AU	Unc	BU
1872	—	350	600	900
1873/2	—	400	700	1,100
1873	—	600	750	—
1874	—	525	850	1,300
1875	—	475	600	1,000
Note:				
1876/5	—	700	1,000	1,300

GOLD RUSH

KM# 14.2 Obverse: Small Indian head above date **Reverse:** 1 DOLLAR CAL inside wreath

Date	XF	AU	Unc	BU
1875	700	900	1,200	—
1876	—	1,000	1,400	—

KM# 14.2

KM# 14.3 Reverse: 1 DOLLAR inside wreath; CALIFORNIA GOLD around wreath

Date	XF	AU	Unc	BU
1876	—	500	750	—

KM# 14.3

DOLLAR (ROUND)

KM# 15.1 Obverse: Liberty head **Reverse:** Large eagle and legends

Date	XF	AU	Unc	BU
1853 Rare	—	—	—	—
Note: Superior sale Sept. 1987 MS-63 $35,200				

KM# 15.1

KM# 15.2 Reverse: Value and date inside wreath; CALIFORNIA GOLD around wreath

Date	XF	AU	Unc	BU
1854	3,000	5,500	—	—
1854	5,000	7,500	—	—
1854 Rare	—	—	—	—
Note: Superior sale Sept. 1988 Fine $13,200				
1857 2 known	—	—	—	—
1870	500	1,250	2,000	—
1871	850	1,450	2,500	—
Note: Coutnerfeits reported				

KM# 15.3 Obverse: Liberty head above date **Reverse:** Value inside wreath; CALIFORNIA GOLD around wreath

Date	XF	AU	Unc	BU
1870	500	1,000	1,400	2,000
1871	500	1,000	1,400	2,000

KM# 15.3

KM# 15.4 Obverse: Goofy Liberty head **Reverse:** Value and date inside wreath; CALIFORNIA GOLD around wreath

Date	XF	AU	Unc	BU
1870	400	1,000	1,500	—

KM# 15.4

KM# 16 Obverse: Large Indian head above date **Reverse:** Value inside wreath; CALIFORNIA GOLD outside wreath

Date	XF	AU	Unc	BU
1872	650	1,100	1,800	2,400

KM# 16

CALIFORNIA LARGE-DENOMINATION GOLD COINAGE

Baldwin & Company. San Francisco jewelers George C. Baldwin and Thomas S. Holman acquired the minting equipment of the Pacific Company in May 1850. California's first $20 piece was among the issues of the resulting Baldwin & Company.

5 DOLLARS

KM# 17

Date	Fine	VF	XF	Unc
1850	4,000	6,500	10,000	25,000

10 DOLLARS

KM# 18

Date	Fine	VF	XF	Unc
1850	15,000	22,500	48,500	85,000
Note: Bass Sale May 2000, MS-64 $149,500				

KM# 19

Date	Fine	VF	XF	Unc
1851	9,000	14,500	28,500	50,000

KM# 18

20 DOLLARS

KM# 20

Date	Fine	VF	XF	Unc
1851	—	—	—	—
Note: Stack's Superior Sale Dec. 1988, XF-40 $52,800; Beware of copies cast in base metals				

Cincinnati Mining and Trading Company. Little is known of this company's origin and location. It is believed it was organized in the East but was forced to abandon most of its equipment while en route to California. Base-metal counterfeits of its coinage are known to exist.

5 DOLLARS

KM# 23

Date	Fine	VF	XF	Unc
1849 Rare	—	—	—	—

KM# 23

GOLD RUSH

10 DOLLARS

KM# 24

Date	Fine	VF	XF	Unc
1849 Rare	—	—	—	—
Note: Brand Sale 1984, XF $104,500				

Dubosq & Company. This company's coinage was popular in California because its intrinsic value was worth more than its face value. The company originated in Philadelphia as a jewelry firm owned by Theodore Dubosq Sr., Theodore Dubosq Jr., and Henry Dubosq. They set up melting and coining equipment in San Francisco in 1849. Some believe they used dies created by U.S. Mint engraver James B. Longacre.

5 DOLLARS

KM# 26

Date	Fine	VF	XF	Unc
1850	25,000	42,500	—	—

10 DOLLARS

KM# 27

Date	Fine	VF	XF	Unc
1850	25,000	45,000	65,000	—

Dunbar & Company. Edward E. Dunbar owned the California Bank in San Francisco and purchased the coining equipment of Baldwin & Company when that firm went out of business.

KM# 27

5 DOLLARS

KM# 28

Date	Fine	VF	XF	Unc
1851	22,500	32,500	55,000	—
Note: Spink & Son Sale 1988, AU $62,000				

Augustus Humbert, U.S. assayer. On September 30, 1850, Congress directed the Treasury secretary to establish an official assay office in California. Moffat & Company was awarded the contract to perform the office's duties; Humbert, a New York watchcase maker, was appointed U.S. assayer of gold in California. Humbert stamped the provisional government mint's first octagonal pieces on January 31, 1851. The $50 pieces were

KM# 28

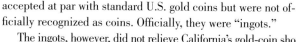

KM# 29.1

KM# 31.1a

accepted at par with standard U.S. gold coins but were not officially recognized as coins. Officially, they were "ingots."

The ingots, however, did not relieve California's gold-coin shortage. Banks did not like them, and the ingots drove overvalued territorial gold $5, $10, and $20 coins from circulation. Eventually, the ingots were discounted 3 percent when accepted in transactions.

Moffat & Company, which had struck gold $5 and $10 coins since 1849, resumed production of those denominations in 1852. The $10 piece was first issued with the Moffat & Company imprint on the Liberty's coronet and later with Humbert's official imprint on the reverse. The $20 piece was issued with the Humbert imprint.

10 DOLLARS
KM# 29.1 Note: AUGUSTUS HUMBERT imprint.

Date	Fine	VF	XF	Unc
1852/1	2,000	3,500	5,500	15,000
1852	1,500	2,500	4,750	11,500

KM# 29.2 Note: Error: IINITED.

Date	Fine	VF	XF	Unc
1852/1 Rare	—	—	—	—
1852 Rare	—	—	—	—

20 DOLLARS
KM# 30

Date	Fine	VF	XF	Unc
1852/1	4,500	6,000	9,500	—

Note: Mory Sale June 2000, AU-53 $13,800; Garrett Sale March 1980, Humbert's Proof $325,000; Private Sale May 1989, Humbert's Proof (PCGS Pr-65) $1,350,000; California Sale Oct. 2000, Humbert's Proof (PCGS Pr-65) $552,000

50 DOLLARS
KM# 31.1 Obverse: 50 D C 880 THOUS, eagle **Reverse:** 50 in center

Date	Fine	VF	XF	Unc
1851	9,500	12,000	22,000	—

GOLD RUSH

KM# 31.1a Obverse: 887 THOUS

Date	Fine	VF	XF	Unc
1851	6,000	9,000	17,500	37,500

KM# 31.2 Obverse: 880 THOUS **Reverse:** Without 50

Date	Fine	VF	XF	Unc
1851	5,000	8,000	16,500	35,500

KM# 31.2a Obverse: 887 THOUS

Date	Fine	VF	XF	Unc
1851	—	14,500	25,000	—

KM# 31.1

KM# 31.3 Note: ASSAYER inverted.

Date	Fine	VF	XF	Unc
1851 Unique	—	—	—	—

KM# 31.4 Obverse: 880 THOUS **Reverse:** Rays from central star

Date	Fine	VF	XF	Unc
1851 Unique	—	—	—	—

KM# 32.1 Obverse: 880 THOUS **Reverse:** "Target"

Date	Fine	VF	XF	Unc
1851	5,000	8,000	16,000	35,000

KM# 32.1

KM# 32.1a Obverse: 887 THOUS

Date	Fine	VF	XF	Unc
1851	5,000	8,000	16,000	35,000
Note: Garrett Sale March 1980, Humberts Proof $500,000				

KM# 32.2 Reverse: Small design

Date	Fine	VF	XF	Unc
1851	5,000	8,000	16,000	—
1852	4,500	7,500	18,500	40,000
Note: Bloomfield Sale December 1996, BU $159,500				

KM# 32.1a

Kellogg & Company. This company struck $20 coins dated 1854 and 1855 – after the closing of the U.S. Assay Office in California in 1853 but before the new San Francisco Mint could begin production. The company was formed by former Moffat & Company employee John G. Kellogg and former U.S. assayer John Glover Richter. After 1855, Augustus Humbert replaced Richter, and the company was reorganized as Kellogg & Humbert Melters, Assayers & Coiners. The Kellogg & Humbert company survived until 1860 but issued only 1855-dated $20 coins.

20 DOLLARS

KM# 33.1 Obverse: Thick date Reverse: Short arrows

Date	Fine	VF	XF	Unc
1854	1,200	2,000	4,000	17,500

KM# 33.2 Obverse: Medium date

Date	Fine	VF	XF	Unc
1854	1,200	2,000	4,000	17,500

KM# 33.3 Obverse: Thin date

Date	Fine	VF	XF	Unc
1854	1,200	2,000	4,000	17,500

KM# 33.4 Reverse: Long arrows

Date	Fine	VF	XF	Unc
1854	1,200	2,000	4,000	17,500
1855	1,200	2,250	4,250	18,500
Note: Garrett Sale March 1980 Proof $230,000				

KM# 33.5 Reverse: Medium arrows

Date	Fine	VF	XF	Unc
1855	1,200	2,250	4,250	18,500

KM# 33.6 Reverse: Short arrows

Date	Fine	VF	XF	Unc
1855	1,200	2,250	4,250	18,500

KM# 33.4

GOLD RUSH

50 DOLLARS

KM# 34

Date	Fine	VF	XF	Unc
1855	—	—	—	—
Note: Heritage ANA Sale August 1977, Proof $156,500				

Massachusetts and California Company. Josiah Hayden, S.S. Wells, Miles G. Moies, and others organized this company in May 1849 in Northampton, Massachusetts. They set up business in San Francisco in 1849. The few pieces extant are heavily alloyed with copper.

5 DOLLARS

KM# 35

Date	Fine	VF	XF	Unc
1849	40,000	65,000	—	—
Note: Proof $125,000.				

KM# 34

Miners Bank. The San Francisco brokerage firm of Wright & Company issued undated gold $10 pieces in fall 1849 under the Miners Bank name. Unlike most territorial gold pieces, the Miners Bank coins were alloyed with copper. Their copper-induced color and low intrinsic value made them unpopular, and the firm dissolved on January 14, 1850.

KM# 35

10 DOLLARS

KM# 36

Date	Fine	VF	XF	Unc
(1849)	—	8,500	17,500	45,000
Note: Garrett Sale March 1980, MS-65 $135,000				

KM# 36

Moffat & Company. Early in 1849, John Little Moffat, a New York assayer, established an office in San Francisco in association with Joseph R. Curtis, Philo H. Perry, and Samuel Ward. The first issues of the Moffat & Company assay office consisted of rectangular $16 ingots and assay bars of various and irregular denominations. In early August 1849, the firm began striking gold $5 and $10 coins resembling official U.S. coinage but with the legend "S.M.V. California Gold" ("S.M.V." meant "standard mint value") on the reverse. Gold $5 pieces of the same design were also issued in 1850.

5 DOLLARS

KM# 37.1

Date	Fine	VF	XF	Unc
1849	1,000	1,500	3,500	12,000

KM# 37.2 Reverse: Die break at DOL

Date	Fine	VF	XF	Unc
1849	1,000	1,500	3,500	12,000

KM# 37.3 Reverse: Die break on shield

Date	Fine	VF	XF	Unc
1849	1,000	1,500	3,500	12,000

KM# 37.4 Reverse: Small letters

Date	Fine	VF	XF	Unc
1850	1,100	1,650	4,200	14,000

KM# 37.5 Reverse: Large letters

Date	Fine	VF	XF	Unc
1850	1,100	1,650	4,200	14,000
Note: Garrett Sale March 1980, MS-60 $21,000				

10 DOLLARS

KM# 38.1 Reverse: Value: TEN DOL., arrow below period

Date	Fine	VF	XF	Unc
1849	1,650	3,500	6,000	15,000

KM# 38.2 Reverse: Arrow above period

Date	Fine	VF	XF	Unc
1849	1,650	3,500	6,000	15,000

KM# 38.3 Reverse: Value: TEN D., large letters

Date	Fine	VF	XF	Unc
1849	2,250	5,000	7,500	16,500

KM# 37.4

KM# 38.2

KM# 38.4 Reverse: Small letters

Date	Fine	VF	XF	Unc
1849	—	5,000	7,500	16,500

KM# 39.1 Note: MOFFAT & CO. imprint, wide date

Date	Fine	VF	XF	Unc
1852	2,500	5,500	10,000	20,000

KM# 39.2 Note: Close date. Struck by Augustus Humbert.

Date	Fine	VF	XF	Unc
1852	2,000	4,250	9,000	18,500

20 DOLLARS

KM# 40 Note: Struck by Curtis, Perry, & Ward.

Date	Fine	VF	XF	Unc
1853	2,150	3,750	6,000	16,500

Norris, Greig & Norris. Thomas N. Norris, Charles Greig, and Hiram A. Norris – members of a New York engineering firm – produced the first California territorial gold coins in 1849. The $5 coins were struck at Benicia City, although they bear the imprint of San Francisco. A unique 1850 variety of this coin has the name "Stockton" beneath the date instead of "San Francisco."

HALF EAGLE

KM# 41.1 Reverse: Period after ALLOY

Date	Fine	VF	XF	Unc
1849	2,250	3,750	7,250	20,000

KM# 41.2 Reverse: Without period after ALLOY

Date	Fine	VF	XF	Unc
1849	2,250	3,750	7,250	20,000

KM# 41.3 Reverse: Period after ALLOY

Date	Fine	VF	XF	Unc
1849	1,750	3,000	6,750	20,000

KM# 41.4 Reverse: Without period after ALLOY

Date	Fine	VF	XF	Unc
1849	1,750	3,000	6,750	20,000

KM# 41.2

KM# 42 Obverse: STOCKTON beneath date

Date	Fine	VF	XF	Unc
1850 Unique	—	—	—	—

J.S. Ormsby. Dr. J.S. Ormsby and Major William M. Ormsby struck undated gold $5 and $10 coins in Sacramento in 1849. They are marked by the initials "J.S.O." The coins were greatly overvalued. The $10 assayed for as little as $9.37.

5 DOLLARS

KM# 43.1

Date	Fine	VF	XF	Unc
(1849) Unique	—	—	—	—

KM# 43.2

Date	Fine	VF	XF	Unc
(1849) Unique	—	—	—	—
Note: Superior Auction 1989, VF $137,500				

10 DOLLARS

KM# 44

Date	Fine	VF	XF	Unc
(1849) Rare	—	—	—	—
Note: Garrett Sale March 1980, F-12 $100,000; Ariagno Sale June 1999, AU-50 $145,000				

Pacific Company. Some mystery surrounds the 1849 gold $5 and $10 coins of this San Francisco company. It is believed its well-struck pattern coins were produced in the East by the Pacific Company organized in Boston and its crude hand-struck pieces by jewelers Broderick and Kohler after they acquired the company's dies. Initially, the coins' intrinsic value exceeded face value, but by the end of 1849, the coins had fallen out of favor. The $10 assayed for as little as $7.86.

5 DOLLARS

KM# 45

Date	Fine	VF	XF	Unc
1849 Rare	—	—	—	—
Note: Garrett Sale March 1980, VF-30 $180,000				

10 DOLLARS

KM# 46.1

Date	Fine	VF	XF	Unc
1849 Rare	—	—	—	—
Note: Waldorf Sale 1964, $24,000				

KM# 46.2

Date	Fine	VF	XF	Unc
1849 Rare	—	—	—	—

1 DOLLAR

KM# A45

Date	Fine	VF	XF	Unc
(1849) Unique	—	—	—	—
Note: Mory Sale June 2000, EF-40 $57,500				

Templeton Reid. Reid moved his coining equipment from Georgia to California when gold was discovered in the West. The only known California Reid $10 piece is in the Smithsonian Institution collection in Washington, D.C. The only known California Reid $25 piece was stolen from the U.S. Mint collection in 1858 and was never recovered.

10 DOLLARS

KM# 47

Date	Fine	VF	XF	Unc
1849 Unique	—	—	—	—

20 DOLLARS

KM# 48

Date	Fine	VF	XF	Unc
1849 Unknown	—	—	—	—
Note: The only known specimen was stolen from the U.S. Mint in 1858 and has never been recovered. For additional listings of Templeton Reid, see listings under Georgia				

Schultz & Company. Judge G.W. Schultz and William T. Garratt of San Francisco operated this brass foundry in the rear of the Baldwin & Company building. Its gold $5 coins are inscribed "Shults & Co.," a misspelling of the company name.

5 DOLLARS

KM# 49

Date	Fine	VF	XF	Unc
1851	—	36,800	50,000	—

KM# 49

KM# 53

KM# 53a

United States Assay Office of Gold. When John L. Moffat left Moffat & Company in 1852, Joseph R. Curtis, Philo H. Perry, and Samuel Ward reorganized the company as the United States Assay Office of Gold. Its 0.900-fine $10, $20, and $50 coins were an attempt to conform to U.S. Mint standards.

10 DOLLARS
KM# 50.1 Obverse: TEN DOLS 884 THOUS Reverse: O of OFFICE below I of UNITED

Date	Fine	VF	XF	Unc
1852	—	—	—	—
Note: Garrett Sale March 1980, MS-60 $18,000				

KM# 51.2 Reverse: O below N, strong beads

Date	Fine	VF	XF	Unc
1852	1,750	2,500	3,850	9,500

KM# 51.3 Reverse: Weak beads

Date	Fine	VF	XF	Unc
1852	1,750	2,500	3,850	9,500

KM# 52 Obverse: TEN D, 884 THOUS

Date	Fine	VF	XF	Unc
1853	5,000	7,750	14,500	—

KM# 52a Obverse: 900 THOUS

Date	Fine	VF	XF	Unc
1853	2,700	4,200	6,500	—
Note: Garrett Sale March 1980, MS-60 $35,000				

20 DOLLARS
KM# 53 Obverse: 884/880 THOUS

Date	Fine	VF	XF	Unc
1853	8,500	12,500	17,500	23,500

KM# 53a Obverse: 900/880 THOUS

Date	Fine	VF	XF	Unc
1853	1,550	2,750	4,250	10,000
Note: 1853 Liberty Head listed under Moffat & Company				

50 DOLLARS
KM# 54 Obverse: 887 THOUS

Date	Fine	VF	XF	Unc
1852	4,000	6,500	13,500	26,500

KM# 54a Obverse: 900 THOUS

Date	Fine	VF	XF	Unc
1852	5,000	7,000	14,500	28,500

GOLD RUSH

Wass, Molitor & Company. This San Francisco company was founded by two Hungarian exiles – S.C. Wass and A.P. Molitor – as a gold smelting and assaying plant. It started producing gold $5 and $10 coins in response to pleas for coinage from the local commercial community.

5 DOLLARS
KM# 55.1 Obverse: Small head, rounded bust

Date	Fine	VF	XF	Unc
1852	2,000	4,000	6,750	16,500

KM# 55.2 Note: Thick planchet.

Date	Fine	VF	XF	Unc
1852 Unique	—	—	—	—

KM# 56 Obverse: Large head, pointed bust

Date	Fine	VF	XF	Unc
1852	2,000	4,500	8,500	17,500

10 DOLLARS
KM# 57 Obverse: Long neck, large date

Date	Fine	VF	XF	Unc
1852	2,750	5,000	8,500	15,500

KM# 58 Obverse: Short neck, wide date

Date	Fine	VF	XF	Unc
1852	1,500	2,650	5,500	13,500

KM# 59.1 Obverse: Short neck, small date

Date	Fine	VF	XF	Unc
1852 Rare	—	—	—	—
Note: Eliasberg Sale May 1996, EF-45 $36,300; S.S. Central America Sale December 2000, VF-30 realized $12,650				

KM# 59.2 Obverse: Plugged date

Date	Fine	VF	XF	Unc
1855	6,000	8,000	12,500	28,500

KM# 59.2

20 DOLLARS
KM# 60 Obverse: Large head

Date	Fine	VF	XF	Unc
1855 Rare	—	—	—	—

KM# 61

KM# 62

KM# 61 Obverse: Small head

Date	Fine	VF	XF	Unc
1855	7,000	11,000	20,000	—

50 DOLLARS

KM# 62

Date	Fine	VF	XF	Unc
1855	—	—	—	—
Note: Bloomfield Sale December 1996, BU $170,500				

COLORADO

Clark, Gruber & Company. When gold was discovered in Colorado Territory, bankers Austin M. Clark, Milton E. Clark, and Emanuel H. Gruber moved from Leavenworth, Kansas, to Denver and established a bank. They issued gold $2.50, $5, $10, and $20 coins in 1860 and 1861 as Clark, Gruber & Company. To protect them against loss of metal from abrasion, the coins were slightly heavier than their value required.

The U.S. government purchased the Clark, Gruber facilities in 1863 and operated it as an assay office until 1906.

2-1/2 DOLLARS

KM# 63

Date	Fine	VF	XF	Unc
1860	750	1,300	2,500	8,500
Note: Garrett Sale March 1980, MS-65 $12,000				

KM# 64.1

Date	Fine	VF	XF	Unc
1861	850	1,500	2,750	11,500

KM# 64.2 Note: Extra high edge.

Date	Fine	VF	XF	Unc
1861	850	1,750	3,500	12,500

KM# 63

GOLD RUSH

5 DOLLARS

KM# 65

Date	Fine	VF	XF	Unc
1860	1,000	1,750	3,000	9,200
Note: Garrett Sale March 1980, MS-63 $9,000				

KM# 66

Date	Fine	VF	XF	Unc
1861	1,500	2,500	4,500	13,500

10 DOLLARS

KM# 67

Date	Fine	VF	XF	Unc
1860	2,750	3,750	8,000	21,500

KM# 68

Date	Fine	VF	XF	Unc
1861	1,500	2,500	4,500	15,500

20 DOLLARS

KM# 69

Date	Fine	VF	XF	Unc
1860	25,000	55,000	75,000	100,000
Note: Eliasberg Sale May 1996, AU $90,200; Schoonmaker Sale June 1997, VCF $62,700				

KM# 70

Date	Fine	VF	XF	Unc
1861	7,000	10,000	21,500	—

KM# 65

KM# 67

KM# 69

KM# 70

KM# 71

J.J. Conway & Company. This Georgia Gulch, Colorado, bank operated the Conway Mint for a short time in 1861. Its undated coins were highly regarded for their scrupulously maintained value.

2-1/2 DOLLARS
KM# 71

Date	Fine	VF	XF	Unc
(1861)	—	45,000	70,000	—

5 DOLLARS
KM# 72.1

Date	Fine	VF	XF	Unc
(1861) Rare	—	—	—	—
Note: Brand Sale June 1984, XF-40 $44,000				

KM# 72.2 Reverse: Numeral 5 omitted

Date	Fine	VF	XF	Unc
(1861) Unique	—	—	—	—

10 DOLLARS
KM# 73

Date	Fine	VF	XF	Unc
(1861) Rare	—	60,000	—	—

KM# 74

John Parsons. Parsons was an assayer at Tarryall Mines. His $2.50 and $5 coins were not dated.

2-1/2 DOLLARS
KM# 74

Date	Fine	VF	XF	Unc
(1861) Rare	—	—	—	—
Note: Garrett Sale March 1980, VF-20 $85,000				

5 DOLLARS
KM# 75

Date	Fine	VF	XF	Unc
(1861) Rare	—	—	—	—
Note: Garrett Sale March 1980, VF-20 $100,000				

GOLD RUSH

GEORGIA

Christopher Bechtler. See North Carolina.

2-1/2 DOLLARS
KM# 76.1 Reverse: GEORGIA, 64 G, 22 CARATS

Date	Fine	VF	XF	Unc
	1,650	2,650	5,000	10,000

KM# 76.2 Reverse: GEORGIA, 64 G, 22 CARATS, even 22

Date	Fine	VF	XF	Unc
	1,850	2,850	5,500	11,500

5 DOLLARS
KM# 77 Obverse: RUTHERF **Reverse:** 128 G, 22 CARATS

Date	Fine	VF	XF	Unc
	2,000	3,500	5,500	11,500

KM# 78.1 Obverse: RUTHERFORD

Date	Fine	VF	XF	Unc
	2,000	3,750	6,000	12,500

KM# 78.2 Reverse: Colon after 128 G:

Date	Fine	VF	XF	Unc
	—	20,000	30,000	—
Note: Akers Pittman Sale October 1997, VF-XF $26,400				

KM# 77

Templeton Reid. This goldsmith and assayer established a private mint at Gainesville and struck the nation's first territorial gold pieces in 1830.

2-1/2 DOLLARS
KM# 79

Date	Fine	VF	XF	Unc
1830	12,500	32,500	55,000	—

KM# 79

KM# 80

5 DOLLARS

KM# 80

Date	Fine	VF	XF	Unc
1830 Rare	—	—	—	—
Note: Garrett Sale November 1979, XF-40 $200,000				

10 DOLLARS

KM# 81 Obverse: With date

Date	Fine	VF	XF	Unc
1830 Rare	—	—	—	—

KM# 82 Obverse: Undated

Date	Fine	VF	XF	Unc
(1830) Rare	—	—	—	—
Note: Also see listings under California				

NORTH CAROLINA

August Bechtler. Christopher Bechtler. German metallurgists Christopher Bechtler Sr., his son August, and his nephew Christopher Jr. established a mint at Rutherfordton in western North Carolina in July 1831. August continued the mint after Christopher Sr. died in 1842. It lasted until 1852, making it the longest surviving private mint in U.S. history.

The Bechtlers issued gold dollar, $2.50, and $5 coins in a wide variety of weights and sizes. The coinage was undated except for three varieties of the $5 piece that carry the inscription "Aug. 1, 1834" to indicate that they conformed to the new weight standard for official U.S. gold coins.

Christopher Sr. also produced gold $2.50 and $5 coins for Georgia.

DOLLAR

KM# 83.1 Reverse: CAROLINA, 27 G. 21C.

Date	Fine	VF	XF	Unc
(1842-52)	450	650	1,150	2,950

KM# 83.2 Reverse: CAROLINA, 27 G. 21C.

Date	Fine	VF	XF	Unc
(1842-52)	450	650	1,150	2,950

5 DOLLARS

KM# 84 Reverse: CAROLINA, 134 G. 21 CARATS

Date	Fine	VF	XF	Unc
(1842-52)	1,750	3,500	6,000	12,500

KM# 84

GOLD RUSH

BIBLIOGRAPHY

Buranelli, Vincent. *Gold, An Illustrated History*.
Hammond Inc., Maplewood, New Jersey. 1979.

Clain-Stefanelli, Elvira and Vladimir. *The Beauty
and Lore of Coins, Currency and Medals*. Riverwood
Publishers Ltd., Croton-on-Hudson, New York. 1974.

Desroches-Noblecourt, Christiane. *Tutankhamen, Life and
Death of a Pharoah*. New York Graphic Society Ltd. 1963.

The Gale Encyclopedia of Science. Bridget Travers, editor.
Gale Research, Detroit. 1996.

Hobson, Burton. *Historic Gold Coins of the World*.
Doubleday & Company Inc., Garden City, New York. 1971.

Hobson, Burton; and Obojski, Robert. *Illustrated
Encyclopedia of World Coins*. Doubleday & Co. Inc.,
Garden City, New York. 1970.

Horn, James. *A Land as God Made It, Jamestown and the
Birth of America*. Basic Books, New York. 2005.

International Monetary Fund. www.imf.org.

Kirkemo, Harold; Newman, William L.; Ashley, Roger P.
U.S. Geological Survey Information Services. Denver.

London Bullion Market Association. www.lbma.org.

Standard Catalog of World Gold Coins, 5th Edition. Colin R.
Bruce II, editor. Krause Publications, Iola, Wisconsin. 2005.

Taxay, Don. *The U.S. Mint and Coinage*. ARCO
Publishing Company Inc., New York. 1983.

United States Department of the Treasury. www.treasury.gov.

U.S. Coin Digest. Dave Harper, editor. Krause
Publications, Iola, Wisconsin. 2007.

Van Ryzin, Robert R. *Crime of 1873, The Comstock
Connection*. Robert R. Van Ryzin and Krause
Publications, Iola, Wisconsin. 2001.

COIN GRADING

In general, grading refers to the amount of wear on a coin. There are two books that offer more detailed and illustrated information on grading U.S. coins: the *Official American Numismatic Association Grading Standards for United States Coins* and *Photograde*. There are almost no grading guides for world coins, but the guidelines that follow combined with experience in examining and valuing particular types of world coins should allow collectors and investors to acquire world coins with confidence.

There are two key factors in grading: (1) overall wear on a coin and (2) loss of design details, such as strands of hair, feathers on eagles, and designs on coats of arms. Coins should be graded by the amount of overall wear and loss of design detail on each side of the coin. The overall grade should be based on the weaker of the two sides. Coins with a moderately small design element that is prone to early wear should be graded by that detail alone.

"Proof" refers to a special process for producing coins, often those intended for direct sale to collectors at a premium above their face values. Proof coins are made from specially prepared dies and receive multiple strikes from the coining press. Proof coins receive their own grading designation (proof-60 and proof-65, for example). A coin does not start out being a proof and then become mint state if it becomes worn. Once a proof coin, always a proof coin.

Following are descriptions of grades commonly used for coins, starting with the lowest grade and proceeding to the highest. The numerical designations added to the descriptive designations are usually used when grading U.S. coins but not world coins.

About good (AG-3). Typically, only a silhouette of a larger design remains. The rim, if any remaining, is worn down into the letters.

Good (G-4). The design is clearly outlined but worn substantially. Some of the larger detail may be visible. The rim may have a few weak spots or wear.

Very good (VG-8). About 25 percent of the original detail is visible, with heavy wear on all of the coin.

Fine (F-12). About 50 percent of the original detail is visible. On a coin with no inner detail, there is fairly heavy wear over all of the coin. Sides of letters are weak. The coin is often dirty or dull. Just under 50 percent of a design detail remains.

Very fine (VF-20). About 75 percent of the original detail is visible. On a coin with no inner detail, there is moderate wear over the entire coin. Corners of letters and numbers may be weak. About two-thirds of a design detail remains.

Extremely fine (EF or XF-40). About 95 percent of the original detail is visible. On a coin with no inner detail, there is light wear over the entire coin. About 90 percent of a design detail remains.

Almost uncirculated (AU-50). All detail is visible. There is wear on only the highest points of the design. Half or more of the original mint luster is present.

Uncirculated (Unc). No visible signs of wear or handling, even under a 30-power microscope. Bag marks, incurred when coins hit against each other when bagged and shipped from the mint, may be present.

Brilliant uncirculated (BU). No visible signs of wear or handling, even under a 30-power microscope. Full mint luster will be present and, ideally, no bag marks.

Mint state (MS): This is another designation for uncirculated used when grading U.S. coins. It is usually followed by a number ranging from 60 to 70. MS-60 is described as "typical uncirculated" and roughly corresponds to grade uncirculated in world coins. MS-65 is described as "choice uncirculated" and roughly corresponds to grade brilliant uncirculated in world coins. The theoretical MS-70 grade is a flawless coin. Professional grading services use all numbers from MS-60 to MS-69 to denote U.S. coins in various states of uncirculated condition.

GOLD BULLION VALUE CHART

The following chart shows the bullion value of various gold weights at various prices for gold per troy ounce.

Oz.	500.00	520.00	560.00	580.00	600.00	620.00	640.00	660.00	680.00	700.00
0.010	5.00	5.20	5.60	5.80	6.00	6.20	6.40	6.60	6.80	7.00
0.050	25.00	26.00	28.00	29.00	30.00	31.00	32.00	33.00	34.00	35.00
0.100	50.00	52.00	56.00	58.00	60.00	62.00	64.00	66.00	68.00	70.00
0.130	65.00	67.60	72.80	75.40	78.00	80.60	83.20	85.80	88.40	91.00
0.150	75.00	78.00	84.00	87.00	90.00	93.00	96.00	99.00	102.00	105.00
0.170	85.00	88.40	95.20	98.60	102.00	105.40	108.80	112.20	115.60	119.00
0.200	100.00	104.00	112.00	116.00	120.00	124.00	128.00	132.00	136.00	140.00
0.230	115.00	119.60	128.80	133.40	138.00	142.60	147.20	151.80	156.40	161.00
0.250	125.00	130.00	140.00	145.00	150.00	155.00	160.00	165.00	170.00	175.00
0.270	135.00	140.40	151.20	156.60	162.00	167.40	172.80	178.20	183.60	189.00
0.300	150.00	156.00	168.00	174.00	180.00	186.00	192.00	198.00	204.00	210.00
0.330	165.00	171.60	184.80	191.40	198.00	204.60	211.20	217.80	224.40	231.00
0.350	175.00	182.00	196.00	203.00	210.00	217.00	224.00	231.00	238.00	245.00
0.370	185.00	192.40	207.20	214.60	222.00	229.40	236.80	244.20	251.60	259.00
0.400	200.00	208.00	224.00	232.00	240.00	248.00	256.00	264.00	272.00	280.00
0.420	210.00	218.40	235.20	243.60	252.00	260.40	268.80	277.20	285.60	294.00
0.450	225.00	234.00	252.00	261.00	270.00	279.00	288.00	297.00	306.00	315.00
0.470	235.00	244.40	263.20	272.60	282.00	291.40	300.80	310.20	319.60	329.00
0.500	250.00	260.00	280.00	290.00	300.00	310.00	320.00	330.00	340.00	350.00
0.510	255.00	265.20	285.60	295.80	306.00	316.20	326.40	336.60	346.80	357.00
0.520	260.00	270.40	291.20	301.60	312.00	322.40	332.80	343.20	353.60	364.00
0.530	265.00	275.60	296.80	307.40	318.00	328.60	339.20	349.80	360.40	371.00
0.540	270.00	280.80	302.40	313.20	324.00	334.80	345.60	356.40	367.20	378.00
0.550	275.00	286.00	308.00	319.00	330.00	341.00	352.00	363.00	374.00	385.00
0.560	280.00	291.20	313.60	324.80	336.00	347.20	358.40	369.60	380.80	392.00
0.570	285.00	296.40	319.20	330.60	342.00	353.40	364.80	376.20	387.60	399.00
0.580	290.00	301.60	324.80	336.40	348.00	359.60	371.20	382.80	394.40	406.00
0.590	295.00	306.80	330.40	342.20	354.00	365.80	377.60	389.40	401.20	413.00
0.600	300.00	312.00	336.00	348.00	360.00	372.00	384.00	396.00	408.00	420.00
0.610	305.00	317.20	341.60	353.80	366.00	378.20	390.40	402.60	414.80	427.00
0.620	310.00	322.40	347.20	359.60	372.00	384.40	396.80	409.20	421.60	434.00
0.630	315.00	327.60	352.80	365.40	378.00	390.60	403.20	415.80	428.40	441.00
0.640	320.00	332.80	358.40	371.20	384.00	396.80	409.60	422.40	435.20	448.00

GOLD RUSH

GOLD BULLION VALUE CHART

Oz.	720.00	740.00	760.00	780.00	800.00	820.00	840.00	860.00	880.00	900.00
0.010	7.20	7.40	7.60	7.80	8.00	8.20	8.40	8.60	8.80	9.00
0.050	36.00	37.00	38.00	39.00	40.00	41.00	42.00	43.00	44.00	45.00
0.100	72.00	74.00	76.00	78.00	80.00	82.00	84.00	86.00	88.00	90.00
0.130	93.60	96.20	98.80	101.40	104.00	106.60	109.20	111.80	114.40	117.00
0.150	108.00	111.00	114.00	117.00	120.00	123.00	126.00	129.00	132.00	135.00
0.170	122.40	125.80	129.20	132.60	136.00	139.40	142.80	146.20	149.60	153.00
0.200	144.00	148.00	152.00	156.00	160.00	164.00	168.00	172.00	176.00	180.00
0.230	165.60	170.20	174.80	179.40	184.00	188.60	193.20	197.80	202.40	207.00
0.250	180.00	185.00	190.00	195.00	200.00	205.00	210.00	215.00	220.00	225.00
0.270	194.40	199.80	205.20	210.60	216.00	221.40	226.80	232.20	237.60	243.00
0.300	216.00	222.00	228.00	234.00	240.00	246.00	252.00	258.00	264.00	270.00
0.330	237.60	244.20	250.80	257.40	264.00	270.60	277.20	283.80	290.40	297.00
0.350	252.00	259.00	266.00	273.00	280.00	287.00	294.00	301.00	308.00	315.00
0.370	266.40	273.80	281.20	288.60	296.00	303.40	310.80	318.20	325.60	333.00
0.400	288.00	296.00	304.00	312.00	320.00	328.00	336.00	344.00	352.00	360.00
0.420	302.40	310.80	319.20	327.60	336.00	344.40	352.80	361.20	369.60	378.00
0.450	324.00	333.00	342.00	351.00	360.00	369.00	378.00	387.00	396.00	405.00
0.470	338.40	347.80	357.20	366.60	376.00	385.40	394.80	404.20	413.60	423.00
0.500	360.00	370.00	380.00	390.00	400.00	410.00	420.00	430.00	440.00	450.00
0.510	367.20	377.40	387.60	397.80	408.00	418.20	428.40	438.60	448.80	459.00
0.520	374.40	384.80	395.20	405.60	416.00	426.40	436.80	447.20	457.60	468.00
0.530	381.60	392.20	402.80	413.40	424.00	434.60	445.20	455.80	466.40	477.00
0.540	388.80	399.60	410.40	421.20	432.00	442.80	453.60	464.40	475.20	486.00
0.550	396.00	407.00	418.00	429.00	440.00	451.00	462.00	473.00	484.00	495.00
0.560	403.20	414.40	425.60	436.80	448.00	459.20	470.40	481.60	492.80	504.00
0.570	410.40	421.80	433.20	444.60	456.00	467.40	478.80	490.20	501.60	513.00
0.580	417.60	429.20	440.80	452.40	464.00	475.60	487.20	498.80	510.40	522.00
0.590	424.80	436.60	448.40	460.20	472.00	483.80	495.60	507.40	519.20	531.00
0.600	432.00	444.00	456.00	468.00	480.00	492.00	504.00	516.00	528.00	540.00
0.610	439.20	451.40	463.60	475.80	488.00	500.20	512.40	524.60	536.80	549.00
0.620	446.40	458.80	471.20	483.60	496.00	508.40	520.80	533.20	545.60	558.00
0.630	453.60	466.20	478.80	491.40	504.00	516.60	529.20	541.80	554.40	567.00
0.640	460.80	473.60	486.40	499.20	512.00	524.80	537.60	550.40	563.20	576.00

GOLD BULLION VALUE CHART

Oz.	500.00	520.00	560.00	580.00	600.00	620.00	640.00	660.00	680.00	700.00
0.650	325.00	338.00	364.00	377.00	390.00	403.00	416.00	429.00	442.00	455.00
0.660	330.00	343.20	369.60	382.80	396.00	409.20	422.40	435.60	448.80	462.00
0.670	335.00	348.40	375.20	388.60	402.00	415.40	428.80	442.20	455.60	469.00
0.680	340.00	353.60	380.80	394.40	408.00	421.60	435.20	448.80	462.40	476.00
0.690	345.00	358.80	386.40	400.20	414.00	427.80	441.60	455.40	469.20	483.00
0.700	350.00	364.00	392.00	406.00	420.00	434.00	448.00	462.00	476.00	490.00
0.710	355.00	369.20	397.60	411.80	426.00	440.20	454.40	468.60	482.80	497.00
0.720	360.00	374.40	403.20	417.60	432.00	446.40	460.80	475.20	489.60	504.00
0.730	365.00	379.60	408.80	423.40	438.00	452.60	467.20	481.80	496.40	511.00
0.740	370.00	384.80	414.40	429.20	444.00	458.80	473.60	488.40	503.20	518.00
0.750	375.00	390.00	420.00	435.00	450.00	465.00	480.00	495.00	510.00	525.00
0.760	380.00	395.20	425.60	440.80	456.00	471.20	486.40	501.60	516.80	532.00
0.770	385.00	400.40	431.20	446.60	462.00	477.40	492.80	508.20	523.60	539.00
0.780	390.00	405.60	436.80	452.40	468.00	483.60	499.20	514.80	530.40	546.00
0.790	395.00	410.80	442.40	458.20	474.00	489.80	505.60	521.40	537.20	553.00
0.800	400.00	416.00	448.00	464.00	480.00	496.00	512.00	528.00	544.00	560.00
0.810	405.00	421.20	453.60	469.80	486.00	502.20	518.40	534.60	550.80	567.00
0.820	410.00	426.40	459.20	475.60	492.00	508.40	524.80	541.20	557.60	574.00
0.830	415.00	431.60	464.80	481.40	498.00	514.60	531.20	547.80	564.40	581.00
0.840	420.00	436.80	470.40	487.20	504.00	520.80	537.60	554.40	571.20	588.00
0.850	425.00	442.00	476.00	493.00	510.00	527.00	544.00	561.00	578.00	595.00
0.860	430.00	447.20	481.60	498.80	516.00	533.20	550.40	567.60	584.80	602.00
0.870	435.00	452.40	487.20	504.60	522.00	539.40	556.80	574.20	591.60	609.00
0.880	440.00	457.60	492.80	510.40	528.00	545.60	563.20	580.80	598.40	616.00
0.890	445.00	462.80	498.40	516.20	534.00	551.80	569.60	587.40	605.20	623.00
0.900	450.00	468.00	504.00	522.00	540.00	558.00	576.00	594.00	612.00	630.00
0.910	455.00	473.20	509.60	527.80	546.00	564.20	582.40	600.60	618.80	637.00
0.920	460.00	478.40	515.20	533.60	552.00	570.40	588.80	607.20	625.60	644.00
0.930	465.00	483.60	520.80	539.40	558.00	576.60	595.20	613.80	632.40	651.00
0.940	470.00	488.80	526.40	545.20	564.00	582.80	601.60	620.40	639.20	658.00
0.950	475.00	494.00	532.00	551.00	570.00	589.00	608.00	627.00	646.00	665.00
0.960	480.00	499.20	537.60	556.80	576.00	595.20	614.40	633.60	652.80	672.00
0.970	485.00	504.40	543.20	562.60	582.00	601.40	620.80	640.20	659.60	679.00
0.980	490.00	509.60	548.80	568.40	588.00	607.60	627.20	646.80	666.40	686.00
0.990	495.00	514.80	554.40	574.20	594.00	613.80	633.60	653.40	673.20	693.00
1.000	500.00	520.00	560.00	580.00	600.00	620.00	640.00	660.00	680.00	700.00

GOLD BULLION VALUE CHART

Oz.	720.00	740.00	760.00	780.00	800.00	820.00	840.00	860.00	880.00	900.00
0.650	468.00	481.00	494.00	507.00	520.00	533.00	546.00	559.00	572.00	585.00
0.660	475.20	488.40	501.60	514.80	528.00	541.20	554.40	567.60	580.80	594.00
0.670	482.40	495.80	509.20	522.60	536.00	549.40	562.80	576.20	589.60	603.00
0.680	489.60	503.20	516.80	530.40	544.00	557.60	571.20	584.80	598.40	612.00
0.690	496.80	510.60	524.40	538.20	552.00	565.80	579.60	593.40	607.20	621.00
0.700	504.00	518.00	532.00	546.00	560.00	574.00	588.00	602.00	616.00	630.00
0.710	511.20	525.40	539.60	553.80	568.00	582.20	596.40	610.60	624.80	639.00
0.720	518.40	532.80	547.20	561.60	576.00	590.40	604.80	619.20	633.60	648.00
0.730	525.60	540.20	554.80	569.40	584.00	598.60	613.20	627.80	642.40	657.00
0.740	532.80	547.60	562.40	577.20	592.00	606.80	621.60	636.40	651.20	666.00
0.750	540.00	555.00	570.00	585.00	600.00	615.00	630.00	645.00	660.00	675.00
0.760	547.20	562.40	577.60	592.80	608.00	623.20	638.40	653.60	668.80	684.00
0.770	554.40	569.80	585.20	600.60	616.00	631.40	646.80	662.20	677.60	693.00
0.780	561.60	577.20	592.80	608.40	624.00	639.60	655.20	670.80	686.40	702.00
0.790	568.80	584.60	600.40	616.20	632.00	647.80	663.60	679.40	695.20	711.00
0.800	576.00	592.00	608.00	624.00	640.00	656.00	672.00	688.00	704.00	720.00
0.810	583.20	599.40	615.60	631.80	648.00	664.20	680.40	696.60	712.80	729.00
0.820	590.40	606.80	623.20	639.60	656.00	672.40	688.80	705.20	721.60	738.00
0.830	597.60	614.20	630.80	647.40	664.00	680.60	697.20	713.80	730.40	747.00
0.840	604.80	621.60	638.40	655.20	672.00	688.80	705.60	722.40	739.20	756.00
0.850	612.00	629.00	646.00	663.00	680.00	697.00	714.00	731.00	748.00	765.00
0.860	619.20	636.40	653.60	670.80	688.00	705.20	722.40	739.60	756.80	774.00
0.870	626.40	643.80	661.20	678.60	696.00	713.40	730.80	748.20	765.60	783.00
0.880	633.60	651.20	668.80	686.40	704.00	721.60	739.20	756.80	774.40	792.00
0.890	640.80	658.60	676.40	694.20	712.00	729.80	747.60	765.40	783.20	801.00
0.900	648.00	666.00	684.00	702.00	720.00	738.00	756.00	774.00	792.00	810.00
0.910	655.20	673.40	691.60	709.80	728.00	746.20	764.40	782.60	800.80	819.00
0.920	662.40	680.80	699.20	717.60	736.00	754.40	772.80	791.20	809.60	828.00
0.930	669.60	688.20	706.80	725.40	744.00	762.60	781.20	799.80	818.40	837.00
0.940	676.80	695.60	714.40	733.20	752.00	770.80	789.60	808.40	827.20	846.00
0.950	684.00	703.00	722.00	741.00	760.00	779.00	798.00	817.00	836.00	855.00
0.960	691.20	710.40	729.60	748.80	768.00	787.20	806.40	825.60	844.80	864.00
0.970	698.40	717.80	737.20	756.60	776.00	795.40	814.80	834.20	853.60	873.00
0.980	705.60	725.20	744.80	764.40	784.00	803.60	823.20	842.80	862.40	882.00
0.990	712.80	732.60	752.40	772.20	792.00	811.80	831.60	851.40	871.20	891.00
1.000	720.00	740.00	760.00	780.00	800.00	820.00	840.00	860.00	880.00	900.00

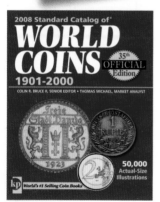
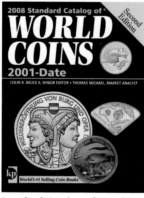
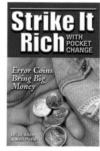